LETTERS OF
PERCY BYSSHE SHELLEY

THE COMPLETE WORKS OF

PERCY BYSSHE SHELLEY

NEWLY EDITED BY ROGER INGPEN AND WALTER E. PECK

IN TEN VOLUMES

CORRESPONDENCE: VOLUMES VIII–IX–X

VOLUME IX

LETTERS

1812 TO 1818

EDITED BY

ROGER INGPEN

GORDIAN PRESS, NEW YORK
ERNEST BENN LIMITED, LONDON
1965

Library of Congress Card No. 65-14696

Published 1965

Reprinted by Arrangement
with Ernest Benn. LTD

Lithographed in U.S.A. by
E D W A R D S   B R O T H E R S ,   I N C .
Ann Arbor, Michigan

CONTENTS OF VOLUME IX

VII

LYNMOUTH, TANYRALLT, AND SECOND VISIT TO DUBLIN, June 30, 1812, to April 3, 1813   *Page* 1

Correspondence with Hookham : "Le Système de la Nature" : On the study of the classics : Godwin invited to Lynmouth : Irish History : Sir James Lawrence : "Queen Mab" : T. L. Peacock's Poems : In London : Shelley reconciled to Hogg : Departure of Miss Hitchener : At Tremadoc : Fanny Imlay and Harriet : Shelley's Book List : "Biblical Extracts" : The Trial of John and Leigh Hunt : Shelley Assaulted at Tanyrallt : Second Visit to Ireland

VIII

LAST DAYS WITH HARRIET, April 5, 1813, to May 14, 1814   *Page* 63

Shelley's Return to London : Negotiations with his Father : The Duke of Norfolk : The birth of his eldest child, Ianthe : John Frank Newton : Revisits the Lakes : At Edinburgh : "The Refutation of Deism" : At Bracknell : Mrs. Boinville and her Daughter : Italian Studies

IX

FIRST VISIT TO THE CONTINENT, August 13, 1814, to June 22, 1815   *Page* 93

Elopement with Mary Godwin : Friendly Letter to Harriet : Continental Tour : Dark Days : Stolen Interviews : Letter from Mary : Isabel Baxter : The Sussex Farmer : The "Ancient Language" : Meeting in Gray's Inn Gardens : Death of Sir Bysshe Shelley : Shelley Refused Admission at Field Place : Receives Income of £1,000 : Pays Income of £200 to Harriet : Tour in Devonshire

X

BISHOPGATE—"ALASTOR," August, 1815, to April 24, 1816   *Page* 113

Improved Health : Thames Excursion to Lechlade : Classical Studies : Financial Correspondence with Godwin : Charles Clairmont : Birth of William Shelley : Negotiations with Timothy Shelley : Deed of Disclaimer : Godwin's "harshness and cruelty" : "Alastor" Published : Letter to Southey : Godwin's "Pecuniary Distress" : Shelley's Tribute to Mary : A "base fee"

XI

SECOND VISIT TO THE CONTINENT, May 3 to August 2, 1816   *Page* 157

The Chancery Decision : Route of Second Continental Journey : Geneva : Villa Diodati : Meeting with Bryon : Excursion round the Lake of Geneva : "History of a Six Weeks' Tour" : "Hymn to Intellectual Beauty" : Yvoire : Evian : Meillerie : Marie Louise : A Narrow Escape : Castle of Chillon : Clarens : Vevai : Lausanne : Gibbon : Seeking a Home : Further Travels Contemplated : Shelley's "Mont Blanc" : Journey to Chamouni : An Avalanche : Glacier des Bossons : Buffon's Theory : Entry in Visitors' Album : Montanvert : Return to St. Martin

CONTENTS

XII

MARLOW, September 8, 1816, to September 22, 1817   *Page* 193

Letters to Byron : Helping Godwin again : "Childe Harold" : Leigh Hunt : His article on Shelley, Reynolds and Keats : "Rimini" : Peacock's Novels : Suicide of Harriet Shelley : Her Life after the Separation : Hunt's Sustaining Friendship : Shelley Marries Mary : Godwin's "Evidence" : Shelley Refused the Custody of his Children : Birth of Allegra : "The Hermit of Marlow" : Letters to Leigh Hunt : Coleridge's "Sybilline Leaves" : "Frankenstein" : Letter to Lord Eldon

XIII

MARLOW—THE REVOLT OF ISLAM, September 24, 1817, to March 12, 1818

     Page 243

"Manfred" : Horace Smith : Shelley in London again : Proposed visit to Italy : Allegra : "Laon and Cythna" Explained : "An Address to the People" : "Rhododaphne" : "Mandeville" : Ill-health : Malthus : Baxter and Booth : "Revolt of Islam" : Ollier's "Altham" : Last Days in England

XIV

EARLY ITALIAN IMPRESSIONS—"ROSALIND AND HELEN," March 13 to November 10, 1818

     Page 287

Leigh Hunt's Poems : The Journey to Italy : Passage of the Echelles : Italian Women : Lake Como : Milan Cathedral : Leghorn : The Gisbornes : The Baths of Lucca : Bathing : Godwin's "Malthus" : "Rosalind and Helen" : Florence : Venice : The Hoppners : Byron : Clare and Allegra : I Cappuccini : Death of Clara Shelley : "Prometheus Unbound" : Journey to Naples : Ariosto and Tasso : Pictures at Bologna

LIST OF SHELLEY'S LETTERS

1812

No.	No. in the last Edition.				Page
2 181a	148	July 5	Lymouth	TO W. GODWIN	4
2 182	149	July 7	Lymouth	,, W. GODWIN	7
2 183	150	July 29	Lymouth	,, T. HOOKHAM	9
2 184	151	July 29	Lymouth	,, W. GODWIN	10
185	2 152	August 11	Lymouth	,, C. NUGENT	16
186	154	August 17	Lymouth	,, SIR J. H. LAWRENCE	17
2 187	155	August 18	Lymouth	,, T. HOOKHAM	18
1 188		November 7	London	,, MRS. E. SHELLEY	21
2 189	156	November 7[?]	London	,, J. WILLIAMS	22
190	1 157	November or December 19	London	,, MRS. HOOPER	26
191	158	December 3	Tanyrallt	,, T. J. HOGG	26
2 192	2 159	December 3	Tanyrallt	,, T. HOOKHAM	28
1 193		December 3	Tanyrallt	,, J. EVANS	29
1 194		[December ?]	Tanyrallt	,, J. EVANS	30
2 195	160	December 10	Ynys-y-Maen-y-Mawr	,, F. IMLAY	30
2 196	2 162	December 17	Tanyrallt	,, T. HOOKHAM	33
1 197		[December 17?]	Tanyrallt	,, T. HOOKHAM	35
198	1 161	December 24	Tanyrallt	,, C. RICKMAN	35
199	163	December 27	Tanyrallt	,, T. J. HOGG	37

1813

No.	No. in the last Edition.				Page
2 200	2 164	January 2	Tanyrallt	,, T. HOOKHAM	39
2 201	2 165	January 26	Tanyrallt	,, T. HOOKHAM	42
202	166	February 7	Tanyrallt	,, T. J. HOGG	43
2 203	167	February 19	Tanyrallt	,, T. HOOKHAM	46
1 204			Tanyrallt	,, T. HOOKHAM	48
2 205	168	March 3	Tanyrallt	,, T. HOOKHAM	49
206	169			,, J. WILLIAMS	50
207	1 170	[After March 5]	Tanyrallt	,, J. WILLIAMS	51
2 208	171	March 6	Tanyrallt	,, T. HOOKHAM	52
209	1 172	[After March 9]	Dublin	,, J. WILLIAMS	54
2 210	173	[March]	Dublin	,, T. HOOKHAM	56
211	1 174	March 21	Dublin	,, J. WILLIAMS	57
2 212	1 175 & 1 177	March 30	[Dublin]	,, J. WILLIAMS	58
213	176	March 31	Dublin	,, T. J. HOGG	61
214	178	April 3[?]	Dublin	,, T. J. HOGG	62
215	179	April 5	London	,, T. J. HOGG	65
2 216	180	May 18	London	,, T. SHELLEY	66
217	181	[May 28]	London	,, DUKE OF NORFOLK	68
218	182	[June 3]	London	,, T. J. HOGG	69

1 Letter added to this edition for the first time.   2 New additions or corrections.

LIST OF SHELLEY'S LETTERS

No.	No. in the last Edition.				Page
219	183	June 16	London	TO T. C. MEDWIN	70
220	² 184	June 21	London	,, T. C. MEDWIN	71
¹ 221		June 27	London	,, J. WILLIAMS	72
¹ 222		[June 27]	London	,, T. J. HOGG	73
² 223	185	June 28	London	,, T. C. MEDWIN	73
² 224	186	July 6	London	,, T. C. MEDWIN	74
225	187	July 9	London	,, T. J. HOGG	75
226	188	July 27	Bracknell	,, T. J. HOGG	75
¹ 227		[October 6]	Warwick	,, T. HOOKHAM	77
² 228	189	November 26	Edinburgh	,, T. J. HOGG	80
² 229	¹ 190	November 28	Edinburgh	,, ———	82
¹ 230			London	,, ———	83
¹ 231			London	,, MR. PIKE	83

1814

² 232	191	March 13	Bracknell	,, T. SHELLEY	84
233	192	March 16	Bracknell	,, T. J. HOGG	85
234	¹ 193	[April 14]		,, J. WILLIAMS	88
¹ 235		May 6	London	,, MR. TEESDALE	89
236	¹ 193a	May 14	London	,, J. WILLIAMS	89
² 237	194	August 13	Troyes	,, H. SHELLEY	95
² 238	195	[? October 24]	[London]	,, M. W. GODWIN	97
² 239	196	[After October 24]	[London]	,, M. W. GODWIN	98
² 240	197	[? October 25]	[London]	,, M. W. GODWIN	100
² 241	198	[? October 27, morning]	[London]	,, M. W. GODWIN	101
² 242	199	[? October 27, night]	[London]	,, M. W. GODWIN	101
² 243	200	[? October 28]	[London]	,, M. W. GODWIN	102
¹ 244		[? November 1]	[London]	,, M. W. GODWIN	104
² 245	201	[? November 2]	[London]	,, M. W. GODWIN	105
² 246	202	[? November 3]	[London]	,, M. W. GODWIN	106
² 247	203	[? November 4]	[London]	,, M. W. GODWIN	108
¹ 248				,, G. B. BALLACHEY	109
² 249	204		[London]	,, M. W. GODWIN	110
² 250	205	[? November 8]	[London]	,, M. W. GODWIN	110

1815

¹ 251		January 17	[London]	,, R. HAYWARD	111
252	¹ 206	April 7	[London]	,, R. HAYWARD	112
253	207	June 22	Torquay	,, J. WILLIAMS	112
254	¹ 208	August	Bishopgate	,, T. J. HOGG	115
¹ 255		September 10	Bishopgate	,, LACKINGTON, ALLEN & CO.	117
¹ 256		September 16	Bishopgate	,, A. B. PERIERA	118
257	209	September	Bishopgate	,, T. J. HOGG	118
258	¹ 210	September 27	London	,, W. LAING	120
¹ 259		October 9	Bishopgate	,, BROOKES & CO.	120
260	211	October 19	Bishopgate	,, R. HAYWARD	121
¹ 261		November 9	Bishopgate	,, LACKINGTON, ALLEN & CO.	122

VIII

LIST OF SHELLEY'S LETTERS

No.	No. in the last Edition.				Page
262	1 212	December 17	Bishopgate	TO LACKINGTON, ALLEN & CO.	122
1 263		December 24	Bishopgate	,, BROOKES & CO.	123

1816

No.	No. in the last Edition.				Page
2 264	213	January 7	Bishopgate	,, W. GODWIN	123
265	1 233a	January 16	Bishopgate	,, J. MURRAY	125
2 266	214	January 18	Bishopgate	,, W. GODWIN	127
2 267	215	January 21	Bishopgate	,, W. GODWIN	128
2 268	216	January 23	Bishopgate	,, W. GODWIN	130
2 269	217	January 25	Bishopgate	,, W. GODWIN	132
2 270	218	January 28	Bishopgate	,, W. GODWIN	134
2 271	1 233b	February 6	Bishopgate	,, CARPENTER & SON	135
272	219	February 16	London	,, W. GODWIN	136
273	220	February 17	London	,, W. GODWIN	138
274	221	February 18	London	,, W. GODWIN	138
275	222	February 21	Bishopgate	,, W. GODWIN	140
2 276	2 223	February 26	Bishopgate	,, W. GODWIN	142
277	224	March 6	London	,, W. GODWIN	145
278	225	March 7	London	,, R. SOUTHEY	146
2 279	226	March 7	London	,, W. GODWIN	147
2 280	227	March 9	London	,, W. GODWIN	149
281	228	March 16	London	,, W. GODWIN	150
1 282		March 18	London	,, W. BRYANT	150
283	229	March 21	London	,, W. GODWIN	151
284	230	March 29	London	,, W. GODWIN	151
285	1 231	April 8	London	,, W. BRYANT	152
286	232	April 14	London	,, W. BRYANT	153
287	1 233	April 24	London	,, W. BRYANT	154
1 288		Saturday	London	,, ———	155
1 289		Thursday morning	London	,, W. BRYANT	155
2 290	234	May 3	Dover	,, W. GODWIN	159
291	235	May 15	Geneva	,, T. L. PEACOCK	161
1 292		June 21	Geneva	,, BROOKES & SON	164
293	236	June 23	Evian	,, W. GODWIN	164
1 294		June 24	Geneva	,, R. HAYWARD	166
295	237	July 12	Geneva	,, T. L. PEACOCK	167
2 296	238	July 17	Geneva	,, W. GODWIN	177
297	239	July 17	Geneva	,, T. L. PEACOCK	178
2 298	240	July 22	Chamounix	,, T. L. PEACOCK	182
1 299		July 22	Chamouni	,, LORD BYRON	191
1 300		August 2	Geneva	,, BROOKES SON & DIXON	192
1 301		September 8	Portsmouth	,, LORD BYRON	195
1 302		September 11	London	,, LORD BYRON	196
1 303	241 [extract]	September 29	Bath	,, LORD BYRON	197
2 304	242	October 2	Bath	,, W. GODWIN	200
305	243	October 2	Bath	,, J. MURRAY	201
306	244	October 30	Bath	,, J. MURRAY	202
307	245	November 9	Bath	,, J. J. PASCHOUD	203
1 308		November 20	Bath	,, LORD BYRON	204
309	246	November 24	Bath	,, W. GODWIN	206
310	2 247	December 8	Marlow	,, L. HUNT	207
2 311	248	December 16	London	,, M. W. GODWIN	211
312	249	December 30	London	,, C. M. J. CLAIRMONT	213

IX

LIST OF SHELLEY'S LETTERS

1817

No.	No. in the last Edition.			TO		Page
² 313	250	*January* 11	London	TO	M. W. SHELLEY	215
² 314	251	[? *January*]	[? London]	,,	M. W. SHELLEY	217
¹ 315		*January* 17	London	,,	LORD BYRON	218
316	252	*January* 30	[London]	,,	C. M. J. CLAIRMONT	220
¹ 317		*February* 22		,,	C. OLLIER	221
² 318	253	*March* 9	Marlow	,,	W. GODWIN	221
¹ 319	254	[*Before March* 14]		,,	C. OLLIER	222
320	255 [Part only]	*March* 14	Marlow	,,	C. OLLIER	223
² 321	256	*March* 22	Marlow	,,	W. GODWIN	224
¹ 322		*April* 20	Marlow	,,	W. HONE	225
¹ 323		*April* 23	Marlow	,,	C. & J. OLLIER	225
¹ 324		*April* 23	Marlow	,,	LORD BYRON	226
¹ 325		[? *April*]	[? Marlow]	,,	T. J. HOGG	228
326	² 257	*June* 29	Marlow	,,	L. & M. HUNT	228
¹ 327		*July* 6	Marlow	,,	T. J. HOGG	230
¹ 328		*July* 9	Marlow	,,	LORD BYRON	232
² 329	¹ 258	*July* 13	Marlow	,,	C. & J. OLLIER	234
² 330	259	*August* 3	Marlow	,,	C. OLLIER	234
² 331	¹ 260	*August* 3	Marlow	,,	L. HUNT	235
² 332	261	*August* 8	Marlow	,,	C. OLLIER	237
333	262	*August* 16	Marlow	,,	M. HUNT	238
334	263	*August* 22	Marlow	,,	LACKINGTON & CO.	240
¹ 335		*September* 20	Marlow	,,	LORD ELDON	241
¹ 336		*September* 22	London	,,	LACKINGTON & CO.	242
¹ 337		*September* 24	London	,,	LORD BYRON	245
² 338	264	*October* 6	London	,,	M. W. SHELLEY	247
² 339	265	*October* 8	London	,,	M. W. SHELLEY	249
340	266	*October* 13	London	,,	A PUBLISHER	250
341	¹ 267	*October* 28	Marlow	,,	LACKINGTON & CO.	252
342	268	*November* 12	London	,,	C. OLLIER	252
343	269	*November* 25	Marlow	,,	C. OLLIER	253
² 344	¹ 288a	*November* 28	Marlow	,,	T. J. HOGG	254
² 345	270	*December* 1	Marlow	,,	W. GODWIN	255
346	¹ 271	*December* 3	Marlow	,,	LACKINGTON & CO.	256
² 347	272	*December* 3	Marlow	,,	C. OLLIER	256
348	273	*December* 7	Marlow	,,	C. OLLIER	257
² 349	274	*December* 7	Marlow	,,	W. GODWIN	258
350	275	*December* 10	Marlow	,,	W. T. BAXTER	261
351	276	*December* 11	Marlow	,,	C. OLLIER	262
² 352	277	*December* 11	Marlow	,,	W. GODWIN	265
353	278	*December* 13	Marlow	,,	C. OLLIER	268
354	¹ 279	*December* 16	Marlow	,,	T. MOORE	269
¹ 355		*December* 17	Marlow	,,	LORD BYRON	270
356	¹ 280	[*December* 22]	Marlow	,,	C. OLLIER	272
¹ 357		*December* 23	Marlow	,,	LACKINGTON & CO.	272
² 358	281	*December* 27	Marlow	,,	C. OLLIER	273
359	282	*December* 30	Marlow	,,	W. T. BAXTER	274

1818

¹ 360		*January* 2	Marlow	,,	C. OLLIER	277
¹ 361		*January* 2		,,	LACKINGTON & CO.	278
¹ 362		*January* 4	Marlow	,,	R. WAITHMAN	278

X

LIST OF SHELLEY'S LETTERS

No.	No. in the last Edition.				Page
363	283	January 11	Marlow	TO C. OLLIER	279
364	284	January 15	Marlow	,, C. OLLIER	279
365	285	January 16	Marlow	,, C. OLLIER	280
2 366	286	January 22	Marlow	,, C. OLLIER	281
367	287	January 22	Marlow	,, C. OLLIER	282
368	288	January 25	Marlow	,, C. OLLIER	282
1 369		January 31	London	,, W. WILLATS	284
370	1 289	March 12	Dover	,, BROOKES & CO.	284
371	290	March 13	Calais	,, L. HUNT	289
372	291	March 22	Lyons	,, L. HUNT	291
373	292	March 26		,, JOURNAL	292
2 374	293	April	Milan	,, T. L. PEACOCK	293
1 375		April 13	Milan	,, LORD BYRON	295
2 376	294	April 20	Milan	,, T. L. PEACOCK	296
1 377		April 22	Milan	,, LORD BYRON	301
1 378		April 30	Milan	,, LORD BYRON	304
2 379	295	April 30	Milan	,, T. J. HOGG	305
2 380	296	April 30	Milan	,, T. L. PEACOCK	308
2 381	297	June 5	Livorno	,, T. L. PEACOCK	309
1 382		June 28	Bagni di Lucca	,, C. OLLIER	311
2 383	298	July 16	Bagni di Lucca	,, J. & M. GISBORNE	311
384	2 299	July 25	Bagni di Lucca	,, T. L. PEACOCK	313
2 385	300	July 25	Bagni di Lucca	,, W. GODWIN	316
386	1 301	July 31	Bagni di Lucca	,, BROOKES & CO.	319
387	302	August 16	Bagni di Lucca	,, T. L. PEACOCK	319
2 388	303	[August 20]	Florence	,, M. W. SHELLEY	322
2 389	304	[August 23]	Venice	,, M. W. SHELLEY	325
1 390		[August]		,, C. OLLIER	330
1 391		September 13	Este	,, LORD BYRON	331
2 392	305	September 22	Padua	,, M. W. SHELLEY	331
2 393	306	[September 25]	[Venice]	,, C. M. J. CLAIRMONT	333
2 394	307	October 8	Este	,, T. L. PEACOCK	334
2 395	308	November 6	Ferrara	,, T. L. PEACOCK	337
2 396	309	November 9	Bologna	,, T. L. PEACOCK	342

XI

VII

JUNE 30, 1812, TO APRIL 3, 1813

LETTERS OF SHELLEY

LYNMOUTH, TANYRALLT, AND SECOND VISIT TO DUBLIN

HARRIET SHELLEY TO CATHERINE NUGENT

Direct *Lymouth, near Barnstaple, Devonshire,*
June 30, [1812].

MY DEAR MRS. NUGENT,

Now that we are again settled[1] I take up the pen in the hopes of giving that pleasure which I received from reading your letter. I received it during my stay at Cwm Elan and a few days after we left that lovely spot, and its amiable hostess for a journey to Chepstow where we were in hopes of finding a house that would suit us, and where we might with pleasure receive the visit ot one whose presence like the sun would make happy those who beheld her. Your letter damped the joy I felt from reading it, by seeing that you could not come to us this summer, for I had hoped tho' we had left Nangwillt that we should have been sure of a visit from you. However, I will say no more about it, as you must be the best judge of your own affairs, and I doubt not that were we to draw you from your own country we should be the means, tho' innocently, of depriving many of your unfortunate countrymen of that relief you know so well how to bestow. I will say this, though I am a loser by it. Continue, oh, amiable woman, the path marked out to thee by virtue and humanity, and let not the whisperings of selfishness in us take thee from so laudable an undertaking. We may yet meet ere this world shall close thy eyes, and that we both desire it our hearts are the best judges. I will now tell you how we came into Devonshire. We arrived at Chepstow. We found the house not half built, and by no means large enough for our family.[2] I did not regret it, as the country was by no means beautiful. We then proceeded into this country, and came to this place in our way to Ilfracombe and the beauty of it has made us residents here for the summer months, when we think of going to London for the winter. It combines all the beauties of our late residence with the addition of a fine bold sea. We have taken the only cottage there was, which is most beautifully situated, commanding a fine view of the sea, with mountains at the side and behind us. Vegetation is more luxuriant here than in any part of England. We have roses and myrtles creeping up the sides of the house, which is thatched at the top. It is such a little place that it seems more like a fairy scene than anything in reality.

---

[1] The Shelleys reached Lynmouth probably by June 25 or 26, and occupied a cottage which has since been pulled down and another built on the site. Their landlady was a Mrs. Hooper, whose niece retained a vivid recollection of Shelley and who pointed out to the late Miss Mathilde Blind the precise situation of the cottage.— Dowden's *Life of Shelley*, Vol. I, pp. 278–9.

[2] Godwin had told Shelley of this "nice cottage" at Chepstow, "near Tintern Abbey and Piecefield."

3

All the houses are built in the cottage style, and I suppose there are not more than 30 in all. We send to Barnstaple for everything, and our letters come but twice a week. It is 18 miles from [here], therefore we ought to be able to [paper torn—? manage] very well on a horse to get there. We have an immense precipice to descend into this valley, about 2 miles in length, which no carriage can come down. It seems as if nature had intended that this place should be so romantic, and shut out from all other intercourse with the neighbouring villages and towns. We still have our Irishman, Daniel [Hill or Healy], whom you may remember in Grafton Street. I am afraid we shall be obliged to part with him, as we do not find him that useful servant we expected he would have [been]. Percy has some thoughts of sending him to Dublin to see after his poems that are at the printers, but whether he will or not is impossible to say. We have not heard from Mr. Lawless now for some time. I suppose his present employment (to my idea not very laudable) fills up his time so much that he cannot think of his absent friends. I hope this is not the case as I should be sorry, knowing him to be an Irishman, if it were true. I think he is a man of very great talent and abilities; but I am afraid that Mr. Curran will never lend him a helping hand. I must now say adieu, my dear friend, and may you ever feel that happiness which springs from conscious integrity and goodness of heart. Percy and Eliza desire to be most kindly remembered, and believe me ever your truly sincere and affectionate friend,

HARRIET.

[Addressed]
MRS. NUGENT,
No. 101 *Grafton Street,*
Dublin, Ireland

CLXXXIa
TO WILLIAM GODWIN
London

Lymouth, Barnstaple,
July 5, 1812.

MY DEAR SIR,

I write to acknowledge the pleasure I anticipate in the perusal of some letters from you and yours, which have not yet reached us. The post comes to Lymouth but twice in the week; and some allowance is to be made for the casualties which attend an event by which we have been unexpectedly unsettled. We were all so much prepossessed in favour of Mr. Eaton's house,[1] that nothing but the invincible objection of scarcity of room would have induced

[1] Some of the names that appear in Shelley's correspondence at this time are confusing owing to their similarity. There were Eaton, the prosecuted bookseller, about whom Shelley addressed his letter to Lord Ellenborough, and Mr. Eton, the landlord of the Chepstow cottage; Mrs. Hooper at Nantgwillt, and Mrs. Hooper, Shelley's Lymouth landlady. Shelley had published through Stockdale in London, and had endeavoured to arrange with a Dublin Stockdale to print his poems.

us, even after seeing it, to resign the predetermination we had formed of taking it. We now reside in a small cottage, but the poverty and humbleness of the apartments is compensated for by their *number*, and we can invite our friends with a consciousness that there is *enclosed* space wherein they may sleep, which was not to be found at Mr. Eaton's. I will, in the absence of other topics, explain to you my reason for fixing upon this residence. I am, as you know, a minor, and as such, depend upon a limited income (£400 per annum) allowed by my relatives. Upon this income justice and humanity have many claims, and the necessary expenses of existing in conformity to some habitudes—which may be said to be interwoven with our being—dissipate the remainder. I might, it is true, raise money on my prospects, but the percentage is so enormous, that it is with extreme unwillingness, I should have recourse to a step, which I might *then* be induced to repeat, even to a ruinous frequency and extent. The involvement of my patrimony would interfere with schemes on which it is my fondest delight to speculate. I may truly therefore be classed *generically* with those minors who pant for twenty one, though I trust that the specific difference is very, very wide. The expenses incurred by the failure of our attempt in settling at Nantgwillt, have rendered it necessary for us to settle for a time in some cheap residence, in order to recover our pecuniary independence. I will still hope, that you and your inestimable family will before much time has elapsed, become inmates of our house. This house boasts not such accommodations as I should feel satisfied in offering you, but I will propose a plan which if it meets your approbation may prove an interlude to our meeting, and become an earnest that much time will not elapse before its occurrence. I have a friend[2]; but first I will make you in some measure acquainted with her. She is a woman with whom her excellent qualities made me acquainted. Though deriving her birth from a very humble source, she contracted, during youth a very deep and refined habit of thinking; her mind naturally inquisitive and penetrating overstepped the bounds of prejudice. She formed for herself an unbeaten path of life.

[2] Eliza Hitchener, who, when passing through London on her way to visit the Shelleys, supped and slept at Godwin's house on July 14.

5

By the patronage of a lady, whose liberality of mind is singular, this woman at the age of twenty was enabled to commence the conduct of a school. She concealed not the uncommon modes of thinking which she had adopted, and publickly instructed youth as a Deist and a Republican. When I first knew her she had not read "Political Justice," yet her life appeared to me in a great degree modelled upon its precepts. Such is the woman who is about to become an inmate of our family. She will pass through London, and I shall take the liberty of introducing to you, one whom I do not consider unworthy of the advantage. As soon as we recover our financial liberty we mean to come to London. Why may not Fanny[3] come to Lymouth with Miss Hitchener (such is her name) and return with us all to London in the autumn? I entreat you to look with a favorable eye upon this request, as indeed and indeed our hearts long for a personal intercourse with those to whom they are devoted; and I fear, from the tenor of Mrs. G[odwin]'s letter, that we must give up the hope of seeing *you*. This disappointed hope determines us to journey to London as *soon as we can*. This place is beautiful. It equals—Harriet says it exceeds—Nantgwillt. Mountains certainly of not less perpendicular elevation than 1,000 feet are broken abruptly into valleys of indescribable fertility and grandeur. The climate is so mild that myrtles of an immense size twine up our cottage, and roses blow in the open air in winter. In addition to these is the sea, which dashes against a rocky and caverned shore, presenting an ever changing view. All "shews of sky and earth, of sea and valley" are here. Adieu. Believe how devotedly and sincerely I must ever remain your's,

P. B. SHELLEY.

I write this letter by return of post, and send purposely to Barnstaple. I have *more* to say but will reserve it until I recieve the letters which are on the way.

[Addressed]
  To MR. WILLIAM GODWIN,
    Skinner Street,
      Ludgate Hill, London
(*Single Sheet*)

[3] Fanny Imlay, the daughter of Mary Wollstonecraft and Gilbert Imlay. She was therefore a kind of step-daughter to Godwin, by whose name she was known.

6

LETTERS

CLXXXII
TO WILLIAM GODWIN

Lymouth,
July 7, 1812.

My dear Sir,

The person whom I sent yesterday to the post-town has returned. He brought those letters from you and yours which have been forwarded from Cwm Elan to Chepstow.

It is a singular coincidence that in my last letter, I entered into details respecting my mode of life, and unfolded to you the reasons by which I was induced, on being disappointed in Mr. Eton's [*sic*] house, to seek an unexpensive retirement. I feel my heart throb exultingly when, as I read the misgivings of your mind concerning my rectitude,[1] I reflect that I have to a certain degree refuted them by anticipation. My letter dated [the] 5th, will prove to you that it is *not* to live in splendor, which I hate—*not* to accumulate indulgences (which I despise) that my present conduct was adopted. Most unworthy indeed should I be of that high destiny which he who is your friend and pupil, must share, if I was not myself *practically* a proselyte to that doctrine, by promulgating which with unremitting zeal and industry, I have become the object of hatred and suspicion.

Our *cottage*, for such not nominally but really it is, exceeds not in its accomodations the dwellings of the peasantry which surround it. Its beds are of the plainest, I may say, the coarsest material ; and from the single consideration that accomodations for personal convenience were glaringly defective did I refrain in my last letter from pressing the request, whose concession is nearest to my desires ; that *you* would come to this lovely solitude, and bring to a conclusion that state of acquaintance which stands between us and *perfect* intimacy. I was beginning a sentence in the middle of the second page of my letter, in which I should have pressed you to come *here*, when Harriet interrupted me, bade me consider that your health was delicate, that our rooms were complete *servants'* *rooms*. I finished the sentence as it stands. She added, that [we]

[1] See note to Letter No. CLXXXIV.

7

would hasten our journey to London, and that *you all* should live with us. It was the thought of the moment; I send it you without comment as it arose. See my defence. Yet, my esteemed and venerated friend, accept my thanks—consider yourself as yet more beloved by me, for the manner in which you have reproved my suppositionary errors; and ever may you, like the tenderest and wisest of parents, be on the watch to detect those traits of vice, which yet undiscovered, are nevertheless marked on the tablet of my character, so that I pursue undeviatingly the path which you first cleared through the wilderness of life.

I said, in my last letter, that there are certain habitudes in conformity to which it is almost necessary that persons who have contracted them, should exist. By this I do not mean that a splendid mansion, or an equipage, is in any degree essential to life; but that if I was employed at the loom, or the plough, and my wife in culinary business and housewifery we should in the present state of society, quickly become very different beings, and, I may add, less useful to our species. Nor, consistently with invincible ideas of delicacy, can two persons of opposite sexes, unconnected by certain ties, sleep in the same apartment. Probably, in a regenerated state of society, agriculture and manufacture would be compatible with the most powerful intellect and most polished manners; probably delicacy, as it relates to sexual distinction, would disappear. Yet now, a ploughboy can with difficulty acquire refinement of intellect; and promiscuous sexual intercourse under the present system of thinking, would inevitably lead to consequences the most injurious to the happiness of mankind. Mr. Eton's house had not sufficient bedrooms, *scarcely* sufficient for ourselves, and you and your family must sleep; for, my dear friend, believe me that I would not willingly take a house for any time, whither you could not come. Have I written desultorily? Is my explanation of *habitudes* incorrect, or indistinct? Pardon me, for I am anxious to lose no time in communicating my sentiments.

Harriet is writing to Fanny. If she is particular in her invitation of Fanny, it is not meant exclusively. There are a sufficient quantity of bedrooms, and if the humbleness of their quality is no objection, I need not say, come, thou venerated and excellent friend, and make us happy. Adieu.

Believe me, with the utmost sincerity and truth,

Ever your's,

P. B. SHELLEY.

[Addressed]
(*Single sheet*)
   MR. WILLIAM GODWIN,
      Skinner Street,
         Ludgate Hill,
            London

CLXXXIII
TO THOMAS HOOKHAM
Old Bond Street, London

Lymouth nr. Barnstaple
July 29, 1812.

SIR

I delayed to answer your very flattering letter until the Printer sent me complete copies of the little work, 25 of which I send you.[1] I beg you to accept of them that you may shew them to any friends who *are not informers*. I shall not persist in my intention of procuring a publisher. Possesing the knowledge I now posess, it would be unjust in me to attempt to draw upon any one the indignation of bigotry and despotism. I have changed, therefore, my former plan to that of gratuitous distribution. In case you could dispose of more than those which I now send, I beg that you will not hesitate a moment in informing me. I have several works, some unfinished, some yet only in contemplation. They are principally in the form of poems or essays. As soon as any one of them is

---

[1] A Letter/to/Lord Ellenborough,/occasioned by the Sentence which he passed on/Mr. D. I. Eaton,/as Publisher of/The Third Part of Paine's *Age of Reason.*/Deorum offensa, Diis curæ./It is contrary to the mild spirit of the Christian Religion, for no/sanction can be found under that dispensation which will warrant a/Government to impose disabilities and penalties upon any man, on/account of his religious opinions. [*Hear, Hear.*]/Marquis Wellesley's Speech. Globe, July 2./The pamphlet, which bears no name of the Printer, place or date, was printed at Barnstaple and was never published. For a reprint of the "Letter" see *Prose Works.*

9

completed I will send it to you, and shall take it as an additional favour if you can, consistently with safety, publish it.

I have received the parcel safe. I would thank you to send in addition "Miltons Prose Works," "Elements of Chemical Philosophy" by Sir H. Davy (to be published 1st of August), "Medical Extracts," "Hartley on Man," "Rights of Woman," by Mary Wollstonecraft (all in boards).

[The signatures, etc., are cut from the original.]

CLXXXIV
TO WILLIAM GODWIN
London

Lymouth,
July 29, 1812.

MY DEAR GODWIN,

I have never seen you[1] and yet I think I know you. I think I knew you even before I ever heard from you; whilst yet it was a question with me whether you were living or dead. It has appeared to me that there are lineaments in the soul as well as in the face; lineaments too, less equivocal and deceptive than those which result from mere physical organization. This opinion may

---

[1] In the undated letter of Godwin to Shelley printed by Hogg in his *Life of Shelley*, Vol. II, p. 141, he says: "Our acquaintance is a whimsical, and, to a certain degree, anomalous one. I have never seen your face,—

'Your face, my Thane, is a book, where men
May read strange matters,'

and till I have seen a man's face, I may say, in good sooth, I do not know him. Would that this whimsical and anomalous state of our acquaintance were brought to a conclusion!" He then continues that not being able to read Shelley's character in a legitimate way, he is reduced to collect traits of his character as they offer themselves in his correspondence. "I am half afraid that I have got a glimpse of a new one—that perhaps I may not altogether approve—this day." It appears that Shelley had addressed a letter to Mr. Eton, at Mrs. Godwin's, declining to take the cottage at Chepstow, of which Eton was the landlord, stating that "the insufficiency of house-room is a vital objection." Godwin, who opened and read this letter, was displeased with Shelley for his motives in rejecting the cottage. With "mild severity" the philosopher rebuked his young friend (with an allowance from his father of "only £200 a year") for his want of prudence and warned him against indulgence in luxuries.

be illusory, if I find it so it shall be retracted. You say three letters of yours have been unanswered. I waited to know whether those of mine contained any topics worthy of notice or discussion. I find they do not; therefore let us pass on.

To begin with Helvetius. I have read La Systeme de la Nature. I suspect this to be Helvetius's by your charges against it.[2] It is a book of uncommon powers, yet too obnoxious to accusations of sensuality and selfishness. Although, like you an irreconcileable enemy to the system of self love, both from a feeling of its deformity and a conviction of its falsehood, I can by no means conceive how the loftiest disinterestedness is incompatible with the strictest materialism. In fact, the doctrine which affirms that there is no such thing as matter, and that which affirms that all is matter, appear to me, perfectly indifferent in the question between benevolence and self love. I cannot see how they interfere with each other, or why the two doctrines of materialism and disinterestedness cannot be held in one mind, as independently of each other, as the two truths that a cricket ball is round, and a box square. Immateriality seems to me nothing but a simple denial of the presence of matter, of the presence of all the forms of being with which our senses are acquainted, and it surely is somewhat inconsistent to assign real existence to what is a mere negation of all that actual world to which our senses introduce us.

I have read Berkeley,[3] and the perusal of his arguments tended more than any thing to convince me that immaterialism, and other words of general usage deriving all their force from mere *predicates* in *non*, were invented by the pride of philosophers to conceal their ignorance, even from themselves. If I err in what I say, or if I differ from you (though in this point I think I do not) Reason stands arbiter between us. Reason (if I may be permitted to personify it) is as much your superior, as you are mine. An hour and a thousand years are equally incommensurate with eternity. With respect to Helvetius's opinion of the omnipotence of education, *there* I submit to your authority, because authority derived from

[2] The book was by Baron D'Holbach. See note, Vol. I, p. 332.
[3] Shelley read Berkeley at Keswick; Southey borrowed a copy belonging to Charles Lloyd (the friend of Lamb and Coleridge), and Shelley was especially struck with Lloyd's marginal notes. See Shelley's Letter to Leigh Hunt, September 27, 1819.

experience such as your's, is reason. I will own that the opinion of
Helvetius until very lately has been mine.

You know that in most points I agree with you. As I see you in
Political Justice, I agree with you. Your Enquirer is replete
with speculations in which I sympathize, yet the arguments there
in favour of classical learning, failed to remove all my doubts on
that point. I am not sufficiently vain and dogmatical to say that
now I have *no* doubts on the deleteriousness of classical education;
but it certainly is my opinion, nor has your last letter sufficed to
refute it, that the evils of acquiring Greek and Latin considerably
overbalance the benefits. But why, because I think so, should it
even be supposed necessary by you to warn me against fearing that
you feel displeasure. Assure yourself that the picture of you in the re-
tina of my intellect, is a standing proof to me that its original is
capable of extending to opinions the most unlimited toleration, and
that he will scan with disgust nothing but a defect of the heart.
Let Reason, then, be arbiter between us; yet sometimes I am
struck with dismay when I consider that, placed where you are,
high up on the craggy mountain of knowledge, you will scarcely
condescend to doubt (even sufficiently for the purposes of discussion) that opinion which you hold, although by that doubting you
might fit me for following your footsteps. Yet I will explain my
reasons for doubting the efficacy of classical learning as a means of
forwarding the interests of the human race.

In the first place, I do not perceive how one of the truths of
Political Justice rest[s] on the excellence of ancient literature.
That Latin and Greek have contributed to form your character it
were idle to dispute, but in how great a degree have they contributed? Are not the reasonings on which your system is founded
utterly distinct from and unconnected with the excellence of Greece
and Rome? Was not the government of republican Rome, and
most of those of Greece, as oppressive and arbitrary, as liberal of
encouragment to monopoly, as that of Great Britain is at present?
And what do we learn from their poets? As you have yourself acknowledged somewhere, "they are fit for nothing but the perpetua-
tion of the noxious race of heroes in the world." Lucretius forms,
perhaps, the single exception. Throughout the whole of their liter-

ature runs a vein of thought similar to that which you have so justly censured in Helvetius. Honor, and the opinion either of cotemporaries, or (more frequently) of posterity, is set so much above virtue as, according to the last words of Brutus, to make it nothing but an empty name. Their politics sprang from the same narrow and corrupted source; witness the interminable aggressions between each other of the states of Greece; and the thirst of conquest with which even republican Rome desolated the Earth. They are our masters in politics, because we are so immoral as to prefer self interest to virtue, and expediency to positive good. You say that words will neither debauch our understandings, nor distort our moral feelings. You say that the time of youth could not be better employed than in the acquisition of classical learning. But *words* are the very things that so eminently contribute to the growth and establishment of prejudice: the learning of *words* before the mind is capable of attaching correspondent ideas to them, is like possessing machinery with the use of which we are so unacquainted as to be in danger of misusing it. But words are merely signs of ideas. How many evils, and how great, spring from the annexing inadequate and improper ideas to words. The words honor, virtue, duty, goodness, are examples of this remark. Besides, we only want one distinct sign for one idea. Do you not think that there is much more danger of our wanting ideas for the signs of them already made, than our wanting these signs for inexpressible ideas. I should think that natural philosophy, medicine, astronomy, and, above all, History, would be sufficient employments for immaturity; employments which would completely fill up the era of tutelage, and render unnecessary all expedients for losing time well by gaining it safely.

Of the Latin language, as a grammar, I think highly. It is a key to the European languages, and we can hardly be said to know our own without first attaining a complete knowledge of it. Still, I cannot help considering it as an affair of minor importance, inasmuch as the science of things is superior to the science of words. Nor can I help considering the vindicators of ancient learning (I except you, not from *politeness*, but because you, unlike them, are willing to subject your opinions to Reason) as the vindicators of a literary despotism; as the tracers of a circle which is intended to shut out from real knowledge, and to which this fictitious knowledge is attached, all who do not breathe the air of prejudice, and who will not support the established systems of politics, Religion, and morals. I have as great a contempt for Cobbet as you can have, but it is because he is a dastard and a time server; he has no humanity, no refinement; but were he a classical scholar, would he have more? Did Greek and Roman literature refine the soul of Johnson, does it extend the [views of the] thousand narrow bigots educated in the very bosom of *classicality?* But

in publica commoda peccem
Si longo sermone morer tua tempora,

says Horace at the commencement of his longest letter.

Well, adieu. All join in kindest love to your amiable family, of whom I have forgotten to speak, but not to think; and I remain,

Very truly and affectionately yours,

P. B. SHELLEY.

[Addressed]
MR. W. GODWIN,
Skinner Street,
Ludgate Hill,
London

HARRIET SHELLEY TO CATHERINE NUGENT

Lynmouth,
August 4 [1812].

MY DEAR MRS. NUGENT,
        Your affectionate letter gave us very great pleasure. To hear from those we love when it is not in our power to see them constitutes one of the greatest joys in existence. You may suppose how we laughed at the idea of the tempter, tho' how such a horrible looking creature should gain admittance to the garden of Eden at once surprises me and turns the sanctity of the whole into a burlesque. I suppose the ingenious discoverer has very good reasons and arguments to support his cause, tho' we may doubt if we like; the idea is truly ridiculous and laughable and how do the people take this new mode of accounting for how all the sin in the world arose. Will they believe it as soon as they would the other? If they do I should be inclined to think their belief is a mere matter of form and not an involuntary act. If they go on in this way we shall next hear, I suppose, of its being a bear or lion or anything else. I thank you in Percy's name for your kind offer of service, tho' at the same time we cannot accept it. The case is this.

14

LETTERS

His printer refuses to go on with his poems until he is paid. Now such a demand is seldom made, as printers are never paid till the profits arising from the sale of the work come in, and Percy agreed with him to this effect, and as long as we staid in Dublin he wore the mask which is now taken off. However, I am in great hope that Mr. Lawless will get them from him. He is coming to London on business and then we shall see him. I wish to think well of him because he is your countryman, tho' there is too much the [man of the world] about him. Perhaps he is different out of the city. If not I shall still admire his talents, tho' I shall have no high opinion of him. What do you think of Cobbett? A man that can change his opinions so quickly I do not admire, and particularly when he could write of Sir F. Burdett in such an abusive and contradictory a way. It seems to me that Cobbett merely changes his sentiments as occasion requires as best suits his interests. I hope I am mistaken, tho' his behaviour looks very like it. Percy has sent you a defense of D. I. Eaton. It must not be published, but you [will] give us your opinion of it. What think you of Lord Stanhope?—divine being, how beautifully he speaks. We have sent him one as well as Sir F. Burdett. Did you see a clergyman enter into his defence? I do not remember his name, but it was a very wonderful thing to hear a clergyman write for universal toleration. He said his standing in the pillory was an honour to him. I think the publick mind is very much in favour of Mr. Eaton. It looks well, does it not? Our friend, Miss Hitchener, is come to us. She is very busy writing for the good of mankind. She is very dark in complexion, with a great quantity of long black hair. She talks a great deal. If you like great talkers she will suit you. She is taller than me or my sister, and as thin as it is possible to be. I hope you will see her some day. I should think that next summer you might take a peep at us. You may judge how much we all wish to see you. Your being an Irish woman must interest us in your happiness independently of our knowing the amiable qualities you possess. I have read Miss Owenson's "Missionary" and much do I admire the author. I am now reading her "Novice of St. Dominick." I regret not having known her when I was in Dublin. Her Patriotic Sketches have won my heart. She speaks so feelingly of your dear country, but I love her for that. Miss Hitchener has read your letter and loves you in good earnest. Her own expression. I know you would love her did you know her. Her age is 30. She looks like as if she was only 24 and her spirits are excellent. She laughs and talks and writes all day. She has seen the Godwins, and thinks Godwin different to what he seems, he lives so much from his family, only seeing them at stated hours. We do not like that, and he thinks himself such a very great man. He would not let one of his children come to us just because he had not seen our faces. Just as if writing to a person in which we express all our thoughts, was not a sufficient knowledge of them. I knew our friend [Miss Hitchener], whom we call Bessy, just as well when we corresponded as I do now. Such excuses sit not well upon so great a literary character as he is. I might have expected such an excuse from a woman of selfish and narrow mind, but not from Godwin. I must now finish. They all unite in love and affection to our dear little Irishwoman, and believe me more than ever your sincerely attached and affectionate friend,

H. S.

[Addressed]
Mrs. Nugent,
No. 101 *Grafton Street,*
Dublin, Ireland

LETTERS

CLXXXV
HARRIET SHELLEY TO CATHERINE NUGENT

Lynmouth,
August 11 [1812].

MY DEAR MRS. NUGENT,

    Your friend and our friend, *Bessy*, has been reading "Pieces of Irish History," and is so much enraged with the characters there mentioned that nothing will satisfy her desire of revenge but the printing and publishing of them to exhibit to the world those characters which are (shameful to say) held up as beings possessing every amiable quality, whilst their hearts are as bad as it is possible to be. They will be shown to the world in a new light, and it will remain to be seen if that world does not repay them as they so eminently deserve. Percy thinks of printing it by subscription. 500 subscribers at seven shillings each will amply repay the printing and publishing. Percy intends to print some proposals for printing Pieces of Irish History, saying that everyone whether Irish or English ought to read them. We depend upon you for many subscribers, as being upon the spot where so many of your exalted and brave countrymen suffered martyrdom. I should think there were very many would be glad to put their names to it. There must be many still smarting under the wounds they have seen their brave companions suffer, and all from this hated country of mine. Good God, were I an Irishman or woman how I should hate the English. It is wonderful how the poor Irish people can tolerate them. But I am writing to one who from her example shows them how they ought to tolerate this barbarous nation of ours. Thank God, we are not all alike, for I too can hate Lord Castlereagh as much as any Irishman. How does my heart's blood run cold at the idea of what he did in your unfortunate country. How is it that man is suffered to walk the streets in open daylight! Oh, if I were to meet him I really think I could fly at him and tear him to pieces! I have drawn a likeness of him and Percy says it is a very good one. You know I have no pretensions to drawing, but sometimes I take up the pen and sketch faces. I have not preserved the horrible countenance, but if I were to meet it I should it for him [*sic*]. I cannot bear Curran; what use is he to your country? Was he active at the time of the Union? No, if he had been, tho' his life had been the sacrifice, Ireland would have been saved. I have no patience with Curran. I shall convert Mr. *Lawless* I hope from his *idol*. It is too sickening to hear him talk of Curran as he does. We are going to the valley of Llangothlin. It is much nearer to Ireland than we are here or even at Nangwillt. If we are there next summer I hope we shall see you. Bessie wishes very much to see you. Your last letter won her heart instantly. Reading "Pieces of Irish History" has made her so low-spirited. She possesses too much feeling for her own happiness. I am in great hopes she will get the better of her low spirits. May I ask how are your spirits and your health? If they are but as good as I wish them to be it will make me very happy. You do not let your feelings get the better of your reason. If you do I am extremely sorry, as I shall know from that you are not so happy as you ought to be. They all unite in the kindest regards to the dear little Irishwoman, and believe me most sincerely your attached friend,

H. S.

[Written by Shelley]

    I shall print proposals for publishing by subscription, and if you could send us any names you would much benefit the *Cause*. We determine at any rate to publish the Irish History. It is a matter of doubt with me whether any bookseller will dare to put his name to it. This will be no obstacle.

LETTERS

TO SIR JAMES HENRY LAWRENCE
Knight of Malta

Lymouth, Barnstaple, Devon,
August 17, 1812.

SIR,

I feel peculiar satisfaction in seizing the opportunity which your politeness places in my power, of expressing to you personally (as I may say) a high acknowledgment of my sense of your talents and principles, which, before I conceived it possible that I should ever know you, I sincerely entertained. Your "Empire of the Nairs,"[1] which I read this Spring, succeeded in making me a perfect convert to its doctrines. I then retained no doubts of the evils of marriage,—Mrs. Wollstonecraft reasons too well for that; but I had been dull enough not to perceive the greatest argument against it, until developed in the "Nairs," viz., prostitution both *legal* and *illegal.*

I am a young man, not yet of age, and have now been married a year to a woman younger than myself. Love seems inclined to stay in the prison, and my only reason for putting him in chains, whilst convinced of the unholiness of the act, was, a knowledge that in the present state of society, if love is not thus villainously treated, she, who is most loved, will be treated worse by a misjudging world. In short, seduction, which term could have no meaning, in a rational society, has now a most tremendous one; the fictitious merit attached to chastity has made that a forerunner of the most terrible of ruins, which, in Malabar, would be a pledge of honour and homage. If there is any enormous and desolating crime, of which I should shudder to be accused, it is seduction.—I need not say how much I admire "*Love;*" and little as a British public seems to appreciate its merit, in never permitting it to emerge from a first edition, it is with satisfaction I find, that justice has conceded abroad what bigotry has denied at home.

[1] "The Empire of the Nairs; or, the Rights of Woman. An Utopian Romance, in twelve Books [and 4 vols.]. By James Lawrence, author of *The Bosom Friend, Love, an Allegory*, etc.," was published by Hookham in 1811. This romance, which deals with the Nair caste in Malabar, was originally written in German and published in 1800; it was afterwards re-written in French and finally in English.

I shall take the liberty of sending you any little publication I may give to the world. Mrs. S. joins with myself in hoping, if we come to London this winter, we may be favoured with the personal friendship of one whose writings we have learnt to esteem.

Yours very truly,

PERCY BYSSHE SHELLEY.

CLXXXVII
TO THOMAS HOOKHAM
Old Bond Street

Lymouth Barnstaple
August 18, 1810 [sic].

DEAR SIR

Your parcel arrived last night for which I am much obliged. Before I advert to any other topic I will explain the contents of mine in which this is enclosed. In the first place I send you 50 copies of the "Letter."[1] I send you a copy of a work which I have procured from America, and which I am exceedingly anxious should be published. It developes, as you will perceive by the most superficial reading, the actual state of republicanized Ireland, and appears to me above all things calculated to remove the prejudices which have too long been cherished of that oppressed country, to strike the oppressors with dismay. I enclose also two pamphlets[2] which I printed and distributed whilst in Ireland some months ago (no bookseller daring to publish them). They were on that account attended with only partial success, and I request your opinion as to the probable result of publishing them with the annexed "suggestions"[3] in one pamphlet, with an explanatory preface, in *London*. They would find their way to Dublin. You confer on me an obligation, and involve a high compliment by your advice. I shall if possible prepare a vol. of essays, moral

---

[1] To Lord Ellenborough.
[2] *An Address to the Irish People,* and *Proposals for an Association of those Philanthropists,* etc.
[3] The unpublished "Suggestion" to which Shelley refers in Letter No. CLIX, Vol I, p. 288.

18

and *religious* by November; but, all my MSS. now being in Dublin, and from peculiar circumstances not immediately obtainable, I do not know whether I can. I enclose also by way of specimen all that I have written of a little poem[4] begun since my arrival in England. I conceive I have matter enough for 6 more cantos. You will perceive that I have not attempted to temper my constitutional enthusiasm in that Poem. Indeed, a Poem is safe: the iron-souled Attorney general would scarcely dare to attack

"genus irritabile vatum."

The Past, the Present, and the Future are the grand and comprehensive topics of this Poem. I have not yet half exhausted the second of them.

I shall take the liberty of retaining the two poems[5] which you have sent me—Mr. Peacock's—and only regret that my powers are so circumscribed as to prevent me from becoming extensively useful to *your friend*. The poems abound with a genius, an information, the power and extent of which I admire, in proportion as I lament the object of their application. Mr. Peacock concieves that commerce is prosperity; that the glory of the British Flag, is the happiness of the British people; that George III. so far from having been a warrior and a Tyrant, has been a Patriot. To me it appears otherwise; and I have rigidly accustomed myself, not to be seduced by the loveliest eloquence or the sweetest strains to regard with intellectual toleration [that] which ought not to be tolerated by those who love Liberty, Truth, and Virtue. I mean not to say that Mr. Peacock does not love them; but I mean to say that he regards

---

[4] Which subsequently developed into *Queen Mab;*/a Philosophical Poem:/with notes./ By/Percy Bysshe Shelley./*Ecrasez l'infame:*/*Correspondence de Voltaire,*/quotations from "Lucretius," and "Archimedes"/London:/Printed by P. B. Shelley,/23 Chapel Street, Grosvenor Square,/1813. This poem was finished by February, 1813, and issued privately. Shelley cut out the title-page, dedication (to Harriet), and the imprint at the end of the volume, of many of the copies circulated by him.

[5] Apparently the following volumes, "*The Genius of the Thames, Palmyra, and other Poems.* By T. L. Peacock. The Second Edition. London. Published by T. Hookham, junior, and E. T. Hookham, Old Bond Street. Gale & Curtis, Paternoster Row, and Ballantyne & Co., Edinburgh. 1812," and "*The Philosophy of Melancholy,* a poem in Four Parts, with a Mythological Ode. By T. L. Peacock, London. Printed by William Bulmer & Co., Shakespeare Press, for T. Hookham, junior, and E. T. Hookham, Old Bond Street, Gale & Curtis, Paternoster Row; and John Ballantyne & Company, Edinburgh, 1812." The first part of *The Genius of the Thames,* and *Palmyra* were originally published respectively in 1810 and 1806.

those means [as] instrumental to their progress, which I regard [as] instrumental to their destruction. See *Genius of the Thames*, p. 24, 26, 28, 76, 98. At the same time I am free to say that the Poem appears to be far beyond mediocrity in genius and versification, and the conclusion of "Palmyra" the finest piece of poetry I ever read. I have not had time to read the Philosophy of Melancholy, and of course am only half acquainted with that genius and those powers whose application I should consider myself rash and impertinent in critisizing, did I not concieve that frankness and justice demand it.

I should esteem it as a favor if you would present the enclosed letter to the Chevalier Lawrence. I have read his Empire of the Nairs,[6] nay, have it. Perfectly and decidedly do I subscribe to the truth of the principles which it is designed to establish.

I hope you will excuse, nay, and doubt not but you will, the frankness I have used. Characters of any liberality are so wondrous rare that the sooner they know each other, and the fuller and more complete that knowledge is, the better.

Dear Sir,
Permit me to remain
Yours very truly
PERCY B. SHELLEY.

I am about translating an old 'French' work, professedly by a *M. Mirabaud*—not the famous one "La Système de la Nature." Do you know any thing of it?

[Addressed]
   MR. HOOKHAM, Jun.
      &c. &c.

---

[6] See note to Letter No. CLXXXVI.

On August 19, the day after this letter was written, Daniel Healey, Shelley's Irish servant whom he had brought with him from Dublin, was arrested at Barnstaple while distributing and posting up copies of Shelley's *Declaration of Rights*. On being brought before the Mayor he gave his name as Hill, and stated that a gentleman had given him five shillings to post up and distribute the papers. The Mayor, not satisfied with Healey's account of how he became possessed of the papers, caused inquiries to be made about the man's master, and learnt that Shelley was viewed with suspicion at Lynton and Lynmouth. The man was convicted in a fine of £200, and in lieu of payment, to go to jail for six months. Shelley, unable to pay this fine, arranged that for the payment of fifteen shillings a week his man should be granted certain immunities and privileges.—Professor Dowden's *Life of Shelley*, Vol. I, p. 297.

LETTERS

TO MRS. ELIZABETH SHELLEY

St. James's Coffee House,
November 7 [1812].

My dear Mother,

I write to request you, if you can, to manage to send me the Galvanic Machine and Solar Microscope[1] which I left at Field Place. The latter instrument being essential to a branch of philosophy which I am now pursuing.

I take this opportunity of sending my love to yourself and my sisters, of assuring you that any thing I can do for you, in town, I will, and that having been rendered by a most disinterested friend to a certain degree independent, my means of serving you in any little matter are by no means so limited as you may suppose.

However you may have felt piqued at the deception which I practised on my marriage, I know you will be glad to hear that I am *now* one of the happiest of men, and that nothing but the idea of this *temporary* estrangement from my family prevents me from becoming the happiest.

My dear Mother,
Very sincerely your Affectionate Son,

Percy B. Shelley.

You can send the things by the coach immediately, as we leave Town, in a day or two for our *Cottage* in the Mountains of Carnarvonshire.

[Addressed]
  Mrs. Shelley,
    Field Place,
    Horsham,
    Sussex

---

[1] See note to Shelley's letter to Mary, October 27, 1814.

LETTERS

CLXXXIX
TO JOHN WILLIAMS
Tremadoc

St. James Coffee House, [*London,*[1]]
November 7, 1812.

MY DEAR WILLIAMS,

I received your long and kind letter, and although press of business does not permit me to answer to its length, I do hope that it may not be considered deficient in kindness. I need not assure you of the pleasure which I receive from the intelligence of the safety and success of the embankment, of the honorable perseverance of the men, or your own good hopes and spirits. You know my feelings on all these things; I have too often expressed my unabated and unconquerable ardour for the success of you and your enterprizes to need repetition now.

On Thursday [November 12] next we set out for Tanyrallt and

---

[1] Corrected from a MS. "copy" of the letter in the Bodleian Library. Shelley, probably aware that he was being watched at Lynmouth, had hastily left that place, apparently towards the end of August, and crossing the Bristol Channel at length settled near Tremadoc, in a house called Tan-yr-allt. This house had been built by William Alexander Madocks (1774–1824), M.P. for Boston, who let it to Shelley at a considerable rent, but on easy terms. Mr. Madocks had reclaimed from the sea a large tract of marsh land in Carnarvonshire, upon which he had built a new town, named Tremadoc, after its enterprising founder. At the time of Shelley's visit to this town the embankment which was being built to protect it was in danger of destruction by the sea. Shelley at once became keenly interested in the fate of the embankment, and not only proceeded to canvass the district for subscriptions, heading the list with a sum of £100, but he went up to London with his wife, Eliza Westbrook and Miss Hitchener, to forward his object. Shelley's object in seeing the Duke of Norfolk was to solicit a subscription for the Tremadoc embankment. Hogg says that he was informed that the Duke politely answered that he had no funds at his immediate disposal.— *Life of Shelley,* Vol. II, p. 173. During this visit of Shelley to London, he was reconciled to his friend Hogg, on whom he called unexpectedly, at his chambers in the Temple, one evening at ten o'clock.

Some three weeks after the Shelleys had left Lynmouth, William Godwin arrived at that place with the object of paying a visit to his young friend. In a letter from Lynmouth to his wife, dated September 19, 1812, Godwin tells her that "The Shelleys are gone! have been gone these three weeks. . . . I have been to the house where Shelley lodged, and I bring good news. I saw the woman of the house [Mrs. Hooper] and I was delighted with her. She is a good creature, and quite loved the Shelleys. They lived here nine weeks and three days. They went away in a great hurry, in debt to her and two more. They gave her a draft upon the Honourable Mr. Lawless, brother to Lord Cloncurry, and they borrowed of her twenty-nine shillings, besides £3 that she got for them from a neighbour, all of which they faithfully returned when they got to Ilfracombe, the people not choosing to change a bank note which had been cut in half for safety in sending it by the post. But the best news is that the woman says they will be in London in a fortnight. This quite comforts my heart."—*Shelley Memorials,* pp. 41–2.

expect to be with you on the ensuing Monday [November 16]. The Duke of Norfolk has just returned to London. I shall call upon him this morning, and shall spare no pains in engaging his interests or perhaps his better feelings in ours and our country's cause.

I see no hope of effecting on my part any grand or decisive scheme until the expiration of my minority. In Sussex I meet with no encouragement. They are a parcel of cold, selfish, and calculating animals, who seem to have no other aim or business, on earth, but to eat, drink, and sleep; but in the mean while my fervid hopes, my ardent desires, my unremitting personal exertions (so far as my health will allow), are all engaged in that cause, which I will desert *but with my life.* Can you hire a trustworthy undermaid-servant, as we shall require three in all? Believe me, I feel the polite attention of the Nanney family very deeply.

Harriet is now writing to Mrs N to express her sense of her kindness. I do think that your country owes infinitely more than I can express to the disinterestedness, activity and patriotism of that admirable lady.

Harriet and the ladies unite with me in sincerest best wishes, and believe me,

> Your true friend,
>
> PERCY BYSSHE SHELLEY.

P.S. I am much better than when you saw me last. If I can find time today I shall write to the Dr.[2] Mr. Bedwell will settle the £70 affair.

[Addressed]
JOHN WILLIAMS, ESQ.,
Embankment Office,
Tre Madoc,
Carnarvonshire

---

[2] "The Dr." may have been William Roberts, a surgeon of Carnarvon, who bailed out Shelley when he was arrested at Carnarvon for a sum of money which he owed. Shelley repaid the money for which he was arrested, but he did not repay another sum which Roberts lent him. See *Shelley in England,* pp. 633-35.

LETTERS

HARRIET SHELLEY TO CATHERINE NUGENT

Lewis's Hotel, St. James's Street, London,
[Undated. ? 1812.]

MY DEAR MRS. NUGENT,

You will smile at my address, wondering how and where we have been during the long interval which has taken place since the receipt of your last letter. I believe I mentioned that we were going to the Vale of Langothlin there to remain at least for the winter season; but I know not how it is that whenever we fix upon any particular place of residence something comes to take us to another. Instead of going to Langothlin we went to a New town which is called Tremadoc. It is built upon [land] that has been saved from the sea by a Mr. Madock, M.P. for Boston. The character of this man is such as to call forth our warmest admiration and esteem. He is what we call a true *patriot* in every sense of the word. He loves his country dearly, and always stands up for the interests and welfare of the poor. He is building an embankment which does honour to him and is an ornament to his country; but unfortunately possessing only a small fortune, when compared with the immense sums that others possess, he has not sufficient to finish the undertaking which has cost him 12 years' hard labour. We came up to London in the hopes of raising a subscription that would finish it; but as yet nothing is done. Bysshe's being a minor lays us under many unpleasant affairs, and makes us obliged to depend upon in a great measure the will of others, in the manner of raising money, and without which nothing is to be done. We have seen the Godwins.[1] Need I tell you that I love them all? You have read his works, therefore you know how you feel towards the author. His manners are so soft and pleasing that I defy even an enemy to be displeased with him. We have the pleasure of seeing him daily, and upon his account we determine to settle near London. For long journeys do not agree with him, having never been in the habit of travelling when a young man. There is one of the daughters [Fanny Imlay] of that dear Mary Wolstoncroft [*sic*] living with him. She is 19 years of age, very plain, but very sensible. The beauty of her mind fully overbalances the plainness of her countenance. There is another daughter of hers, who is now in Scotland. She is very much like her mother, whose picture hangs up in his study. She must have been a most lovely woman. Her countenance speaks her a woman who would dare to think and act for herself. I wish you could share the pleasure we enjoy in his company. He is quite a family man. He has one son by his present wife, a little boy of nine years old. He is extremely clever, and will, I have no doubt, follow the same enlightened path that Godwin has before him. Godwin is particularly fond of Curran and I am to be introduced to Miss Curran on Sunday. How comes he [(paper torn)] in England, can you solve this [problem]? You know that Mrs. Godwin keeps a [bookseller's] shop. She conducts the whole herself. [I am] in great hopes she will succeed. They are sometimes very much pressed for enough ready money. They require such an immense capital; but taking everything as it goes, I think they will succeed. The many trials that Mrs. Godwin has had to encounter makes me very much inclined to believe her a woman of great fortitude and unyielding temper of mind. There is a very great sweetness marked in her countenance. In many instances she has shown herself a woman of very great magnanimity and independence of character. Oh, if you could see them all to-morrow. I am going to stay all day with them. G. is very much taken with Percy. He seems to delight so much in his society. He has given up everything for the sake of our society. It gives me so much pleasure to sit and look at him. Have you ever seen a bust of Socrates, for his head is very much like that? Percy, Bessey and Eliza desire to be remembered most affectionately to you. Percy says he wishes you to go to Stockdale's, and get all his manuscript poems and other pieces. I am afraid you will be obliged to use a little manœuvre to get them. In

[1] Mary Godwin had been in Scotland on a visit to her friends the Baxters since June, 1812. She returned home, however, by November 10, and on the following day the Shelleys dined at the Godwins, when it is possible Shelley may have first seen his future wife.

24

the first place, you can say you wish to look at them, and then you may be able to steal them away from him. I leave it all to you, knowing you will do your best in the way to obtain them, and believe me ever most sincerely your attached friend,

H. SHELLEY.

P.S.—If I have said anything wrong pray forgive me.

[Addressed]
MRS. NUGENT,
No. 101 *Grafton Street,*
Dublin, Ireland

HARRIET SHELLEY TO CATHERINE NUGENT

Stratford-upon-Avon,
November 14 [1812].

MY DEAR MRS. NUGENT,
My last letter to you was from London, which place I left on Friday the 13th, and am now in my way to Tanyrallt, our beautiful Welsh cottage. The reason of your silence I am at a loss to account for, unless your answer has not been delivered to me, a circumstance not at all impossible, considering the hotel we lodged at. Do not think from this that we were backward in our enquiries every day respecting letters. They are and always will be the first objects of our solicitude, when coming from so dear a friend as yourself. The lady I have so often mentioned to you, of the name of Hitchener, has to our very great happiness left us. We were entirely deceived in her character as to her republicanism, and in short everything else which she pretended to be. We were not long in finding out our great disappointment in her. As to any noble disinterested views, it is utterly impossible for a selfish character to feel them. She built all her hopes on being able to separate me from my dearly loved Percy, and had the artfulness to say that Percy was really in love with her, and was only his being married that could keep her within bounds now. Percy had seen her once before his marriage. He thought her sensible but nothing more. She wrote continually, and at last I wrote to her, and was very much charmed with her letters. We thought it a thousand pities that such a mind as hers appeared to be should be left in a place like that she inhabited. We therefore were very urgent for her to come and live with us; which was no sooner done than we found out our mistake. It was a long time ere we could possibly get her away, till at last Percy said he would give her £100 per annum. And now, thank God, she has left us never more to return. We are much happier now than all the time she was with us. Have you been able to get the poems from Stockdale? If not it cannot be helped, but do pray write to us, for we are quite uneasy at not hearing from you for so long a time. Direct your letters to me at Tanyrallt, near the town of Tremadoc (in Carnarvonshire, North Wales). It is 260 miles from London, but the loveliest place I have seen many a day. We are not very far from Ireland. If you could so manage it as to come to us in the Spring, you know not the happiness you would confer upon our little circle, which is now just as you beheld it in your own native air. I have got the Irish Melodies. which I intend to study. If you know of any good old Irish song I should esteem it a favor to hear of it. I must now say adieu, and believe me truly your affectionate friend,

H. S.

Percy and Eliza desire not to be forgotten.

[Addressed]
MRS. NUGENT,
No. 101 *Grafton Street,*
Dublin, Ireland

LETTERS

London,
December [? *November*] 19, 1812.

DEAR MRS. HOOPER,

I send you £20, out of the debt of £30 that I owe you. The remainder I will send as soon as I can.

Your well-wisher,

P. B. SHELLEY.

CXCI
TO THOMAS JEFFERSON HOGG

Tanyrallt [*Tremadoc*],
Dec. 3, 1812.

MY DEAR FRIEND,

Your letter begins with the Duke of Norfolk.[1] I stared, when I saw his name; from the very moment I parted from you to the moment of the receipt of your letter, I had thought no more of the Duke of Norfolk than of the man in the moon. I will this instant sit down, and do penance for my involuntary crime by writing a long and wheedling letter to his Grace, and you shall be duly informed of the success of the experiment. I have no hopes, however, of bending my father, but by the mere force of gross interest, and therefore suppose it equally impossible, that he should come to terms before I am of age, as that he should hold out at the expiration of my minority. Be it as it may, I will give him a fair chance, I will put on my most good-humoured and conciliatory

---

[1] Shelley was apparently very short of money, and had perhaps applied for a loan to Hogg, who suggested that he should write to the Duke. In an unpublished letter to John Williams at Ynys Towyn, dated December 4, 1812, Shelley says: ". . . not having a sixpence of ready money, I am placed in a most awkward situation by this mistake."

countenance, which Heaven knows, will in this case have something of the Grimgriffinhoff in it after all. When I see him, though I shall say the civilest things imaginable, yet I shall not look as if I liked him, because I do not like him.

You think that, because your reasonings on the subject of moral and political science have led you wide of me, you are regarded by me with less complacency; but good intention is the essence of merit, and any qualification so involuntary as belief, or opinion, is surely a defective standard by which to measure out esteem. It is only when conviction is influenced by debasing and unworthy motives, that it becomes in any degree criminal.

Of such motives I do not accuse you, and you appear tainted with some portion of that illiberality, of which you indirectly accuse me, by the very spirit of suspicion, which produces that accusation.

You misinterpret my feelings on the state of the moral world, when you suppose that the bigotry of commonplace republicanism, or the violence of faction, enters into them at all.

I certainly am a very resolved republican (if the word applies), and a determined sceptic; but although I think their reasonings very defective, I am clearly aware that the noblest feelings might conduct some few reflecting minds to Aristocracy and Episcopacy. Hume certainly was an aristocrat, and Locke was a zealous Christian.

The Brown Demon,[2] as we call our late tormentor and schoolmistress, must receive her stipend. I pay it with a heavy heart and an unwilling hand; but it must be so. She was deprived by our misjudging haste of a situation, where she was going on smoothly: and now she says that her reputation is gone, her health ruined, her peace of mind destroyed by my barbarity; a complete victim to all the woes mental and bodily, that heroine ever suffered! This is not all fact; but certainly she is embarrassed and poor, and we being in some degree the cause, we ought to obviate it. She is an artful, superficial, ugly, hermaphroditical beast of a woman, and my astonishment at my fatuity, inconsistency, and bad taste was

[2] Miss Elizabeth Hitchener, who seems, from an entry in Godwin's diary, to have left the Shelleys on or before November 8.

27

never so great, as after living four months with her as an inmate. What would Hell be, were such a woman in Heaven?

The society in Wales is very stupid. They are all aristocrats and saints: but that, I tell you, I do not mind in the least: the unpleasant part of the business is, that they hunt people to death, who are not so likewise.

Miss Westbrook is perfectly well. Harriet unites with me in wishing you all possible good, and I am your very sincere friend,

PERCY B. SHELLEY.

Write soon, for your letters amuse us ALL.

CXCII
TO THOMAS HOOKHAM
Old Bond Street

Tanyrallt,
December 3, 1812.

MY DEAR SIR,

The parcel is not yet arrived. I own I am rather anxious concerning it, as the irregularity of the coaches to this solitude among mountains frequently causes mistakes.

I have read Mr. Peacock's verses. Independently of their poetical merit, they are accurately descriptive, of the exquisite souls by whom I am encompassed. Bigotry is so universally pervading that the best are deeply tainted; I was speaking of Mr. Peacock to a Lady[1] who knew him during his residence in Wales. In many respects she is a woman of considerable merit; and except in religious matters a model of toleration. "Ah!" said she "there Mr. Peacock lived in a cottage near Tan y bwlch, associating with no one, and hiding his head like a murderer"; "but" she added, altering her voice to a tone of appropriate gravity, "he was *worse than that*, he was an *Atheist*." I exclaimed much against the in-

---

[1] Probably the lady was Mrs. Madocks, the wife of Shelley's landlord. Mr. Madocks was absent from Tremadoc during the period of Shelley's stay at Tanyrallt.

28

tolerance of her remark, without producing the slightest effect. She knows very well that I am an infidel and a democrat, but perhaps *she does not do me justice.* There is more philosophy in one square inch of your counter than in the whole of Cambria; it is the last stronghold of the most vulgar and commonplace prejudices of aristocracy. Lawyers of unexampled villainy rule and grind the poor whilst they cheat the rich; the peasants are mere serfs and are fed and lodged worse than pigs, the gentry have all the ferocity and despotism of the ancient barons without their dignity and chivalric disdain of shame or danger. The poor are as abject as Samoyads, the rich as tyrannic as Bashaws.

Make my best Compts to Mr. Peacock. If he extends not the curse he has pronounced on Merion to Carnarvon, we should be always happy to see him.

When do you concieve it probable that you will be able to gratify us with a visit. Assure yourself that the sooner you come the more [. . .]²

When does God save [. . .] I am anxious for th[. . .] There is a new w[. . .] at *Daniel Isaac* [Eaton] to secure for me [. . .] parcel.

I conclude as Ve[. . .]
       F.C. [. . .]
[Part of Postscript] The Ladies unite in [. . .]

CXCIII
TO JOHN EVANS
Carnarvon

Tanyrallt, Tremadoc,
3 *Dec.,* 1812.

Your name is subscribed to the amount of £50 towards the Embankment . . . and tho' a stranger, I assume the liberty of reminding you of the propriety of its immediate payment.

You came forward with this support, impelled, I doubt not, by the most elevated and generous feeling for the public good, the

The letter is torn and the words within the square brackets are missing.

backwardness of subscribers in general I must own has considerably surprised me. . . . That you share not the latter disgrace
everyone will believe when your money is paid.

CXCIV
TO JOHN EVANS
Carnarvon

Tanyrallt,
Friday Ev. [*?Dec.,* 1812].

In reply to a message which I sent you by Mr. John Williams, you asserted that you had never received my letter.
To obviate the repetition of so singular an occurrence I sent this
by a personal messenger.
The substance of my former letter was to remind you, by right
of being a fellow subscriber, of your debt to the Tremadoc Embankment, which, being a debt of honor, ought to be of all others
the most imperious and to press the necessity of its immediate
payment, to lament also the apathy and backwardness of defaulters
in such a cause.

CXCV
TO FANNY IMLAY

Ynys-y-Maen-y Mawr,
December 10, 1812.

Dear Fanny,
So you do not know whether it is *proper* to write to me. Now,
one of the most conspicuous considerations that arise from such a
topic is—who and what am I? I am one of those formidable and
long clawed animals called a *man*, and it is not until I have assured
you that I am one of the most inoffensive of my species, that I live
on vegetable food, and never bit since I was born, that I venture

to intrude myself on your attention. But to be serious. I shall feel much satisfaction in replying, with as much explicitness as my nature is capable of, to any questions you may put to me. I know that I have in some degree forfeited a direct claim to your confidence and credit, and that of your inestimable circle; but if you will believe me as much as you can, I will be as sincere as I can. I certainly am convinced that, with the exception of one or two isolated instances, I am so far from being an insincere man that my plainness has occasionally given offence, and caused some to accuse me of being defective in that urbanity and toleration which is supposed to be due to society. Allow me, in the absence of the topics which are eventually to be discussed between us, to assume the privilegde [*sic*] which you have claimed, and ask a question. How, is Harriet a *fine lady?* You indirectly accuse her in your letter of this offence—to me the most unpardonable of all. The ease and simplicity of her habits, the unassuming plainness of her address, the uncalculated connexion of her thought and speech, have ever formed in my eyes her greatest charms; and none of these are compatible with fashionable life, or the attempted assumptions of its vulgar and noisy eclat. You have a prejudice to contend with in making me a convert to this last opinion of yours, which, so long as I have a living and daily witness of its futility before me, I fear will be insurmountable. The second accusation (the abruptness of our departure) has more foundation, though in its spirit it is not less false or futile than the first. It must, indeed, I confess it, have appeared insensible and unfeeling, it must have appeared an ill return for all the kind greetings we had recieved at your house, to leave it in haste and coldness, to pass over the enlightened and zealous benevolence of Godwin, ever inventive for good, and never deterred or discouraged in schemes for rectifying our perplexed affairs—to bid not one adieu to one of you. But had you been placed in a situation where you might justly have balanced all our embarrassments, qualms and fluctuations; had seen the opposite motives combating in our minds for mastery, had felt some tithe of the pain with which at the length we submitted to a galling yet unappealable necessity, you would have sympathized rather than condemned, have pitied rather than criminated, us unheard. Say the truth; did not a sense of the in-

31

justice of our supposed unkindness add some point to the sarcasms which we found occasionally in your last letter; and some strength [to] the sus[picion] of our inconstancy that dictated some of its [—]?

If all my laughs were no[t] dreadful, Sardonic grins, disgraceful to the most hideous of Cheshire cats, I should certainly laugh at two things in your last letter. The one is, "not knowing whether it is *proper* to write to me," lest—God knows what might happen; and the other is, comparing our movement to that of a modern novel. Now a novel (modern or antient) never moves but as the reader moves, and I, being a reader, if I take up one of these simi-litudes of our progress, never can get beyond the third line in the second page; therefore you ought rather to have compared a novel to a snail, than to us.

Now, my dear Fanny, do not be angry at either my laughs, my critisisms, or my queries. They proceed from levity, my proper views of things and my desire of setting them to you in what I consider a right light.

Your questions shall be answered with precision, and the [?] of hope that in my *quality* as a man be not too tremendous, I shall acquire from the result an interesting and valuable correspondent.

With much esteem, Your true friend,

P. B. SHELLEY.

[Addressed]
Miss FANNY GODWIN,[1]
Skinner Street,
Ludgate Hill,
London

---

[1] See note to Letter CLXXXI, Vol. II, p. 6.

LETTERS

Tanyralt,
December 17, 1812.

MY DEAR SIR,

I do not know whether I informed you that our last parcel from your house has arrived: the Translation of the Georgeics you sent is not precisely *in my way;* but I shall keep it: any works except those absolutely cosmopolitical or anti-Christian I shall not want until I write for.

You will receive the "Biblical Extracts "[1] in a day or two by the twopenny post. I confide them to the care of a person going to London. Would not Daniel I. Eaton publish them? Could the question be asked him in any manner?

I am also preparing a Volume of Minor Poems. Respecting whose publication I shall request your judgment, both as publisher and friend. A very obvious question would be.—Will they sell or not?

Subjoined is a list of books which I wish you to send me very soon. I am determined to apply myself to a study that is hateful and disgusting to my very soul, but which is above all studies, necessary for him who would be listened to as a mender of anti-quated abuses. I mean that record of crimes and miseries—History. You see that the metaphysical works to which my heart hankers are not numerous in this list. One thing will you take care of for me—that those standard and reputable works on History etc. be of the cheapest possible editions? With respect to metaphysical works I am less scrupulous ['on this point' deleted].

Spinosa you may or you may not be able to obtain. Kant is translated into Latin by some Englishman; I would prefer that the Greek Classics should have Latin or English versions printed oppo-site. If not to be obtained thus, they must be sent otherwise. Mrs. Shelley is attacking *Latin* with considerable resolution, and can

---

[1] Evidently the Manuscript of this work. There is another reference to the *Biblical Ex-tracts* in Harriet Shelley's letter to Hookham of January 31, which implies that Shelley expected Hookham to print them. Daniel I. Eaton was the publisher whom Shelley de-fended in his *Letter to Lord Ellenborough.*

already read many Odes in Horace. She unites with her sister and myself in best wishes to yourself and brother.

Your very sincere friend,

P. B. SHELLEY.

*Kant.

Spinosa.

Gibbons Decline & Fall of the Rom. Emp. (Cheapest poss. Edit.)

*Hume's Hist of England (Cheapest poss. Edit.)

Humes Essays

Darwins Zoonomia.

Vertot (French) Histoire de la Rome.

Gillie's History of Greece

Herodotus
Thucidydes
Zenophon with Latin or English Translations subjoined
*Plutarch

Adolphus's continuation of the History of England (Cheapest poss. Edit.)

Moor's Indian Pantheon.[2]

Rumford on Stoves.

Spencers Works Fairy Queen &c. (Cheapest poss. Edit.)

Southey's History of the Brazil

Do you know anything of the famous French Encyclopedie composed by Voltare, D'Alembert etc.? It is a Book I should much wish to have. Is it to be obtained? Could you obtain it?

The parcel will come safe if directed as usual. To these (which will take some stiff reading) you may add any thing new that you conceive of sufficient worth.—You will receve [sic] a parcel directed to us which you would much oblige us by enclosing with the books.

There is a work by a French Physician Cabanis, that I wish you also to send.

[Addressed]
MR. T. T. HOOKHAM, Junr.,
 Bookseller,
  Old Bond Street,
   London

[2] This book is quoted by Southey in his notes to *The Curse of Kehama*. All the books in the List except those marked with an asterisk, have been scored through apparently to denote that they have been supplied.

LETTERS

[*Tanyrallt,*
? December 17, 1812].

MY DEAR SIR,
I write hastily again today because I hear from Ireland of my MSS. You can include it in the box of books.
I wish you to add to them
Marcus Antoninus.
Seneca's Works.
Plato (with a translation)
Nicholson's Enclopedia [*sic*] (Boards)

CXCVIII
TO CLIO RICKMAN
London

Tanyrallt, Tremadoc, Carnarvonshire, North Wales
December 24, 1812.

SIR,
In a letter which I received from you on a different subject, you expressed your willingness to receive my orders.—I am now in want of some books, a list of which I enclose, and I prefer employing a countryman,[1] and a man of a liberal and enlightened mind, to a stranger.—I should wish for such editions of the classics I have mentioned as have translations subjoined; or, if such are not obtainable, translations separate.—I prefer them in the cheapest form.
Sir, I remain,
Your very ob[edien]t s[ervant],
PERCY BYSSHE SHELLEY.

P.S.—If the box which contains the books is sent to Mr. Bedwell,

[1] This fragment of nine lines only undated and without address, in the Bodleian Library, was doubtless written to Hookham and on the same date as the preceding letter.
[1] Rickman, like Shelley, was a Sussex man.

35

6 Tooley St., Canterbury Square, Southwark, it will reach me safely (directed as above).

Turn over.

I would prefer the books in boards.

[Addressed]
> MR. CLIO RICKMAN,
>> *Bookseller,*
>>> *No. 7 Upper Marylebone St.,*
>>> *London*

Postmark, 28. 12. 1812. [The seal bears the word] Liberty.

Original and translation,
 if possible, united—
Æschylus
Epicurus
Celsus
Ptolemæus
Confusius (a translation only)
Euripides
Polybius
Tacitus
Procopius
Hippocrates
Diodorus Siculus
Lucius Florus
Justin of Samaria (the original only)
Pythagoras
Theophrastus
Titus Livius
Josephus
Sappho

———

Shakespeare's works (cheap edition)
Cowley's works
Blackstone's "Commentaries"
Sir W. Jones's works
Lord Monboddo "on the origin and progress of language"
Robertson's "History of Scotland"
 do. "History of America"

Robertson's "Historical Disquisition on India."
Bishop Berkeley's works
Garcilaso de la Vega
Spallanzani's works (either English or Italian)
Les Ouvres de Diderot
 do. do. Condorcet
Roscoe's "History of the Houses of Medicis"
Sir W. Drummond's Essay on a Punic Inscription"
Darwin's "Temple of Nature"
Trotter on "Nervous Temperament"
 do. "Essay on "Drunkenness"

———

Poems by Clio Rickman
"Metrical Tales" by Southey
Southey's "Thalaba"
Wordsworth's Poems, 4 vols.
Coleridge's Poems
Tooke's "Diversions of Purley"
Godwin's "Enquirer"
 do. "Caleb Williams"
 do. "St. Leon"
 do. "Fleetwood"

LETTERS

TO THOMAS JEFFERSON HOGG

Tanyrallt [*Tremadoc*],
Dec. 27, 1812.

My dear Friend,
Your letter to Harriet contains some hints of the possibility of your being at leisure in a short time. I sincerely hope that your schemes will allow a visit to Tanyrallt. The advantage of a mail within seventeen miles would entirely obviate any hitch in the affair. We all anxiously wish you would come, and hope that your hint was something better than a mere lure for the opportunity of refusal.

We are all surprised at the complaints of cold which issue from London. For a day or two, indeed, it bit a little in the first of the morning, but nothing more.

Believe me that I sympathize in your feelings on Buonaparte and Peace, very warmly. Buonaparte is a person to whom I have a very great objection; he is to me a hateful and despicable being. He is seduced by the grossest and most vulgar ambition into actions which only differ from those of pirates by virtue of the number of men and the variety of resources under his command. His talents appear to me altogether contemptible and commonplace; incapable as he is of comparing connectedly the most obvious propositions, or relishing any pleasure truly enrapturing. Excepting Lord Castlereagh, you could not have mentioned any character but Buonaparte whom I contemn and abhor more vehemently. With respect to those victories in the North; if they tend towards peace, they are good; if otherwise, they are bad. This is the standard by which I shall ultimately measure my approbation of them. At the same time, I cannot but say that the first impression which they made on me was one of horror and regret.[1]

Brougham's defence was certainly not so good as it might have been; it was fettered by the place wherein he stood. Entire liberty

[1] The *Examiner* for December 20, 1812, says: "If the Russian Bulletins are to be believed, Buonaparte has not now a corporal's guard left out of his whole 'grand army,' and they are without shoes, according to the ministerial papers. Considering that Napoleon and his army have been so completely surrounded by the Russians, the news of their capture is rather tardy in its arrival."

of speech was denied. He could not speak treason; he could not commit a libel; and therefore his client was not to be defended on the basis of moral truth. He was compelled to hesitate when truth was rising to his lips; he could utter that which he did utter only by circumlocution and irony. The speech of the Solicitor-General appeared to me the consummation of all shameless insolence, and the address of Lord Ellenborough so barefaced a piece of time-servingness, that I am sure his heart must have laughed at his lips as he pronounced it.[2]

I have as yet received no answer from the Duke of Norfolk. I scarcely expect one. I do not see that it is the interest of my father to come to terms during my non-age; perhaps even not after. Do you know, I cannot prevail upon myself to care much about it. Harriet is very happy as we are; and I am very happy. I question if intimacy with my relations would add at all to our tranquillity. They would be plotting and playing the devil, or showing us to some people who would do so; or they would be dull; or they would take stupid likes or dislikes, and they certainly might cramp our liberty of movement. In fact, I have written to the Duke. I can say to my conscience, "I have done my best;" but I shall not be very unhappy, if I fail.

I continue vegetable; Harriet means to be slightly animal, until the arrival of Spring. My health is much improved by it; though partly perhaps by my removal from your nerve-racking and spirit-quelling metropolis.

[2] On Wednesday, December 9, 1812, in the Court of King's Bench, John Hunt, the printer, and Leigh Hunt, the Editor of the *Examiner*, were charged before Lord Ellenborough and a special jury for having "With intention to traduce and vilify his Royal Highness the Prince of Wales, Regent of the United Kingdom, and to bring his Royal Highness into hatred, contempt and disgrace on the 22nd of March [1812] in the 52nd year of the King, published a libel against the Prince Regent." Then followed a passage quoted from the *Examiner* article entitled "The Prince on St. Patrick's Day," in which certain phrases of unmeasured panegyric applied to the Prince Regent in the Tory press, appeared with Leigh Hunt's unflattering comments, concluding with the following : ". . . This Adonis in Loveliness *was a corpulent gentleman of fifty! In short, that this* delightful, blissful, wise, pleasurable, honourable, virtuous, true, *and immortal* PRINCE *was a violator of his word, a libertine over head and ears in debt and disgrace, a despiser of domestic ties, the companion of gamblers and demireps, a man who has just closed half a century without one single claim on the gratitude of his country or the respect of posterity."* Although ably defended by their friend Brougham, who had succeeded in obtaining an acquittal of the Hunts on a previous Government prosecution, in 1811, he was prohibited, from the nature of the case, from producing any proofs on behalf of his clients, and they were pronounced guilty, sentence being deferred.

We are divided between two opinions: Whether you really will allow us the heartfelt pleasure of seeing you here this winter: or whether your suggestion was a quiz.

My dear friend, I remain,

Yours very affectionately,

PERCY B. SHELLEY.

CC

TO THOMAS HOOKHAM
Old Bond Street

Tanyralt [*Tremadoc*],
Jan. 2, 1813.[1]

MY DEAR SIR,

On reflection I feel rather chagrined that I excepted against the Georgics. I fear it may withhold your hand when you would otherwise send me some really valuable work. I assure you I am quite reconciled to Professor Martyn.[2] Harriet will probably derive some assistance from his translation when she has mastered Horace. Now to answer your questions. The Tractatus Theologico Politicus and the Opera Posthuma of Spinoza will fully suf-

---

[1] Shelley's letter, to which the following was a reply, is not forthcoming:—

TIMOTHY SHELLEY TO P. B. SHELLEY

Field Place,
Jan. 1814 [? 1813].

Dᴿ BYSSHE,
        I am oblig'd by your kind enquiries, & good wishes of the New Year, we all join in returning them tenfold to you & yours, & that you may see many & more happy ones.
        I lament exceedingly that there shd. have been cause for the present difficulties. I hope the mountains in Wales may produce Reflections that you well know would be so congenial to my own sentiments, as well as those of yr. Mother. We shall be glad to hear of yr. welfare, & yr. address.
                With our united Sentiments of Love & Affection to you & yrs.
                        I am Yr. Affecte. Father
                                T. SHELLEY.

[2] Dr. Thomas Martyn (*d.* 1816), Physician at Chelsea, and Professor of Botany at Cambridge, author of *Dissertations and Critical Remarks on the Æneids of Virgil, with a life of the author,* 1770.

fice, at least for the present. With respect to Kant, there is a work of his, and as I judged the only one which has been translated into Latin by some Dr. This, which is his most celebrated work, is the only one I require; and I have no choice between a Latin, a French, or an English Translation. My Poems will, I fear, little stand the criticism even of friendship. Some of the later ones have the merit of conveying a meaning in every word, and these all are faithful pictures of my feelings at the time of writing them. But they are, in a great measure, abrupt and obscure—all breathing hatred to government and religion, but I think not too openly for publication. One fault they are indisputably exempt from, that of being a volume of *fashionable literature*. I doubt not but your friendly hand will clip the wings of my Pegasus considerably. I think that the type and size of Godwin's Essay on Sepulchres would be a good model for The Biblical Extracts. At all events I would wish them to be sent to the press. If you cannot have access to Eaton 250 copies would suffice. Small Christmass or *Easter offerings* of a neat little book have frequently a surprising effect. The Emperors of China seem to form a singular exception to the usual doltishness of the regal race.[3] I sympathise with his imperial majesty, but might not a preface be as efficacious in preventing the circulation of Biblical poison as a penal law?

Accept my warmest thanks for your kindness respecting the money affair. I may, in a future letter, trouble you with a few more enquiries on the subject.

The Post is just going out. We hope to see you here *early* in the spring. Harriet and her sister unite with me in best wishes to yourself and brother.

Yours very truly,

P. B. SHELLEY.

[Addressed]
MR. T. S. HOOKHAM, Junr.,
    Bookseller,
        Old Bond Street,
            London

---

[3] "In China the circulation of the Old and New Testaments had been proscribed by Imperial Edicts."—Dowden's *Life of Shelley*, Vol. I, p. 339.

LETTERS

HARRIET SHELLEY TO CATHERINE NUGENT

Tan-y-rallt,
Jany 16. [1813.]

MY DEAR MRS. NUGENT,

The sight of your well-known hand was like intelligence from the dead to the living. Shall I say that it gave me only pleasure? no, that is too cold a word to convey the feelings of happiness, in which we all alike participated. I am sorry to hear you have been so much engaged, as I cannot bear the idea of a woman like yourself being obliged to do that which so many are better qualified to perform. I saw with very great sorrow the ruin of so many of your valuable manufactories. I knew how many of your unfortunate countrymen suffered all the miseries of famine before, and now there must be many more. That the wounds of thy beloved country may soon be healed for ever, is the first wish of an Englishwoman who only regrets her being born among those inhuman beings who have already caused so much misery wherever they turn their steps. All the good I wrote of Mr. Madocks I recant. I find I have been dreadfully deceived respecting that man. We are now living in his house, where formerly nothing but folly and extravagance reigned. Here they held their midnight revels, insulting the spirit of nature's sublime scenery. The sea which used to dash against the most beautiful grand rocks, for grand indeed they are, and the mind is lost in the contemplation of them towering above one another, and on the opposite side the most jagged mountains, whose peaks are generally covered in clouds, was, to please his stupid vanity and to celebrate his name, turned from its course, and now we have for a bold fine sea, which there used to be, nothing but a sandy marsh uncultivated and ugly to the view. How poor does this work of man seem when standing on one of the mountains we see them all rising one behind the other as tho' they had stood the iron grasp of time many centuries. Then to look down on this embankment which viewed from the height looks as if a puff of wind from the mountains would send it to oblivion like its founder's name. The harm that man has done through his extravagance is incalculable. Here he built the town of Tremadoc, and then almost ruined its shopkeepers by never paying their just debts. We have been the means of saving the bank from utter destruction, for which I am extremely glad, as that person who purchases it will reap very great benefit from it. I admire your song much, and am determined to set it to some very plaintive tune. I have seen Miss Curran: she resides in England. What I saw of her I did not like. She said begging was a trade in Dublin. To tell you the truth, she is not half such an Irishwoman as myself, and that is why I did not feel disposed to like her. Besides, she is a coquette, the most abominable thing in the world. I met her at Godwin's house, alas [paper torn] Godwin he, too, is changed, and [filled] with prejudices, and besides, too, he expects such universal homage from all persons younger than himself, that it is very disagreeable to be in company with him on that account, and he wanted Mr. Shelley to join the Wig [*sic*] party and do just as they pleased, which made me very angry, as we know what men the Wigs [*sic*] are, now. He is grown old and unimpassioned, therefore is not in the least calculated for such enthusiasts as we are. He has suffered a great deal for his principles, but that ought to make him more staunch in them, at least it would me. Eliza and Percy desire their kind regards to you, with many thanks for your embassy to Stockdale, who will hear from Mr. S. soon. Adieu, dearest friend to liberty and truth, and that you may ever be happy is the first prayer of your affectionate friend,

H. SHELLEY.

LETTERS

CCI
TO THOMAS HOOKHAM[1]

Tanryallt,
Tremadoc, Jan. 26, [1813].

MY DEAR SIR.

I answer your letter hastily, by return of Post because I am provoked at the stupidity of the people who were to send the box. I wish you by no means to wait for it. The Waggon goes from the Castle and Falcon, Aldersgate Street. It had better be directed "to be forwarded from Bangor, by the Carnarvon Coach." I certainly wish to have all Kants works. My question concerning the Encyclopedie was more one of curiosity than want.

I expect to have Queen Mab, and the other Poems finished by March. Queen Mab will be in ten cantos and contain about 2800 lines.[2] The other poems probably contain as much more. The notes to Q.M. will be long and philosophical. I shall take that opportunity which I judge to be a safe one of propagating my principles, which I decline to do syllogistically in a poem. A poem very didactic is I think very stupid.[3]

I do not think that Sir W. Drummonds arguments have much weight. His Œdipus has completely failed in making me a convert.

When may we expect the pleasure of seeing you at Tanyrallt? Before or after March? I hope your brother will likewise be able to come.

My dear Sir
Your very faithful friend,

P. B. SHELLEY.

The thermometer is 12 degrees below freezing. This is Russian cold.

---

[1] There is no address to this letter, which is now printed in full from the original in the Bodleian Library.
[2] In its printed form *Queen Mab* is divided into nine cantos and consists of 2,289 lines.
[3] Compare Preface to *Prometheus Unbound*, 1820; "Didactic poetry is my abhorrence; nothing can be equally well expressed in prose that is not tedious and supererogatory in verse."

42

LETTERS

HARRIET SHELLEY TO THOMAS HOOKHAM

Tanyrallt,
Jany. 31st, [1813].

DEAR SIR,
In reading the Paper I perceived that Coleridge has just published a play called Remorse. I wish you to send us two copies of it also a copy of the Rejected Addresses and one of Campbell's Gertrude of Wyoming for a neighbour of ours. Mr. Shelley hopes to find some copies of the Biblical Extracts in the Box. I wish you to send me the song of Robin Adair and Kate of Kearney; they are very old songs but they may be better for that as our new music is generally very stupid. I see by the Papers that those poor men who were executed at York have left a great many children.[1] Do you think a subscription would be attended to for their relief? If you think it would, pray put down our names and advertise it in the Papers. Put down my Sister's name, Mr. Shelley's and mine for two guineas each; if this meets with your approbation we will enclose the sum.

Dear Sir,
Yours &c. &c. &c.
H. SHELLEY.

[Addressed]
MR. T. HOOKHAM, Junr.,
Old Bond Street,
London

CCII
TO THOMAS JEFFERSON HOGG

Tanyrallt,
Feb. 7, 1813.

MY DEAR FRIEND,
I have been teased to death for the last fortnight. Had you known the variety of the discomfitures I have undergone, you would attribute my silence to anything but unkindness or neglect. I allude to the embankment affairs,[1] in which I thoughtlessly engaged; for when I come home to Harriet, I am the happiest of the happy. I forget whether I have expressed to you the pleasure which you know I must feel at your visit in March.[2] I hope it will

[1] Alluding to the recent execution of fourteen of the riotous frame-makers, known as Luddites, at York.
[1] Shelley's zeal for the "embankment affairs" was such that, according to Mrs. Williams, he helped her husband to write letters, "and was in the office from morning to night, using every means in his power to show his kind interest."—Quoted by Professor Dowden, *Life of Shelley*, Vol. I, 319.
[2] Hogg had promised to visit the Shelleys at Tanyrallt "during the Spring Circuit, that is to say, at the beginning of March."

43

be early in the month, and that you will arrange matters so in London, that it may be protracted to the utmost possible length.

We simple people live here in a cottage extensive and tasty enough for the villa of an Italian Prince.[3] The rent, as you may conceive, is large, but it is an object with us that they allow it to remain unpaid till I am of age.

What said Harriet of America?[4]

You must take your place in the mail as far as Capel Cerrig, and inform me of the time you mean to be there, and I will meet you. I do not think that you have ever visited this part of North Wales. The scenery is more strikingly grand in the way from Capel Cerrig to our house than ever I beheld. The road passes at the foot of Snowdon; all around you see lofty mountain peaks, lifting their summits far above the clouds, wildly-wooded valleys below, and dark tarns reflecting every tint and shape of the scenery above them. The roads are tremendously rough; I shall bring a horse for you, as you will then be better able to see the country than when jumbled in a chaise.

"Mab"[5] has gone on but slowly, although she is nearly finished. They have teased me out of all poetry. With some restrictions, I have taken your advice, though I have not been able to bring myself to rhyme. The didactic is in blank heroic verse, and the descriptive in blank lyrical measure. If an authority is of any weight in support of this singularity, Milton's "Samson Agonistes," the Greek Choruses, and (you will laugh) Southey's "Thalaba" may be adduced. I have seen your last letter to Harriet. She will answer it by next post. I need not say that your letters delight me, but all your principles do not. The species of pride which you love to encourage appears to me incapable of bearing the test of reason.

[3] Tanyrallt is built in the Italian style, or what would now be known as a commodious bungalow with one storey and a verandah.

[4] Did Shelley ever think of going to America? We know that he sympathized with the Mexican Revolution, and he had been told that America was a place where beggars practically were unknown (Letter No. CLX). In a letter to C. Kirkpatrick Sharpe, printed in Lady Charlotte Bury's *Diary Illustrative of the Times of George the Fourth*, 1838, Vol. I, p. 91, he says, in writing from Christ Church, Oxford, October, 1811, "The ingenious Mr. Shelley hath been expelled from the University on account of his atheistical pamphlet. Was ever such bad taste and barbarity known? He behaved like a hero, he 'showed to Fortune's frowns a brow serene,' and declared his intention of emigrating to America."

[5] *Queen Mab*.

44

Now, do not tell me that Reason is a cold and insensible arbiter. Reason is only an assemblage of our better feelings—passion considered under a peculiar mode of its operation. This chivalric pride, although of excellent use in an age of Vandalism and brutality, is unworthy of the nineteenth century. A more elevated spirit has begun to diffuse itself, which, without deducting from the warmth of love, or the constancy of friendship, reconciles all private feelings to public utility, and scarce suffers true Passion and true Reason to continue at war. Pride mistakes a desire of being esteemed for that of being really estimable. I scarce think that the mock humility of ecclesiastical hypocrisy is more degrading and blind. I remember when over our Oxford fire we used to discuss various subjects; fancy me present with you in spirit, and own "how vain is human pride!" Perhaps you will say that my Republicanism is proud; it certainly is far removed from pot-house democracy, and knows with what smile to hear the servile applauses of an inconsistent mob. But though its cheeks could feel without a blush the hand of insult strike, its soul would shrink neither from the scaffold nor the stake, nor from those deeds and habits which are obnoxious to slaves in power. My Republicanism, it is true, would bear with an aristocracy of chivalry and refinement before an aristocracy of commerce and vulgarity; not, however, from pride, but because the one I consider as approaching most nearly to what man ought to be. So much for Pride!

Since I wrote the above, I have finished the rough sketch of my poem. As I have not abated an iota of the infidelity or cosmopolicy of it, sufficient will remain, exclusively of innumerable faults, invisible to partial eyes, to make it very unpopular. Like all egotists, I shall console myself with what I may call, if I please, the suffrages of the chosen few, who can think and feel, or of those friends whose personal partialities may blind them to all defects. I mean to subjoin copious philosophical notes.

Harriet has a bold scheme of writing you a Latin letter. If you have an Ovid's "Metamorphoses,"[6] she will thank you to bring it. I do not teach her grammatically, but by the less laborious method

[6] Shelley's copy of Ovid's *Metamorphoses*, with his signature on the title-page, was formerly in the collection of the late H. B. Forman.

45

of teaching her the English of Latin words, intending afterwards to give her a general idea of grammar. She unites with me in all kindest wishes.

CCIII

TO THOMAS HOOKHAM[1]

Old Bond Street

[*Tanyrallt, near Tremadoc*],
[*Postmark*], 19 *February*, 1813.

MY DEAR SIR,

I am boiling with indignation at the horrible injustice and tyranny of the sentence[1] pronounced on Hunt and his brother, and it is on this subject that I write to you. Surely the seal of abjectness and slavery is indelibly stamped upon the character of England.

Although I do not retract in the slightest degree my wish for a subscription for the widows and children of those poor men hung at York, yet this £1,000 which the Hunts are sentenced to pay is an affair of more consequence. Hunt is a brave, a good, and an enlightened man. Surely the public for whom Hunt has done so much will repay in part the great debt of obligation which they owe the champion of their liberties and virtues; or are they dead, cold, stone hearted, and insensible, brutalized by centuries of unremitting bondage? However that may be, they surely may be excited into some slight acknowledgement of his merits. Whilst hundreds of thousands are sent to the tyrants of Russia, he pines in a dungeon far from all that can make life to be desired.

Well I am rather poor at present but I have £20 which is not immediately wanted. Pray begin a subscription for the Hunts; put [down] my name for that sum, and, when I hear that you have complied with my request I will send it you. Now if there are

---

[1] Lord Ellenborough had passed sentence on Leigh and John Hunt, on February 4, 1812, of a fine of £500 each, imprisonment of two years, John Hunt in Coldbath Fields, and Leigh Hunt in the Surrey County Jail, and at the expiration of that term each were to give a security, in £500 each and two sufficient securities in £250, for their good

46

any difficulties in the way of this scheme of ours, for the love of liberty and virtue overcome them. Oh that I might wallow for one night in the Bank of England!

I am sorry to hear that we are not to have the pleasure of your company before August. I expected that June would have been the latest date of your kind visit. Surely many families *who read* do not swelter in London then?

Queen Mab is finished and transcribed. I am now preparing the Notes which shall be long and philosophical. You will recieve it with the other poems. I think that the whole should form one volume; but of that we can speak hereafter.

As to the French Encyclopedie, it is a book which I am desirous very desirous of posessing; and, if you could get me a few months' credit (being at present rather low in cash), I should very much desire to have it.

How *long* will the Poems be printing after you receive them?

My dear sir, excuse the earnestness of the first part of my letter. I feel warmly on this subject, and I flatter myself that, so long as your own independance and liberty remains uncompromised, you are inclined to second my desires.

Mrs. S. and Miss W. unite in best wishes to yourself and brother and I remain

Your very sincere friend,

P. B. SHELLEY.

[P.S.] If no other way can be devised for this subscription, will you take the trouble on yourself of writing an appropriate advertisement for the paper, inserting by way of stimulant, my subscription.

On second thoughts, I enclose the £20.

You would very much oblige me if you would collect all possible documents on the Precession of the Equinoxes, as also anything that may throw light upon the question of whether or no the Posi-

behaviour during five years. The Hunts, however, refused to accept any assistance and paid the fine. Shelley not only proposed this subscription, but he also wrote to Leigh Hunt, who tells us in his *Autobiography*: "It was [this] imprisonment that brought me acquainted with my friend of friends, Shelley. I had seen little of him before; but he wrote to me making me a princely offer, which at the time I stood in no need of."

tion of the Earth on its poles is not yearly becoming less oblique? It is an astronomical affair.[2]

[Addressed]
   Mr. T. HOOKHAM, Junr.,
     Bookseller,
      Old Bond Street,
      London

CCIV
TO THOMAS HOOKHAM

[Fragment]

Tanyralt Tremadoc Carnarvonshire
for letters.
Tanyralt Tremadoc Carnarvonshire
to be left at Capel Curig Inn
for parcels.

MY DEAR SIR,
    You will recieve a parcel directed to me at your House. Open it and you will find the Essay on Atheism; Queen Mab, and the Biblical Extracts. Keep the former for yourself (it is the only one I have) and send the others carefully packed by the Mail: directed to be forwarded with *care* and *speed*. If you have got any thing new or Paine's Works send it with them. Oh! and is God Save the King done. My loyal soul pants for its arrival.

---

[2] The original of this paragraph is on a slip fastened to Shelley's letter to Hookham of January 2, but it is probably a postscript to *this* letter. The originals of both letters are in the Bodleian Library.

LETTERS

[*Tanyrallt, Tremadoc,
March 3, 1813.*]

MY DEAR SIR

I have just escaped an atrocious assassination. Oh send the 20£ if you have it—you will perhaps hear of me no more.

[1] friend,

PERCY SHELLEY

[*Written by Harriet Shelley.*]

Mr Shelley is so dreadfully nervous today from having been up all night that I am afraid what he has written will alarm you very much. We intend to leave this place as soon as possible as our lives are not safe so long as we remain. It is no common robber we dread but a person who is actuated by revenge & who threatens my life & my sisters as well. If you can send us the money it will greatly add to our comfort.

Sir, I remain your sincere friend,

H SHELLEY

[Addressed]
T. HOOKHAM, Esq.

---

[1] "Your" was entirely omitted in Shelley's frantic state of mind!
The assault on Shelley referred to in this letter (on the night of Friday, February 26), and related in detail by Harriet Shelley in her letter to Hookham of March 11, 1813, p. 56, remained for ninety-two years one of the inexplicable incidents of the poet's life, and was variously described by his biographers as either an hallucination of Shelley's brain or a trick to escape from his creditors at Tremadoc. To the *Century Magazine* for October, 1905, however, Miss Margaret L. Crofts contributed the following well-attested account of Shelley's adventure. It appears that "Shelley was in the habit of climbing up the Roman steps near Tanyrallt to the rocky height, which was a grazing place for sheep. Here Shelley had more than once put an end to the life of a sheep affected with scab or some other lingering disease. It was his habit to carry pistols, and in his pity for the helpless creatures he would put an end to them by a kindly shot. This habit of Shelley's had so exasperated a rough specimen of the Welsh mountain sheepfarmer, named Robin Pant Evan, that he and his friends came down to Tanyrallt on

LETTERS

TO JOHN WILLIAMS
Tremadoc

MY DEAR WILLIAMS,

I am surprised that the wretch who attacked me has not been heard of. Surely the inquiries have not been sufficiently general, or particular?

Mr. Nanney requests that you will order that some boards should be nailed against the broken window of Tanyrallt. We are in immediate want of money. Could you borrow twenty-five pounds in my name, to pay my little debts? I know your brother could lend me that sum. I think you could ask him on such an occasion as this.

My dear Williams, yours very truly,

P. B. SHELLEY.

---

that wild February night, and Evan fired a shot through the window, not meaning to murder anyone, but to give the inconvenient meddler a good fright. Shelley's pistol flashed in the pan. Robin entered the room, wrestled with him, knocked him down, and then escaped through the window. It was his rough face and form that Shelley afterwards saw standing near the beech-tree; and when Shelley gazed out, all bewildered with the night alarm and the shaking, he thought he saw the devil. Robin gained his end, for Shelley and Harriet and her sister left the place next day never to return." When trying to describe the assault to Mrs. Williams, Shelley sketched on a screen a figure of the man by whom he had been attacked; the screen has unhappily disappeared, but a reproduction from a copy of the sketch accompanies the article. Some years after the event, the same Robin Pant Evan confessed his part in this night adventure to certain members of the Greaves family who were living at Tanyrallt between 1847 and 1865. Miss Greaves, who occupied Tanyrallt, very courteously communicated to me some interesting particulars of the house. Peacock, who visited Tanyrallt in the summer of 1813, stated that he "heard the matter much talked of. Persons who had examined the premises on the following morning had found that the grass of the lawn appeared to have been much trampled and rolled on, but there were no footmarks on the wet ground except between the beaten spot and the window; and the impression of the ball on the wainscot showed that the pistol had been fired towards the window, and not from it."

LETTERS

CCVII
TO JOHN WILLIAMS
Tremadoc

[Postmark], Bangor,
[After March 5, 1813.]

MY DEAR WILLIAMS,

I have received a letter from Leeson,[1] which I enclose. His statement of this fact I know on reflection to be perfectly correct, with the exception of the latter part of his letter which is twisted in this way by his malice.

Did I not know the unalterable goodness of your heart, and had I not a confidence not to be shaken in your general rectitude, I should feel staggered at this deceit.

But I can trace all the springs of your conduct—all the windings of your mind are known to me.

In justice to the good, I, whilst I pity the bad I find, I am still obliged to disapprove.—I should not have been offended with you, had you told me the truth. You know me but little, whilst I know you very well.

---

[1] The following—

ROBERT LEESON[(1)] TO P. B. SHELLEY

Morfa Lodge,
March 5, 1813.

SIR,—Having heard from several quarters that you lie under a mistake relative to the manner in which I was put in possession of a pamphlet signed "P.B.Shelley," I think it a pity that you should not be undeceived. I beg to tell you that it was not given to me by Mr. Ashstone, nor taken by him from John Williams' house,—*but* was handed to me by *John Williams* with a remark that it contained matter dangerous to the State, and that you had been in the practise of haranguing 500 people at a time when in Ireland. So much for your friend.

Sir, I remain yours,
ROB. LEESON.

(1) Robert Leeson, as we see from Harriet's letter of March 11, was supposed to have had a hand in the Tanyrallt outrage. This Professor Dowden discredited in his *Life of Shelley*, although he was, of course, without the facts that have recently come to light. He describes Leeson as "an eminently loyal and disagreeable Englishman, who had learnt in the early Tremadoc days from effusive Miss Hitchener of Shelley's authorship of a seditious pamphlet and the risk of a Government prosecution." "An envious, un-feeling sort of man," declares Mrs. Williams, "not very particular what he said of any-one," and who had charged Shelley to the face with his utterance of sedition. Mrs. Williams said that "when Mr. Shelley asked for his informant, Mr. Leeson pointed to my husband; but when the three met, Mr. Leeson made an apology, and confessed he had been told by Miss Hitchener."

Hence you suspect, and I confide. Let me have the comfort of knowing that when I vouch for your word, I vouch for what is true. As I told you when we parted unless you are explicit and unreserved to me I am fighting in the dark. I am and shall continue to be your friend, but I should be your friend to little purpose unless I were also your confidant.

You will hear from us again soon in Dublin. I shall believe you in future, but never deceive me again.

My dear Williams,
Your true friend,
P. B. SHELLEY.

[Addressed]
MR. JOHN WILLIAMS,
Ynnis Towyn,
Tremadoc

CCVIII
TO THOMAS HOOKHAM
London

Bangor Ferry,
March 6, 1813.

MY DEAR FRIEND,

In the first stage of our journey towards Dublin we met with your letter. How shall I express to you what I felt of gratitude, surprise and pleasure—not so much that the remittance rescued us from a situation of peculiar perplexity but that one there was who by disinterested and unhesitating confidence made amends to our feelings, wounded by the suspicion, coldness, and villainy of the world. If the discovery of truth be a pleasure of singular purity, how far surpassing is the discovery of virtue!

I am now recovered from an illness brought on by watching, fatigue, and alarm, and we are proceeding to Dublin, to dissipate the unpleasing impressions associated with the scene of our alarm.

We expect to be there on the 8th.[1] You shall then hear the detail

---

[1] The Shelleys arrived at Dublin on March 9.

of our distresses. The ball of the assassins pistol (he fired at me twice) penetrated my night gown and pierced the wainscot. He is yet undiscovered though not unsuspected as you will learn from my next.

Unless you knew us all more intimately, you could not concieve with what fervour and sincerity my wife and sister join with me to you in gratitude and esteem.

Yours ever faithfully and affectly

PERCY B. SHELLEY.

P.S.—Though overwhelmed by our own distresses, we are by no means indifferent to those of liberty and virtue. From the tenor of your letter I augur that you have applied the £20 I sent to the benefit of the Hunts. I am anxious to hear further of the success of this experiment. My direction is—35 Great Cuffe Street, Dublin, Ireland.[2] By your kindness and generosity we are perfectly relieved from all pecuniary difficulties. We only wanted a little breathing time, which the rapidity of our persecution was unwilling to allow us. [I will] readily repay the £20 when I hear from my correspondent in London, but when can I repay the friendship, the disinterestedness, and the zeal of your confidence?

[Addressed]
MR. T. HOOKHAM, Junr.,
Bookseller,
Old Bond St.,
London

---

[2] This was the address of Shelley's friend, John Lawless.

CCIX
TO JOHN WILLIAMS
Tremadoc

50 *Great Cuffe St[reet], Dublin,*
[? *after March* 9], 1813.

MY DEAR WILLIAMS,

I write to tell you that we have safely arrived in Dublin. Our passage was very tedious and stormy. It made us all so ill that we are scarcely recovered. Well, we are arrived in Dublin, but so poor that, unless we find some friend, I know not what we shall do. I do not think that we can manage to live until the arrival of Mr. Caldecott's expected loan. We are in a foreign country where our name even is scarcely known, and where no one will give us credit for a farthing. You are surrounded by your friends, and though poor have some hope of refuge in necessity. You would oblige me by asking your brother to lend me £25.[1] I know that if you wish to do this you can do it. Your brother is a man worth £5,000, and surely it would be an act of common friendship only to accommodate me with this sum until the arrival of the amount of Caldecott's loan.

I shall know by your compliance with this request whether the absence of friends is a cooler for friendship or not.

I remain, with the greatest zeal for your interests,

Your sincere friend,

P. B. SHELLEY.

[Addressed]
MR. JOHN WILLIAMS,
Tremadoc,
Carnarvon

---

[1] Apparently Williams's brother Owen lent £100 to Shelley, who gave Williams a bond stipulating for the payment of £200 on the deaths of his father and grandfather. See *Shelley in England*, p. 635.

LETTERS

HARRIET SHELLEY TO THOMAS HOOKHAM

35 Cuffe Street, Stephen's Green, Dublin,
March 12 [1813].

MY DEAR SIR,
We arrived here last Tuesday [March 9] after a most tedious passage of forty hours, during the whole of which time we were dreadfully ill. I'm afraid no diet will prevent us from the common lot of suffering when obliged to take a sea voyage.

Mr. S. promised you a recital of the horrible events that caused us to leave Wales. I have undertaken the task, as I wish to spare him, in the present nervous state of his health, every thing that can recal to his mind the horrors of that night, which I will relate.

On Friday night, the 26th of February, we retired to bed between ten and eleven o'clock. We had been in bed about half an hour, when Mr. S. heard a noise proceeding from one of the parlours. He immediately went downstairs with two pistols, which he had loaded that night, expecting to have occasion for them. He went into the billiard room, where he heard footsteps retreating. He followed into an other little room, which was called an office. He there saw a man in the act of quitting the room through a glass window which opens into the shrubbery. The man fired at Mr. S., which he avoided. Bysshe then fired, but it flashed in the pan. The man then knocked Bysshe down, and they struggled on the ground. Bysshe then fired his second pistol, which he thought wounded him in the shoulder, as he uttered a shriek and got up, when he said these words: By God, I will be revenged! I will murder your wife. I will ravish your sister. By God, I will be revenged. He then fled—as we hoped for the night. Our servants were not gone to bed, but were just going, when this horrible affair happened. This was about eleven o'clock. We all assembled in the parlour, where we remained for two hours. Mr S. then advised us to retire, thinking it impossible he would make a second attack. We left Bysshe and our man-servant, who had only arrived that day, and who knew nothing of the house, to sit up. I had been in bed three hours when I heard a pistol go off. I immediately ran down stairs, when I perceived that Bysshe's flannel gown had been shot through, and the window curtain. Bysshe had sent Daniel to see what hour it was, when he heard a noise at the window. He went there, and a man thrust his arm through the glass and fired at him. Thank Heaven! the ball went through his gown and he remained unhurt, Mr. S. happened to stand sideways; had he stood fronting, the ball must have killed him. Bysshe fired his pistol, but it would not go off. He then aimed a blow at him with an old sword which we found in the house. The assassin attempted to get the sword from him, and just as he was pulling it away Dan rushed into the room, when he made his escape.

This was at four in the morning. It had been a most dreadful night; the wind was as loud as thunder, and the rain descended in torrents. Nothing has been heard of him; and we have every reason to believe it was no stranger, as there is a man of the name of Leeson, who the next morning that it happened went and told the shop-keepers of Tremadoc that it was a tale of Mr. Shelley's to impose upon them, that he might leave the country without paying his bills. This they believed, and none of them attempted to do anything towards his discovery.

We left Tanyrallt on Saturday, and staid till every thing was ready for our leaving the place, at the Sol[icitor]General of the county's house, who lived seven miles from us. This Mr. Leeson had been heard to say that he was determined to drive us out of the country. He once happened to get hold of a little pamphlet which Mr. S. had printed in Dublin; this he sent up to Government.([1]) In fact, he was for ever saying something against us, and that because we were determined not to admit him to our house, because we had heard his character and from many acts of his we found that he was malignant and cruel to the greatest degree.

([1]) See Shelley's letter No. CCVII to Williams and footnote.

The pleasure we experienced at reading your letter you may conceive, at the time when every one seemed to be plotting against us. When those whom we had . . . the horrible suspicion . . . from the task when called upon in a moment like that.([2]) Pardon me if I wound your feelings by dwelling on this subject. Your conduct has made a deep impression on our minds, which no length of time can erase. Would that all mankind were like thee.

Mr. Shelley and my sister unite with me in kind regards; whilst I remain,

Yours truly,

H. SHELLEY.

[Addressed]

MR. T. HOOKHAM, Junr.,
   Bookseller,
     Old Bond Street, London.   [Postmark] Mar. 12.

CCX
TO THOMAS HOOKHAM
London

[*Cuffe Street, St. Stephen's Green, Dublin,*
March, 1813.]

MY DEAR SIR

    Harriet related to you the mysterious events which caused our departure from Tanyralt. I was at that time so nervous and unsettled as to be wholly incapable of the task. Do not however concieve that for one moment I lose the grateful recollection of your kindness and attention.

    I send you my Poem.[1] To your remarks on its defects I shall listen and derive improvement. No duty on a friend is more imperious than an utter sincerity and unreservedness and criticism; none of which a candid mind can be the object with more inward complacency and satisfaction. At the same time in spite of its various errors, I am determined to give it to the world.[2] . . . If you do not dread the arm of the law, or any exasperation of public opinion

([2]) The gaps here are due to the absence in the Bodleian original of a quarter of the last leaf of the letter—involving the absence on the verso of the last sentence ("Mr. Shelley and my sister") and the subscription, which are here printed from Hogg's transcript.

[1] *Queen Mab*, which was printed in Post octavo without either the motto from Shakespeare or a preface.

[2] Here, for the sake of Shelley's signature on the other side, an autograph hunter has snipped out a piece of the letter: the words remain, "I shall know at what a loss . . . all my future literary worth . . . erase the memory of its deficiencies."

against yourself, I wish that it should be printed and published immediately.

The notes are preparing and shall be forwarded before the completion of the printing of the Poem. I have many other Poems which shall also be sent.

The notes will be long, philosophical, and Anti Christian. This will be unnoticed in a Note.

Do not let the title page be printed before the body of the Poems. I have a motto to introduce from Shakespeare, and a Preface.

I expect no success. Let only 250 copies be printed, a small neat Quarto, on fine paper, and so as to catch the aristocrats: they will not read it, but thier sons and daughters may.

All join in best feelings towards you.

Your faithful friend[3]

CCXI
TO JOHN WILLIAMS

35 *Cuff Street, Stephen's Green, Dublin,*
March 21, 1813.

MY DEAR WILLIAMS,

I have received your letter. Nothing less entered my mind than the accusing, or even in the slightest degree suspecting, you of treachery. The contents of my letter from Bangor is the amount of my charge against you. You, like all other men, are to a certain degree defective and inconsistent. True friendship bears to hear, and bears to tell, of faults.

Bedwell has written to tell me that all my bills are returned protested. I know not what to do. If Caldicott will advance £400, I must commission you to discharge the demands at Tremadoc against me: if he will not, I must be content that Leeson's lies should gain credit, and never return again.

Have you heard again from the mortgagees? Does Bedwell press on you for his debt? How go on your concerns?—Mine are in a

[3] See note 2.

bad state. I have no friends in Ireland who are not poorer than myself.

Enclosed is a——, which Ellen took as the price of a ——.[1]

There is a box of books directed to me at Carnarvon, which I am extremely anxious to receive. Could you see to forward it, and pay the duty—2d. per lb.? The other box I wish to be sent to the care of Mrs. Nanney.

Harriet and Eliza desire to be kindly remembered.

Your sincere friend,

P. B. SHELLEY.

[Addressed]
JOHN WILLIAMS, Esq.,
    Tremadoc, Carnarvonshire,
    North Wales

CCXII
TO JOHN WILLIAMS

35 *Gt. Cuffe St.*,
[*Stephen's Green, Dublin*],
March 30: 1813.

MY DEAR WILLIAMS

I feel much obliged by your friendly exertions to procure the small sum I stand in need of; I did not devise the request as a test of your goodness; and, if I said so, it was the dictate rather of our extreme distress than any doubt I entertained of you. I have recieved a very dictatorial and unpleasant letter from Mr. Bedwell, which I have answered in an unbending spirit. He is a friendly and well meaning man, but I must not be treated like a school-boy. I told him in my letter that "I pay friendship with friendship, and money with money."

The letter which you have sent me of Miss H[itchener]'s is the most artful production I ever read. It is suited to what she be-lieves to be your character, and to my supposed ignorance of law.

---

[1] [Letter torn.]

58

But in truth she is a woman of desperate views and dreadful passions but of cool and undeviating revenge. Her affected contempt of this feeling puts me in mind of the man who said "Damn my body and blood if I ever swear—damn me if I do." Her artifice, in one part of the letter, is too palpable for success. She can assume the character of Christian or Infidel as it suits her purpose; I laughed heartily at her day of retribution, and at her idea of bringing you, me and herself before a Being whom a few months ago she was the most active to deny. If you write to her you may tell her (but not from me) that her threats of confiscation and death savour so little of vengeance or intimidation that my heart is quite subdued by the bewitching benevolence of her intentions but that I fear the government (tho' perhaps the weakest is [*sic*] the world) is not so miserably silly or wicked as to help the wiles of a scorned and disappointed woman. With respect to her friendliness to Harriet in her answers to yours of that you are the best judge. And to that you will answer "with the fear of the Lord before your eyes."

Altho my dear Williams I am a very hardened sinner, and without doubt shall be damned to all eternity, yet in this life I am ready to do any thing for my country and my friends that will serve them, and among [the] rest for you

Whose affectionate friend I continue to remain

PERCY B SHELLEY

Harriet and Eliza unite in kind remembrance. Perhaps it were as well to send this letter to Miss Hitchener. I am above all secrecy and her threats are surely calculated rather than [*sic*] to amuse than alarm any but little boys and girls.

[*Two postscripts by Harriet Shelley*]

(*a*) Do not send this Letter to Miss H. and do not answer hers.

(*b*) DEAR SIR,

Will you have the goodness to call upon Mr. Wakeman at Carnarvon, to receive the sum of £2 which he has had to pay for a Box of ours. But the Box has been sent to Chester therefore he is to pay you the money. I find the carrier has a little Bill against us. Will you pay him and send the Box which he retains to *London* to Mr. Westbrook's, 23 Chapel Street, Grosvenor Square, *London*. If it came to us the Custom house men would take it, as it contains G[—].[1]

[Addressed by Harriet Shelley]
MR. JOHN WILLIAMS,
   Ynnis y Towyn,
     Tremadoc,
      Carnarvonshire,
       North Wales

---

[1] The following letter throws an interesting sidelight on the foregoing correspondence—

FROM CAPTAIN PILFOLD TO JOHN WILLIAMS

Nelson Hall, Lindfield, Sussex,
Jany. 6, 1814.

SIR,
   There is an old proverb "Better late than never," I therefore take this opportunity to thank you for your letter of the 21 of Feby., 1813, in which you completely refuted Miss Hitchener's charge against Miss Westbrook and Mrs. Shelley of having offered you the least possible insult. Mr. Shelley is my nephew, and I need not tell you *how* difficult I found it, to reconcile Miss Hitchener's story with their known moral and virtuous good characters. My only having heard this story has given such offence that I have never heard from them since. Wishing you all possible health and happiness to enjoy their delightful company,

I am yours, etc.,
JOHN PILFOLD.

P.S. I was also pleased to find from your letter that Mr. Shelley had so honourably and on the first application discharged his debt to your brother, whom Miss H[itchener] did not describe as a poor man, but one to whom such a loss would be serious. Your expressions of gratitude towards Mr. and Mrs. Shelley for their great kindness towards you, does credit to you as a man of feeling.

LETTERS

CCXIII
TO THOMAS JEFFERSON HOGG

Cork Hotel, Dublin,
March 31, 1813.

MY DEAREST FRIEND,

We have just arrived in Dublin[1]—had you remained here but one day, you would have seen us. We travelled night and day, from the receipt of your note. My Harriet insisted on accompanying me. Her spirits, and the hope of seeing you here, supported her through two days and nights of hard travelling: 240 English miles.

You falsely supposed that her note was in answer to yours. We did not receive yours until Monday noon. Monday evening we began travelling on Irish roads with Irish horses and Chaise. We reached Cork at one the next day—took the Mail, and to-day, Wednesday, at 3 o'clock arrived. We shall soon be with you in London; Eliza and our servant remain in Killarney.[2]

You ought not to accuse me of reserve towards you. It is the inconceivable blindness and matter of fact stupidity of Lawless that deserves your reprehension; but had you staid one day longer, you would have heard the words of sincerity and friendship from my own lips. As soon as I shall consider the fatigue as overcome, I shall come to London. I must by some means raise money for the journey here, but I am not one to shirk at difficulties.

---

[1] Hogg's promised visit to Tanyrallt had been abandoned owing to the assault on Shelley at that place, and his flight to Ireland. As a compensation, Hogg was invited to Dublin, from whence several letters (since lost) were addressed to him, pressing him to come. When Hogg arrived at 35 Cuffe Street, Dublin, he was informed that Shelley, Harriet, Miss Westbrook, and the servant, probably Daniel Healey, had gone off to Killarney. After spending a week or ten days in Dublin, Hogg, vexed at his fruitless journey, returned in the Post Office Packet for Holyhead. (Hogg's *Shelley*, Vol. II, p. 217 *et seqq.*) According to Hogg, Shelley had occupied a cottage on the lake at Killarney. This place made a deep and lasting impression on the poet, for in a letter to Peacock from Milan on April 20, 1818, Shelley says that "Lake (Como) exceeds anything I ever beheld in beauty, with the exception of the Arbutus Islands of Killarney."

[2] "At the end of March, 1813, Shelley and Harriet came from Killarney in great haste, leaving Miss Westbrook there, with a large library, but without money, that there might be no temptations to discontinue her studies."—Hogg's *Shelley*, Vol. II, p. 389.

61

Do not write to us here. We shall be on our way before your letter could arrive.

Harriet unites in kind remembrances.

Your very sincere friend,
PERCY B. S.

Harriet will write to-morrow.

[Addressed]
T. J. HOGG,
170 *Chancery Lane*

CCXIV
TO THOMAS JEFFERSON HOGG

Dublin,
April 3, [? 1], 1813.

MY DEAR FRIEND,

I wrote yesterday before I had seen Lawless, under the one and only impression of disappointment at not meeting you here. That, however, shall speedily be remedied. I have raised a small sum of money, and to-morrow evening we embark for Holyhead.

I have been very much pleased at what Lawless has said of you. The first ten words he spoke entirely dissipated all the ill-humour I had cherished against him. He had done what I could not conceive any one, who dined with you, could have neglected. He had been open with you.

Of course you will not write to us here. Above all do not send, or dream of procuring for us any money; we will do those matters well. The property of friends at least is in common. On Monday evening we shall be in London.

I write from Lawless's. I am very much pleased and flattered by his account of you.

Harriet is quite well. She writes to-day.

My dear friend, all happiness attend you.

Yours affectionately,
PERCY B. SHELLEY.

VIII
APRIL 5, 1813, TO APRIL 14, 1814

LAST DAYS WITH HARRIET

CCXV
TO THOMAS JEFFERSON HOGG

[23 *Chapel Street, London,*
April 5, 1813.]
[*No date.*]

MY DEAR FRIEND,[1]
We have just arrived. We are now at 23 Chapel Street,
but will see you, or write to-morrow morning.

Yours affectionately,

P. B. S.

[1] There was some anxiety on the part of Mr. Lawless at the Shelleys' sudden departure
from Dublin, and not hearing from him for a month he at length wrote to Hogg for tidings of his friend. The following correspondence is printed by Hogg in his *Life of Shelley*,
Vol. II, p. 259—

TO THOMAS JEFFERSON HOGG

35 *Great Cuffe Street, Dublin,*
May 3, 1813.

DEAR SIR,
I take the liberty of troubling you with these few lines to be informed by you how
our good friends the Shelleys are, from whom I have heard but once since they left this
country. I did flatter myself with a letter from my friend long before this, and now begin
to apprehend some serious cause for his not writing. I hope no such cause has inter-
posed, and if not, you will much oblige me by telling him how anxious both Mrs. Lawless and I are to hear from him and Mrs. Shelley. I suppose Miss Westbrook has long
since arrived with you.

I remain,
Your very humble servant,
JOHN LAWLESS.

[*First Indorsement*]
TO HARRIET SHELLEY

Sunday Morning.

DEAREST HARRIET,
I am very sorry that Bysshe is unwell. It is hard that his heart should be so good,
and his head so bad : I wish you had as much influence over the latter as over the former. Mr. Lawless has had the goodness to send me the paper, on which I write. Bysshe

LETTERS

CCXVI
TO TIMOTHY SHELLEY

Cooke's Hotel,
Albermarle Street, [London],[1]
Tuesday Mor.,
Recd. 4 o'ck., 18th May, 1813.

MY DEAR FATHER,

I once more presume to address you, to state to you my Sincere desire of being consider'd as worthy of a Restoration to the intercourse with yourself and my Family which I have forfeited by my Follies. Some time since I stated my feelings on this Subject in a letter to the Duke of Norfolk. I was agreeably surprised by a visit from him the other day and much regretted that illness prevented me from keeping my appointment with him on the succeeding morning. If however, I could convince you of the change that has taken place in some of the most unfavourable traits of my Character and of my willingness to make any Concessions that may be judg'd for the Interest of my Family, I flatter myself that there would be little further need of his Grace's Interference. I hope the time is approaching when we shall consider each other as Father and Son with more confidence than ever, and that I shall no longer be a

---

will answer him. I met Mr. and Mrs. Newton, as I returned last night; they ordered me to tell you that they would take tea with you this evening. Adieu!

Yours truly,
T. J. H[OGG.]

[Second Indorsement]
TO THOMAS JEFFERSON HOGG

Bysshe is better now, and wishes for your company this evening, at eight o'clock, to meet the Newtons.

HARRIET.

[1] From a copy, apparently made by Timothy Shelley, in the Bodleian Library. Dowden gives the date of this letter as May 4. Hogg says (Vol. II, p. 389) that the Shelleys "remained a few days at a hotel in Dover Street, and then Harriet took lodgings in Half-Moon Street, accounting the situation fashionable; they stayed there several months, and then went to Pimlico to be near the B[oinville]s, which was esteemed very desirable; and there I think Ianthe was born. In August following Shelley came of age. There was a little projecting window in Half-Moon Street, in which Shelley might be seen from the street all day long, book in hand, with lively gestures and bright eyes; so that Mrs. N[ewton] said, he wanted only a pan of clear water and a fresh turf to look like some young lady's lark, hanging outside for air and song." I have not seen any letters of Shelley addressed from Half-Moon Street, or Pimlico; it seems possible that after he left the hotel he may have continued to use it as an address for letters.

cause of Disunion to the Happyness of my Family.[2] I was happy to hear from John Grove who din'd with us yesterday that you continue in good Health. My Wife unites with me in respectful regards and I remain

Your very affecte
and Dutyfull Son,
PERCY B. SHELLEY.

[Addressed]
To
T: SHELLEY, ESQR.

HARRIET SHELLEY TO CATHERINE NUGENT

Cooke's Hotel, Albemarle Street, London,
May 21 [1813].

MY DEAR MRS. NUGENT,
I find the longer a time elapses before I make my apology for not having written before, the more awkward I feel at the idea of addressing you. My greatest consolation, however, is derived from this—that you will not attribute my silence to neglect, but to the hurry and bustle of a city. I am ashamed to say I have written to no one since I arrived here, if that can extenuate my crime. You would pardon me if you knew in what a state of confusion I live. To give a description of it is impossible. Even now there are two waiters in the room to lay our cloth for dinner, and you well know the movements of a waiter are far from silent. I have been in London a long time, though it seems to me that I have only been here a few days. Mr. Shelley's family are very eager to be reconciled to him, and I should not in the least wonder if my next letter was not sent from his Paternal roof, as we expect to be there in a week or two. His father has been in town, when, at the earnest solicitation of his cousin, Bysshe wrote to him. He has not yet answered the letter; but we expect it daily. Their conduct is most surprising, after treating us like dogs they wish for our Society. I hope it will turn out well, tho' I hardly dare suppose so. My sister has joined me some time. You may suppose I was not a little pleased to see her again. We have not got our boxes yet that were sent from Cork to Bristol, and when we shall see them again is uncertain. Mr. Ryan dines with us to-day. I give him meat, but we have all taken to the vegetable regimen again, which I shall not leave off, for I find myself so much better for it, that it would be very great injustice to eat flesh again. Have you seen Mr. Lawless? He wrote to us from Prison a few weeks ago, but I do not suppose he was there, because Ryan knew nothing about it, and he is only just arrived from there. This is franked by La Touche, for I feel it is not worth postage. I hope to hear from you soon, tho' I feel I do not deserve it; but you are too kind to take any advantage over me. Mr. Shelley continues perfectly well, and his Poem of "Queen Mab" is begun [apparently, to be printed], tho' it must not be published under pain of death, because it is too much against every existing establishment. It is to be privately distributed to his friends, and some copies sent over to America. Do you [qy. know]

---

[2] In the following letter to Catherine Nugent, Harriet alludes to Shelley's negotiations with his father for a reconciliation, and it would appear from Harriet's letter of June 22, 1813, that Shelley's mother and sisters wished him and Harriet to visit Field Place. Unhappily the terms of peace, laid down by his father, made this reconciliation impossible.

any one that would wish for so dangerous a gift? If you do, tell me of them, and they shall not be forgotten. Adieu! All unite in kind regards to you, and I remain your sincerely attached friend,

H. SHELLEY.

Direct to this hotel

[Addressed]
MRS. NUGENT,
   No. 101 *Grafton Street,*
      St. Stephen's Green, Dublin

CCXVII
TO CHARLES, DUKE OF NORFOLK
Norfolk House

Cooke's Hotel, Albemarle Street [*London*],
Friday Morning [*May* 28, 1813].

MY LORD DUKE,

I sincerely regret that any of your valuable time should have been occupied in the vain and impossible task of reconciling myself and my father. Allow me, however, to express my warmest gratitude for the interest you have so kindly taken in my concerns, which have thus unexpectedly terminated in disunion and disappointment.

I was prepared to make my father every reasonable concession, but I am not so degraded and miserable a slave as publicly to disavow an opinion which I believe to be true. Every man of common sense must plainly see that a sudden renunciation of sentiments seriously taken up is as unfortunate a test of intellectual uprightness as can possibly be devised. I take the liberty of enclosing my father's letter[1] for your Grace's inspection. I repeat what I have said

[1] TIMOTHY SHELLEY TO P. B. SHELLEY

Miller's Hotel [*London*].
26 *May,* 1813,

MY DEAR BOY,

I am sorry to find by the contents of your letter of yesterday that I was mistaken in the conclusion I drew from your former letter, in which you assured me a change had taken place in some of the most unfavourable Traits in your Character, as what regards your avow'd opinions are in my Judgment the most material parts of Character requiring amendment; and as you now avow there is no change effected in them, I must de-from the commencement of this negociation, in which private communications from my father first induced me to engage, that I am willing to concede anything that is reasonable, anything that does not involve a compromise of that self-esteem without which life would be a burthen and a disgrace.

Permit me to repeat the unalterable recollection I cherish of your kindness, and to remain,

My Lord Duke,
Your very faithful obt. Servt.,

PERCY BYSSHE SHELLEY.

CCXVIII
TO THOMAS JEFFERSON HOGG
London

Cooke's Hotel [London],
Wednesday Morn. (June [3], 1813).

MY DEAREST FRIEND,

Harriet writes in this. I only desire that I were always as anxious to confer on you all possible happiness, as she is. She tells you, that she invites you this evening. It will be better than our lonesome and melancholy interviews.

Your very affectionate,

P. B. SHELLEY.

I am very sure that Harriet will be as kind as ever. I could see, when I spoke to her (if my eyes were not blinded by love), that it was an error, not of the feelings, but of reason. I entreat you to come this evening. I send this by the servant, that there may be no delay.

cline all further Communication, or any Personal Interview, until that shall be Effected and I desire you will consider this as my final answer to anything you may have to offer.

If that Conclusion had not operated on my mind to give this answer, I desire you also to understand that I should not have received any Communication but through His Grace the Duke of Norfolk, as I know his exalted mind will protect me at the moment and with the World.

I beg to return all usual remembrance.

I am, Yr. Affecte. Father,
T. SHELLEY.

LETTERS

TO THOMAS CHARLES MEDWIN
Horsham

Cooke's Hotel, Albemarle Street, [London, Postmark], 16 June, 1813.

MY DEAR SIR,

It is some time since I have addressed you, but as our interests are interwoven in a certain degree by a community of disappointment, I shall do so now without ceremony.

I was desirous of seeing you on the subject of the approaching expiration of my minority, but hourly expecting Mrs. Shelley's confinement, I am not able to leave her for the present.

I wish to know whether at that epoch, you would object to see me through the difficulties with which I am surrounded.

You may depend on my grateful remembrance of what you have already done for me, and suffered on my account, whether you consent or refuse to add to the list of my obligations to you. The late negotiations between myself and my father have been abruptly broken off by the latter. This I do not regret, as his caprice and intolerance would not have suffered the wound to heal.

I know that I am heir to large property. How are the papers to be seen? Have you the least doubt but that I am the safe heir to a large landed property? Have you any certain knowledge on the subject?

If you are coming to town soon, I should be most happy to see you; or, after Mrs. Shelley's confinement, I will visit you at Horsham.

Mrs. S. unites in her remembrances to all your family.

Yours very sincerely,

P. B. SHELLEY.

LETTERS

Cooke's Hotel, Dover Street [London],
June 21, 1813.

MY DEAR SIR,

Mrs. Shelley's confinement may take place in one day, or not until six weeks. In this state of uncertainty, I would unwillingly leave town even for a few hours. I therefore should be happy to see you so soon as you could make a journey to town convenient. Depend upon it that no artifice of my father's shall seduce me to take a life interest in the estate. I feel with sufficient force, that I should not by such conduct be guilty alone of injustice to myself, but to those who have assisted me by kind offices and advice during my adversity.

Mrs. S. unites in best wishes to you and yours.

My dear Sir,
Your very obliged
PERCY B. SHELLEY.

[Addressed]
T. C. MEDWIN, Esq.,
Horsham,
Sussex

HARRIET SHELLEY TO CATHERINE NUGENT

Cooke's Hotel, Dover Street, Piccadilly,
June 22nd [1813].

MY DEAR MRS. NUGENT,

The kind expressions contained in your last letter gave me sincere pleasure, feeling as I did that I had not acted according to my ideas of right and wrong in delaying to write to you. I am sorry to hear that poor Lawless is confined [in prison]. If he had taken his friend's advice all his debts would have been settled long ago; but pride, that bane of all human happiness, unfortunately stepped in and marred all his good prospects. Mr. Ryan is still in London; but I expect to hear daily of his leaving us. Have you had any good weather, for ours is miserable? Our summer has not yet commenced. The fruit is still sour for want of sun, and will continue so from the present appearance of the weather. Our Irish servant [Daniel Healey] is going to leave us. Poor fellow, he pines after his dear Ireland, and is at the same time very ill. He was never of any use to

71

us; but so great was his attachment that we could not bear to send him away. Mr. Shelley has broken off the negotiation, and will have no more to say to his son, because that son will not write to the people of Oxford, and declare his return to Christianity. Did you ever hear of such an old dotard? It seems that so long as he lives, Bysshe must never hope to see or hear anything of his family. This is certainly an unpleasant circumstance, particularly as his mother wishes to see him, and has a great affection for him. What think you of Bonaparte? To most of the Irish he is a great favourite. I only wish we had peace. So long a war as this has been is indeed too dreadful to continue much longer. How is your health? I am afraid you sit too close to your business [paper torn, word lost] to enjoy good health; yet, as the winter is gone, surely you need not make any more warm tippets! That will be time enough next November. We have not seen much of Godwin, for his wife is so dreadfully disagreeable that I could not bear the idea of seeing her. Mr. S. has done that away, tho', by telling G. that I could not bear the society of his darling wife. Poor man, we are not the only people who find her troublesome. Mr. S. joins me and Eliza in kind regards to you, and believe me yours with esteem

H. S.

[Addressed]
   Mrs. Nugent,
     No. 101 *Grafton Street,*
      St. Stephen's Green, Dublin

CCXXI
TO JOHN WILLIAMS
London

Cook's Hotel
Dover Street, Piccadilly.
June 27, 1813.

My dear Williams,

    I am very happy to hear that you are in Town. If you can call any time before two o'clock, I shall be at home, if afterwards, Mrs. S. will be very happy to see you. I dine out to-day

I remain
Your very sincere friend,

P. B. Shelley.

Dan will show you the way.

[Addressed]
   To John Williams,
     White Hart Coffee House,
     Holborn

LETTERS

CCXXII
TO THOMAS JEFFERSON HOGG[1]

[? *Cook's Hotel, Dover Street,*
June 27, 1813.]

MY DEAR FRIEND,
I have lost or mislaid the letter of which I spoke to you.
I return your Flaxman with many thanks.—I believe I must break
my engagement with you to walk today, as I am going to see
Williams the Welchman. I will be at your lodgings about four
o'clock.

Yours affectionately

P. B. SHELLEY.

[Addressed]
T. JEFFERSON HOGG, Esq.,
No. 70 *Chancery Lane*

CCXXIII
TO THOMAS CHARLES MEDWIN
Horsham

Cooke's Hotel, Dover Street,
June 28, 1813.

MY DEAR SIR,
I am happy to inform you that Mrs. Shelley has been safely
delivered of a little girl,[1] and is now rapidly recovering.—
I could not however, leave her in her present state, and therefore
still consider your proposal of fixing the interview in London as the
most eligible.

---

[1] In Mr. Carl H. Pforzheimer's collection.

[1] Shelley's eldest child, born shortly before the date of this letter, was named Ianthe
Elizabeth. Ianthe is the name of the lady in *Queen Mab*, which also saw the light this
year; the name of Elizabeth was that of Shelley's favourite sister, and also of Harriet's
sister. Ianthe Shelley, who became Mrs. Esdaile, died in June, 1876, and was buried in
Cothelstone Churchyard, near Taunton. Her descendants are Shelley's only living
representatives.

I need not tell you, that the sooner I have the pleasure of seeing you, the sooner my mind and that of my wife will be relieved from a most unpleasant feeling of embarrassment and uncertainty.—You may entirely confide in my secrecy and prudence.—

I desire [my] very best remembrances to all yours, and remain

Dear Sir

Very faithfully yours, per scribe

P. B. Shelley.

[Addressed]
    T. C. Medwin, Esqre.,
      Horsham,
      Sussex

CCXXIV
TO THOMAS CHARLES MEDWIN
Horsham

Cooke's Hotel, Dover Street,
July 6, 1813.

My dear Sir,

    I shall be most happy to see you at six o'clock, to dinner, to-morrow. I think this plan is the better as the Horsham Coach will come nearer to this part of the town. Mrs. Shelley unites with me in best remembrances to all your family.

I remain, Dear Sir.

Yours very faithfully,

P. B. Shelley.

[Addressed]
    T. C. Medwin, Esq.,
      Horsham, Sussex

LETTERS

CCXXV
TO THOMAS JEFFERSON HOGG

Cooke's Hotel,
Friday [July 9, 1813].

MY DEAR FRIEND,
Medwin, the attorney of Horsham, stayed so late on the night of my promised visit, that I could not come. Last night your short note arrived, also beyond its hour, and the N[ewton]s[1] had already taken me with them. This night the N[ewton]s have a party at Vauxhall; if you will call here at *nine* o'clock we will go together.

What can your notes mean; how suspicious you have become. I will not insert *one but*. Leonora[2] has arrived. Medwin dines with me. Harriet is quite well, and her infant better.

Your affectionate friend,
P. B. SHELLEY.

CCXXVI
TO THOMAS JEFFERSON HOGG

High Elms, Bracknell,
July 27, 1813.

MY DEAR FRIEND,
I was disappointed at being unable to call on you on Sunday morning [July 25]. My presence was required at home, but as I shall be in town in a few days, I expect still to have the pleasure of seeing you before your journey to the North.

[1] Shelley made the acquaintance of John Frank Newton (author of *The Return to Nature, or a Defence of the Vegetable Regimen,* 1811) through the Godwins, when he visited London in October and November, 1812. Shelley made use of Newton's book in his vegetarian note to *Queen Mab*, which he afterwards reprinted in 1813 as a separate pamphlet. At the Newtons' house in Chester Street, Shelley was admitted to a circle of very charming people, among whom were Mrs. Boinville (sister to Mrs. Newton), and her daughter Cornelia, who afterwards became Mrs. Turner. When the Shelleys took a furnished house at Bracknell and Mrs. Boinville went to live in the same village, the intimacy of the two families continued.
[2] Does this relate to *Leonora*, the novel so called, jointly produced by Shelley and Hogg while at Oxford? The theory gains probability from Mrs. Newton's reference (Hogg's *Life of Shelley*, Vol. II, 477) to having "read the first part of an early work" of Hogg's, at Bracknell or London some time before October 21, 1813.

75

LETTERS

Tell me when you depart from London. I am anxious to see you, or if I cannot, to write to you at greater length. It is far more probable that we shall remain here until the Spring.

I know you will be happy even to receive these few lines, and therefore I do not wait until to-morrow, when I should write a longer letter.

Your very affectionate Friend,

PERCY B. SHELLEY.

HARRIET SHELLEY TO CATHERINE NUGENT

High Elms House, Bracknell, Berkshire,
August 8 [1813].

MY DEAR MRS. NUGENT,

I confess I have been guilty of seeming unkindness in not writing before; but such a multiplicity of business has occupied me ever since the receipt of your last that I have not had a moment to spare, even to you, my good friend. The babe is quite well, and very much grown. She is indebted to you for many kind enquiries, which one day she will thank you for in person. Mr. S. is of age, but no longer heir to the immense property of his sires. They are trying to take it away, and will I am afraid succeed, as it appears there is a flaw in the drawing up of the settlement, by which they can deprive him of everything. This is a beautiful idea, and well worthy the noble men who have formed it, among whom I suspect a certain *great personage*. They have put it into Chancery, though I fancy it can and will be kept an entire secret. You may suppose that we will do everything to prevent this shameful abuse of property, as we are convinced that more good would be effected if we have it, than if they regain it. We are now in a house 30 miles from London, merely for convenience. How long we remain is uncertain, as I fear our necessities will oblige us to remove to a greater distance. Our friends the Newtons are trying to do everything in their power to serve us; but our doom is decided. You who know us may well judge of our feelings. To have all our plans set aside in this manner is a miserable thing. Not that I regret the loss, but for the sake of those I intended to benefit. Mr. S. unites with me and Eliza in kind regards, whilst believe me your firmly attached friend,

H. S.

LETTERS

HARRIET SHELLEY TO CATHERINE NUGENT

High Elms House, Bracknell, Berks.
Sep. 10 [1813].

MY DEAR MRS. NUGENT,
I hasten to answer your last letter and to give you the same hopes which we entertain about the subject of my last. Mr. Shelley has seen his father and told him of what he heard, which he denied, and received him very kindly. Since then his lawyer has employed a council (*sic*). His opinion is at present tending (*sic*). I have no doubt now, tho' I had at first, that they can take it away. I have a very bad opinion of all lawyers in general, and I rather think Mr. S.'s lawyer was either told so by someone, or he thought it necessary to employ a council. They are forever playing a losing game into each other's hands. I am very sorry to hear you have been so ill. I hope sincerely you will soon recover, and do not, I pray you, sit so close to your business; for it is not one that contributes to the happiness of the many, only the few, who ought not, in my opinion, to indulge in such useless luxuries at the expense of so many who are even now at a loss for food. Of late we have had many arguments concerning the respect that all men pay to property. Now what do you think of this affair? I wish much to know if your ideas on this subject correspond with ours! I will not tell you what they are yet as I have an excellent reason which you will acknowledge when you hear it. The post has just brought me a letter from Mr. Shelley's sister, who says that her father is doing all in his power to prevent his being arrested. I think even his family pride must long to give way on the present occasion. [*Paper torn*] keeps everything a secret, but Mrs. Shelley tells her son everything she hears. I will write again soon and tell you everything that takes place. With every good wish for your happiness, in which we all unite, believe me most affectionately your friend,

H. SHELLEY.

We think of going to our favourite Nantgwillt, but not yet. You will certainly hear from me again at this house before we can go. Let me hear from you soon.

CCXXVII
TO THOMAS HOOKHAM

Warwick, Monday Night.
[*Endorsed Oct.* 6, 1813.]

MY DEAR HOOKHAM,
We are on our way to the Lakes. We shall take our first station at Lowood Inn on the banks of Windermere.

You will recieve [*sic*] a package from Chapel-House, which I w[oul]d thank you to send on to Lowood Inn directed to Peacock, together with his small trunk now at your House containing books. These may be sent by the Coach, and sent immediately, as the contents of the former are required. It formed part of our luggage and was too heavy for the Carriage.[1]

I very much regret that I did not see you on Saturday with Starling. I had wished to converse with you on a subject of some import. All I will tell you now is that I gave Starling a Post Obit of 2000£ in return for 500£ advanced. I shall [*altered to* wish you to] consider all communications made to you on this subject as secret. I may confide to you surmises probably rash, and possibly ill founded. To your secrecy and friendship I shall commit them.

Direct to us at Lowood Inn, Ambleside, Westmoreland. I am anxious to hear from you.

I hope your knee now suffers you to walk.

Adieu.

We all unite in best wishes.

I remain
Yours very sincerely,
P. B. SHELLEY.

Direct
Lowood Inn. Ambleside. Westmoreland.

HARRIET SHELLEY TO CATHERINE NUGENT

[*Low Wood Inn, Westmoreland*],
Sunday, October 11 [1813].

MY DEAR MRS. NUGENT,

We are again among our dear mountains. One week has sufficed to perform a journey of more than 300 miles, with my sweet babe, who I am most thankful to say has received no injury from the journey. I am now staying at Low Wood Inn, which is close to the Lake of Winandermere in Westmoreland. We do not wish any one to know where we are. Therefore if any one should ask you I rely upon [your] friendship for not satisfying their curiosity. Have you seen Daniel? We were obliged to discharge him, for his conduct was so unprincipled that it was impossible to have him in our service any longer. Is Mr. Lawless out of prison yet? Had he not taken us in as he did, Bysshe would have done something for him; but his behaviour was altogether so dishonest that Mr. Shelley will not do anything for him at present. If he wished it he could not, for he is obliged to pay 3 for 1, which is so ruinous that he will only raise a sufficient [sum] to pay his debts. In November he is to see his father; but I do not expect they will settle

[1] The carriage which Shelley procured some months before was called into service for this journey. The party consisted of Shelley, Harriet, her little daughter Ianthe, Eliza Westbrook, and Peacock.

anything, for Mr. S. will never give way to his son in the least. How has your health been since I heard from you last; I sincerely hope you are better, and that you will take care of yourself, I wish you could see my sweet babe. She is so fair, with such blue eyes, that the more I see her the more beautiful she looks. Some day, my dear friend, I hope you will come to England, and pay us a visit. When we get our dear Nantgwillt, then I may make sure of you. Mr. S. joins me and Eliza in kind regards to you, and may you ever be happy is the best and first wish of your sincere friend,

H. SHELLEY.

Direct your letter to me at Mrs. Calvert's, Greta Bank, Keswick, *Cumberland*.

HARRIET SHELLEY TO CATHERINE NUGENT

Edinburgh,
October 20 [1813].

MY DEAR MRS. NUGENT,
My last letter was written from the lakes of Cumberland, where we intended to stay till next Spring; but not finding any house that would suit us we came on to this far-famed city. A little more than two years has passed since I made my first visit here to be united to Mr. Shelley. To me they have been the happiest and longest years of my life. The rapid succession of events since that time make the two years appear unusually long. I think the regular method of measuring time is by the number of different ideas which a rapid succession of events naturally give rise to. When I look back to the time before I was married I seem to feel I have lived a long time. Tho' my age is but eighteen, yet I feel as if I was much older. Why are you so silent, my dear friend? I earnestly hope you are not ill. I am afraid it is nearly a month since I heard from you. I know well you would write oftener if you could. What is your employment on a Sunday? I think on those days you might snatch a few minutes to gratify my wishes. Do not direct your letter to me at Mrs. Calvert's; but to the post office in this city. We think of remaining here all this winter. Tho' by no means fond of cities, yet I wished to come here, for when we went to the lakes we found such a set of human beings living there that it took off all our desire of remaining among the mountains. This City is, I think, much the best. The people here are not so intolerant as they are in London. Literature stands on a higher footing here than anywhere else. My darling babe is quite well, and very much improved. Pray let me hear from you soon. Tell me if I can do anything for you. Mr. Shelley joins me and Eliza in kind regards to you, whilst I remain your affectionate friend,

H. S.

Do not tell anyone where we are.

LETTERS

HARRIET SHELLEY TO CATHERINE NUGENT

No. 36 Frederick Street, Edinburgh,
[*Postmark*, "23 Nov., 1813."]

MY DEAR MRS. NUGENT,

Your letter called forth the most lively feelings of regret. It is so long a time since I received a letter from you that I began to feel the greatest anxiety on your account. How much do I feel for your ill state of health. Tell me if I can be of any service to you. How are you situated with respect to personal comfort and attendance? Have you anyone by you who can sympathize with you? If you have not let me come and attend you. It is the office of a friend to soothe the languid moments of illness. The mind looks for sympathy more at such a time than when in perfect health. I am afraid Lawless has practised upon you, as he did upon us. Some time back he wrote to Mr. S. about Daniel, who lived with us, saying we had not treated him well. Now the truth is this—we were very fond of this man: he appeared so much attached to us, with so much honesty and simplicity, that we kept him tho' of no use whatever. For the whole time he stayed with us he never did anything. Afterwards he turned out very ungrateful, and behaved so insolent that we were obliged to turn him away. This is the man Lawless wrote about; but do not think I am offended at what you say of him, as I know it proceeds from the goodness of your heart, and I only wish the object were more deserving of your kindness. There has been no conciliation between Mr. [S. and ?] his father. Their opinions are so contrary, that I do not think there is the least chance of their being reconciled. His father is now ill with the gout; but there is no danger I suppose. If there was he would send for his son and be reconciled to him. I sincerely hope this will find you better. You know what pleasure it would give me to render you any service. Therefore do not let a false opinion of justice keep you from applying to me in anything in which I can serve you. Mr. Shelley and Eliza join me in all good wishes for the recovery of your health, and believe me most firmly, your attached friend,

H. SHELLEY.

CCXXVIII
TO THOMAS JEFFERSON HOGG

Edinburgh,
Nov. 26, 1813.

MY DEAR FRIEND,

I have written to you several times since I received your letter at Bracknell. My letters were directed to you at Stopton in Durham, but I suppose that you had nothing particular to communicate in return—as, indeed, their contents were not of extraordinary importance.

I am happy to hear that you have returned to London, as I shall

LETTERS

shortly have the pleasure of seeing you again. I shall return to
London alone. My evenings will often be spent at the Newtons,
where I presume you are no infrequent visitor.

Your novel is now printed[1] I need not assure you with what pleasure this extraordinary and animated tale is perused by me. Every
one to whom I have shown it agrees with me in admitting that it
bears indisputable marks of a singular and original genius. Write
more like this. Delight us again with a character so natural and en-
ergetic as Alexy—vary again the scene with an uncommon combination of the most natural and simple circumstances: but do not
persevere in writing after you grow weary of your toil; "aliquando
bonus dormitat Homerus;" and the swans and the Eleutherarchs
are proofs that you were a little sleepy.

I have for some time given myself to study. I have read "Tacitus," many of Cicero's philosophical works (who is, in my estimation, one of the most admirable characters the world ever produced),
and Homer's "Odyssey." I am now studying Laplace, " Systeme
du Monde," and am determined not to relax until I have attained
considerable proficiency in the physical sciences.

I have examined Hume's reasonings with respect to the non-
existence of external things, and, I confess, they appear to me to follow from the doctrines of Locke. What am I to think of a philosophy which conducts to such a conclusion?—*Sed hæc hactenus.*

Mr. Peacock is on a visit with us this winter. He is a very mild
agreeable man, and a good scholar. His enthusiasm is not very
ardent, nor his views very comprehensive: but he is neither superstitious, ill-tempered, dogmatical, or proud.

I have translated the two Essays of Plutarch, περὶ σαρκοφαγίας,
which we read together. They are very excellent. I intend to
comment upon them, and to reason in my preface concerning the

[1] Hogg's novel, "Memoirs/of/Prince Alexy. Haimatoff./Translated from/the original
Latin MSS./under the inspection of/the Prince,/By/John Brown, Esq./London:/
Printed for T. Hookham,/15 Old Bond Street,/1813." pp. 236, 12 mo., published Nov-
ember 8, 1813. Although a copy of this rare little book was secured by the British
Museum in 1878, Professor Dowden was the first to identify it as Hogg's, and he made
known the discovery in his article, "Some Early Writings of Shelley," published in the
Contemporary Review, September, 1884, when he also drew attention to the fact that
Shelley had reviewed the book in the *Critical Review* for December, 1814. Shelley's review, and a part of Professor Dowden's article, were issued together in 1886 as one of
the Shelley Society's publications under the editorship of Mr. Thomas J. Wise.

Orphic and Pythagoric system of diet.[2] Adieu! Believe me to be ever sincerely attached to you. My dear friend,

I am yours affectionately,

P. B. SHELLEY.

CCXXIX

TO———[1]

36 *Frederic Street,*
Edinburgh,
[28 *Nov.*, 1813
in another hand].

DEAR SIR,

I have been compelled, since I last wrote yesterday, to draw upon you for £30 for short date. I have to request that you would not return it, as the consequence would be, *our being driven out of our lodgings.* As the emergency is very pressing I doubted not but that I might depend upon your friendly assistance until the raising of £5,000.

We all unite in best respects to yourself and Mr. S.

I remain your very faithful St.

PERCY BYSSHE SHELLEY.

---

[2] Shelley apparently is here referring to his work, "/A/Refutation/of/Deism:/in/a/ Dialogue./ΣΥΝΕΤΟΙΣΙΝ/London:/Printed by Schulze and Dean,/13 Poland Street,/1813,"/ where he quotes from Plutarch's essay on eating flesh. There is no reference to the subject in the short preface. The British Museum copy of this book, formerly the property of Thomas Hookham, bears his name on the fly-leaf. An extract from this work was printed in *The Model Republic* for February, 1843. My friend, Mr. John A. Hookham, informs me that his cousin, Thomas Hookham, a son of Shelley's friend, was a contributor to the *Model Republic* at about this date; it is not unlikely that he may have supplied the extract from his father's copy of *A Refutation of Deism*, which was printed in that periodical.

[1] Now printed in full by permission of Mr. A. Edward Newton.

LETTERS

CCXXX
TO——

41 Skinner Street,
? Dec. 1813.

DEAR SIR,
   I have some hopes still remaining of raising money. The person with whom I am negotiating desires to know where the attested copy of the settlement is;—you would much oblige me by inclosing the address.
   I shall call upon you before I leave town.

Dear Sir,
Your ob: h: sert.
P. B. SHELLEY.

CCXXXI
TO MR. PIKE[1]

41 Skinner Street,
Snow Hill.

Mr. Shelley requests that Mr. Pike would give the Bearer the copy of the settlement in his possession. Mr. S. will return it in the course of the week.

[Addressed]
MR. PIKE,
   Gate Street,
     Lincoln's Inn

---

[1] A money-lender with whom Shelley was in negotiation in October 1814. The original is owned by Mr. A. Edward Newton.

LETTERS

CCXXXII
TO TIMOTHY SHELLEY

Bracknell, Berks.,
March 13, 1814.

MY DEAR FATHER

Permit me to return you my grateful acknowledgements for the polite reception with which you favored Mr. Amory,[1] and the kind interest you expressed to him concerning my embarrassments. Whatever may be the result of my present situation, I am consoled by reflecting that it will not be indifferent to my nearest, and most honored connexions.

I lament to inform you that the posture of my affairs is so critical that I can no longer delay to raise money by the sale of Post Obit bonds to a considerable amount. I trust that the many expedients which I have employed to avoid this ruinous measure, will testify the reluctance with which my necessities compel me at length to have recourse to it. I need not urge the vast sacrifizes which money lenders require, nor press upon your attention that I put it out of my power to resettle the estate in any manner by conceding to their demands. Upon your good wishes, and consoling assurances I rely with the most entire confidence. I know that you do not want the will, but only the power of doing everything which I could reasonably expect. But surely my grandfather must perceive that his hopes of preserving and perpetuating the integrity of the estate will be frustrated by neglecting to relieve my necessities, he knows that I have the power, which however reluctantly I shall be driven to exert of dismembering the property should I survive himself and you. I do not take the liberty of frequently addressing you, but I hope the urgency of this occasion will be thought sufficient to excuse the present exercise of the licence you permitted.

---

[1] Mr. Amory was Shelley's solicitor. In his negotiations with the money-lenders Shelley probably realised how important it was that the validity of his marriage as a minor in Edinburgh should not be questioned. Perhaps he remembered that he had not fulfilled the conditions of the Scottish marriage laws. On March 22 Shelley and Godwin went to Doctor's Commons to obtain a licence, and on March 24, Shelley and Harriet were married at St. George's, Hanover Square, by Edward Williams, curate, in the presence of Harriet's father, Mr. John Westbrook, and another witness.

I hope my mother and sisters, to whom I desire to be affectionately remembered continue as well as at Mr. Amory's visit.

Believe me, my dear Father,
Your very dutiful Son,

P. B. SHELLEY.

[Addressed]
T. SHELLEY, Esq., M.P.,
Field Place,
Horsham,
Sussex

CCXXXIII
TO THOMAS JEFFERSON HOGG

Bracknell,
March 16, 1814.

MY DEAR FRIEND,
I promised to write to you, when I was in the humour. Our
intercourse has been too much interrupted for my consolation. My
spirits have not sufficed to induce the exertion of determining me to
write to you. My value, my affection for you, have sustained no
diminution; but I am a feeble, wavering, feverish being, who requires support and consolation, which his energies are too exhausted to return.
I have been staying with Mrs. B[oinville][1] for the last month; I

[1] The following description of Mrs. Boinville is derived from Professor Dowden's
charming sketch of that lady in his *Life of Shelley*, Vol. I, p. 378 *et seqq.*, to which the
reader is referred. Harriet Boinville and her sister Cornelia, Mrs. Newton, were daughters of Mr. Collins, a cultured, liberal-minded and wealthy West Indian planter who resided in England. His house was visited by many of the constitutional emigrants from
France, among whom was M. de Boinville, an *émigré*, formerly a *fermier général*, whose
property had been confiscated by the revolutionary government. When M. de Boinville declared his love to Miss Collins, and her father objected to the match on the score
of his poverty, she decided to elope with her lover to Gretna Green, where she was
united to him by the blacksmith; the couple afterwards married a second time according to the rites of the Church of England. Mrs. Boinville had an income of her own
on which she and her husband managed to live. Their daughter Cornelia, born in
1795, afterwards became Mrs. Turner. In 1812 M. de Boinville went to Russia with
Napoleon and died during the retreat from Moscow in February, 1813, shortly after the
death of his wife's father, Mr. Collins. The sorrow that had clouded the life of Mrs.

have escaped, in the society of all that philosophy and friendship combine, from the dismaying solitude of myself They have revived in my heart the expiring flame of life. I have felt myself translated to a paradise, which has nothing of mortality, but its transitoriness; my heart sickens at the view of that necessity, which will quickly divide me from the delightful tranquillity of this happy home—for it has become my home. The trees, the bridge, the minutest objects, have already a place in my affections.

My friend, you are happier than I. You have the pleasures as well as the pains of sensibility. I have sunk into a premature old age of exhaustion, which renders me dead to everything, but the unenviable capacity of indulging the vanity of hope, and a terrible susceptibility to objects of disgust and hatred.

My temporal concerns are slowly rectifying themselves; I am astonished at my own indifference to their event. I live here like the insect that sports in a transient sunbeam, which the next cloud shall obscure for ever. I am much changed from what I was. I look with regret to our happy evenings at Oxford, and with wonder at the hopes which in the excess of my madness I there encouraged. Burns says, you know,

> Pleasures are like poppies spread,
> You seize the flower—the bloom is fled;
> Or like the snow-falls in the river,
> A moment white—then lost for ever.

Eliza[2] is still with us—not here!—but will be with me when the

Boinville had turned her hair quite white, but a certain youthful beauty of her face was still retained. In allusion to her appearance, Shelley named her Maimuna in recollection of the mysterious spinner in Southey's *Thalaba*, for

> "Her face was as a damsel's face,
> And yet her hair was gray."

In a letter from Bracknell to Hogg, dated March 11, 1814, Mrs. Boinville says in allusion to Shelley's visit: "I will not have you despise homespun pleasures. Shelley is making a trial of them with us, and likes them so well that he is resolved to leave off rambling, and to begin a course of them himself. Seriously, I think his mind and body want rest. His journeys after what he has never found have racked his purse and his tranquillity. He is resolved to take a little care of the former in pity to the latter, which I applaud, and shall second with all my might. He has deeply interested us. In the course of your intimacy he must have made you feel what we now feel for him. He is seeking a house close to us; and, if he succeeds, we shall have an additional motive to induce you to come among us in the summer."

[2] A month later Eliza Westbrook took her final departure from the Shelley household. Mrs. Boinville, again writing to Hogg from Bracknell, on April 18, 1814, says: "Mrs. N[ewton] is wonderfully recovered. Air and exercise, and friendly conversation, are just

infinite malice of destiny forces me to depart. I am now but little inclined to contest this point. I certainly hate her with all my heart and soul. It is a sight which awakens an inexpressible sensation of disgust and horror, to see her caress my poor little Ianthe, in whom I may hereafter find the consolation of sympathy. I sometimes feel faint with the fatigue of checking the overflowings of my unbounded abhorrence for this miserable wretch. But she is no more than a blind and loathsome worm, that cannot see to sting.

I have begun to learn Italian again. I am reading Beccaria, "Dei delitti e pene."[3] His essay seems to contain some excellent remarks, though I do not think that it deserves the reputation it has gained. Cornelia assists me in this language. Did I not once tell you that I thought her cold and reserved? She is the reverse of this, as she is the reverse of everything bad. She inherits all the divinity of her mother.

What have you written? I have been unable even to write a common letter. I have forced myself to read "Beccaria" and Dumont's "Bentham." I have sometimes forgotten that I am not an inmate of this delightful home—that a time will come which will cast me again into the boundless ocean of abhorred society.

I have written nothing, but one stanza, which has no meaning, and that I have only written in thought:

> Thy dewy looks sink in my breast;
> Thy gentle words stir poison there;
> Thou hast disturbed the only rest
> That was the portion of despair!
> Subdued to Duty's hard control,
> I could have borne my wayward lot;
> The chains that bind this ruined soul
> Had cankered then—but crushed.it not.

This is the vision of a delirious and distempered dream, which passes away at the cold clear light of morning. Its surpassing ex-

restoring her good looks. Shelley is again a widower; his beauteous half went to town on Thursday with Miss Westbrook, who is gone to live, I believe, at Southampton."
[3] Cesare Marchese de Beccaria (1735?-1794). The book which Shelley was reading (on Crimes and Punishments) is an argument against capital punishment and tortures, published in 1764, and was the outcome of Beccaria's studies of the French encyclopædists. The essay was received in France with enthusiasm, notably by Voltaire and Diderot, who published commentaries.

cellence and exquisite perfections have no more reality than the colour of an autumnal sunset. Adieu!

> Believe me truly and affectionately yours,
>
> P. B. SHELLEY.

I hear that you often see the N[ewton]s. Present my kindest regards to Mrs. N[ewton]; remember me also to her husband, who, you know, has quarrelled with me, although I have not consented to quarrel with him.

CCXXXIV
TO JOHN WILLIAMS

[*April* 14, 1814.]

[FRAGMENT]

DEAR WILLIAMS,

If I were not absent from London I would certainly see you. But I have gone to some distance.

It is perfectly impossible that I should meet the bill in September next. I have no prospect of getting money until my Grandfather's death. I should only deceive [sic] you, and increase your distress by signing such a bond.[1]

I wish that you would call upon my Solicitor, Mr. Amory, 59 Old Bond Street, as I am unable to come to town. He would instruct you in the best possible security I can give you, and that you shall have. He is averse to my granting any *post-obits*. I am willing, however, to do so to three times the amount of the sum, therefore if this proposal pleases you, do not go to Mr. Amory.

.   .   .   .

[Addressed]
JOHN WILLIAMS, Esq.

[Endorsed, P. B. SHELLEY, Esq.
April 14, 1814.]

[1] See footnote, Vol. II, p. 54.

LETTERS

Old Bond Street,
May 6, 1814.

SIR,

I beg to inform you that to the best of my knowledge, having made every enquiry on the subject, there has been no portion of the Shelley Estate sold under the Settlement of 1791 except that to Lord George Cavendish. As to any transaction of my own I have raised no money on the reversion unless in one instance the sum of £500, and I assure you on my word of honour that I shall engage n no transactions that can be any way prejudicial to the interest of Mr. Nash, the purchaser.

Yours, &c.,

PERCY B. SHELLEY.

CCXXXVI
TO JOHN WILLIAMS
Tremadoc

15 *Old Bond Street* [*London*],
May 14, 1814.

MY DEAR WILLIAMS,

I have just arrived in Town and find your letter. I earnestly entreated you to refer me to some person here, to whom I would give all that you wish on receiving a receipt in full of everything to which I stand bound. I now repeat this request, and beg you to appoint such a person with the least possible delay.

[1] On March 4, 1814, Shelley had made the sale of a *post-obit*—£8000 for £2593 10s.— the purchaser being Andrew John Nash and George Augustus Nash. His object in raising the money was primarily, if not entirely, to assist Godwin. The indenture, however, was not made until July, and the transaction, therefore, was not then complete at the date of Shelley's letter to his father of March 13. Mr. Teesdale was Messrs. Nash's solicitor. Shortly after the death of Sir Bysshe in 1815 Shelley filed a Bill in Chancery against Messrs. Nash to have the Indenture dated July 12, 1814, rescinded, but the case went against the poet, judgment being given in favour of the defendants on May 28, 1818.

LETTERS

I sincerely sympathise in your distresses which are increased by your own remissness, at least in this instance—I regret that I did not see you when in Town.

Yours faithfully,

P. B. SHELLEY.

[Addressed]
MR. JOHN WILLIAMS,
Ynys-y-Towyn,
Tremadoc, Carnarvonshire,
North Wales

Eliza Westbrook, who had lived with the Shelleys during the whole of their married life, must be reckoned as an important factor in our consideration of Shelley's separation from Harriet. Had she left their house some months earlier, events might have ordered themselves differently. The intense loathing with which Shelley regarded his sister-in-law finds expressions in his letter to Hogg on March 16, 1814, and a month later she departed from the Shelley household. The cold and unsympathetic manner that Harriet assumed towards Shelley at this time may have been caused by his undisguised dislike of her beloved sister. "His violent antipathy," says Hogg, with regard to Shelley's aversion to Eliza Westbrook, "was probably not less unreasonable than his former excess of deference, and blind compliance and concession towards a person whose counsels and direction could never have been prudent, safe or judicious." At this most critical period Harriet foolishly allowed herself to be influenced by Eliza Westbrook, and she was probably acting under her advice when some months earlier she prevailed upon Shelley (whose affairs were extremely embarrassed) to provide her with a carriage, silver-plate and expensive clothes. The idea that she should care for such things was altogether repugnant to him, who had formerly said of Harriet that "the ease and simplicity of her habits" constituted in his eyes her greatest charm. After the birth of her first child (whom she refused to suckle, notwithstanding Shelley's desire that she should do so), Harriet's manner underwent a change. "Her studies," Hogg tells us, "which had been so constant and exemplary, had dwindled away to nothing, and Bysshe had ceased any interest in them, and to urge her, as of old, to devote herself to the cultivation of her mind. When I called upon her, she proposed a walk, if the weather was fine, instead of the vigorous and continuous readings of preceding years. The walk commonly conducted us to some fashionable bonnet-shop; the reading, it is not to be denied, was sometimes tiresome, the contemplation of bonnets was always so. When I called upon Bysshe, Harriet was often absent; she had gone out with Eliza,—gone to her father's. Bysshe himself was sometimes in London, and sometimes at Bracknell, where he spent a good deal of his time in visiting certain friends [Mrs. Boinville and her daughter] with whom at this period he was in close alliance, and upon terms of the greatest intimacy, and by which connection his subsequent conduct, I think, was much influenced." (*Life of Shelley,* Vol. II, pp. 500–1.) According to Mrs. Boinville's letter to Hogg of April 18, 1814 (*Life of Shelley,* Vol. II, p. 533), Shelley was then at Bracknell. Harriet had gone to town, presumably to her father's, and Eliza Westbrook had taken her departure. Although Harriet had now become cold and proud, Shelley still hoped to regain her love, and in some verses inscribed "To Harriet, 1814" (first printed in Professor Dowden's *Life of Shelley,* Vol. I, p. 413), he makes a pathetic appeal for her affection. Whether Harriet was moved by this appeal or not, we do not know. She evidently never intended to alienate herself from Shelley, but she was living in Bath during the early days of July, while Shelley had remained in London since the end of May, excepting for a period of ten days from June 8th to the 18th. Shelley, however, still continued to correspond with Harriet, as is shown by the following letter which she addressed to Thomas Hookham on July 6 or 7, 1814, from 6 Queen's Square, Bath.

LETTERS

"My dear Sir
    "You will greatly oblige me by giving the enclosed to Mr Shelley. I would not trouble you but it is now four days since I have heard from him which to me is an age. Will you write by return of post and tell me what has become of him as I always fancy something dreadful has happened if I do not hear from him. If you tell me that he is well I shall not come to London; but if I do not hear from you or him I shall certainly come as I cannot endure this dreadful state of suspence. You are his friend and can feel for me.

"I remain yours truly
H S."

6 *Queens Square*
  Bath

The above letter sheet is postmarked 7 Jy. 1814, & endorsed (later) with the same date : Robt.

Although Shelley's own pecuniary affairs in 1814 were most unsatisfactory, his admiration for Godwin was such that he engaged to help him out of his embarrassments by assisting him to raise a sum of money, said to be no less than three thousand pounds. This was the first of these negotiations on behalf of Godwin which continued to be such a source of trouble to Shelley almost till his last days. He had not been to Godwin's house since March 22, when he went with him to procure his marriage licence. But it was now necessary for Shelley to be much in Godwin's company, and after he returned to London on July 18 he joined the Skinner Street household each day at dinner. It was during these days that Shelley first came into contact with Mary Godwin, who had just returned from Scotland on a visit to the Baxters. On June 8, the date of Lord Cochrane's trial, Hogg first saw Mary Godwin. He met Shelley in Cheapside, and walked with him through Newgate Street to Godwin's shop in Skinner Street. Shelley enquired for Godwin, who was not at home, and while he was waiting for the philosopher in his bookroom, "the door was partially and softly opened. A thrilling voice called 'Shelley!' A thrilling voice answered 'Mary!' And he darted out of the room, like an arrow from the bow of the far-shooting king. A very young female, fair and fair-headed, pale indeed, with a piercing look, wearing a frock of tartan, an unusual dress in London at the time, had called him out of the room. He was absent a very short time—a minute or two, and then returned. 'Godwin is out; there is no use in waiting.' So we continued our walk along Holborn. 'Who was that, pray?' I asked; 'a daughter?' 'Yes.' 'A daughter of William Godwin?' 'The daughter of Godwin and Mary.' "
    Suggestions have been made that Harriet was unfaithful to Shelley before their separation, and that she was in love with a Major Ryan who is mentioned in her correspondence with Miss Nugent. Apparently there is nothing to support this supposition; on the contrary, the evidence is entirely in her favour, Peacock, Hogg and Hookham, all of whom knew her intimately, believed her to be perfectly innocent of any guilt, and Thornton Hunt and Trelawny shared the same belief. On the other hand, Shelley is said to have been convinced to the contrary in July, 1814, and to have held this opinion to the day of his death. But if Shelley had not thought her guilty, the fact that he was certain she no longer loved him was sufficient in his sight to make it impossible for him to live with Harriet as her husband.
    The convictions on the subject of marriage that he had expressed in *Queen Mab* in 1813 remained his convictions in 1814. He felt he was free to give his heart to Mary, with whom he was now deeply in love. Harriet did not realise that she had lost Shelley, and she came to London at his request on July 14, when Shelley disclosed to her his position. Peacock says, "The separation did not take place by mutual consent. I cannot think that Shelley ever so represented it. He never did so to me: and the account which Harriet herself gave me of the entire proceeding was decidedly contradictory to any such supposition. He might well have said, after seeing Mary Wollstonecraft Godwin, '*Ut vidi! ut perii!*' Nothing that I ever read in tale or history could ever present a more striking image of a sudden, violent, irresistible, uncontrollable passion, than that

91

under which I found him labouring when, at his request, I went up from the country to call on him in London. Between his old feelings towards Harriet, *from whom he was not then separated*, and his new passion for Mary, he showed in his looks, in his gestures, in his speech, the state of a mind, suffering, 'like a little Kingdom, the nature of an insurrection.' His eyes were bloodshot, his hair and dress disordered. He caught up a bottle of laudanum and said, 'I never part from this.' He added, 'I am always repeating your lines from Sophocles—

' Man's happiest lot is not to be :
    And when we tread life's thorny steep
    Most blest are they, who earliest free
    Descend to earth's eternal sleep.'

Again he said more calmly : 'Everyone who knows me must know that the partner of my life should be one who can feel poetry and understand philosophy. Harriet is a noble animal, but she can do neither.' I said, 'It always appeared to me that you were very fond of Harriet.' Without affirming or denying this, he answered : ' But you did not know how I hated her sister.' "—*Fraser's Magazine*, January, 1860.

In connection with this subject, an important letter—dated November 20, 1814—should be consulted giving Harriet Shelley's version of the causes that led to her separation from Shelley. (See Appendix.)

IX

AUGUST 13, 1814, TO JUNE 22, 1815

FIRST VISIT TO THE CONTINENT

CCXXXVII
TO HARRIET SHELLEY[1]

Troyes, 120 miles from Paris on the way to Switzerland,
August 13, 1814.

MY DEAREST HARRIET,

I write to you from this detestable Town; I write to shew you that I do not forget you. I write to urge you to come to Switzerland, where you will at least find one firm and constant friend, to whom your interests will be always dear, by whom your feelings will never wilfully be injured. From none can you expect this but me. All else are either unfeeling and selfish, or have beloved friends of

[1] Corrected from a MS. copy of the letter in the Bodleian Library, Oxford. Shelley eloped with Mary Godwin from London on July 28, 1814. She left her father's shop in Skinner Street, before five o'clock that morning, accompanied by Jane Clairmont (the second Mrs. Godwin's daughter by her first marriage), and a few steps brought them to the corner of Hatton Garden, where Shelley was waiting with a postchaise. It is said that Jane was unaware of Mary's intended elopement, until she was persuaded to enter the chaise; and that she accompanied the lovers because she knew how to speak French, and they did not. At Dartford they took four horses, so as to gain speed. Dover was reached by four o'clock in the afternoon, and by six a small boat had been engaged and was ready to take them to Calais, a journey which they were informed would only take them two hours. After a long, stormy, and somewhat perilous passage, Calais was reached the next morning. Mrs. Godwin, who arrived at Calais shortly after the fugitives, had followed them down from London, and she endeavoured to persuade her daughter, Jane, to return with her, but without success. Shelley and these two young girls, in silk dresses, then resumed their journey. Passing through Boulogne and Abbeville, they reached Paris on August 2, and being detained there for some days for want of funds, they left again on August 8. Shelley purchased an ass to carry the luggage and Mary when she was tired, he and Jane intending to foot it to Switzerland. The ass proved useless and was sold, and a mule was purchased in its place. The journey then continued, but Shelley, having sprained his ankle on August 12, was compelled to ride. The same night Troyes was reached, where the travellers found accommodation at a filthy inn, and where Shelley wrote the above letter to Harriet. Here the mule was sold and an open carriage was purchased for five napoleons, and an incompetent driver was engaged. A week later they were at Neuchâtel inquiring in vain for letters. A small supply of money was obtained, and with it Shelley pressed on to the Lake of Lucerne, and took two rooms in a château at Brunnen at a guinea a month for six months. They did not, however, stay there more

95

their own as Mrs. Boinville to whom their attention and affection is confined.

I will write at length from Neufchatel or Uri. Direct your letters "d'etre laissees à la Bureau de Poste Neufchatel" until you hear again. We have journe[ye]d from Paris on foot with a mule to carry our baggage, and Mary who has not been sufficiently well to bear the fatigue of walking. We passed through a fertile country, neither interesting from the character of the inhabitants or the beauty of the scenery. We came 120 miles in four days. The last two days we past over the country that was the seat of war. I cannot describe to you the frightful desolation of this scene. Village after village entirely ruined and burned; the white ruins towering in innumerable forms of destruction among the beautiful trees. The inhabitants were famished. Families once perfectly independant now beg their bread in this wretched country. No provisions, no accommodation; filth, misery and famine every where. (You will see nothing of this in your route to Geneva.) I must remark to you that dreadful as these calamities are, I can scarcely pity the inhabitants. They are the most unamiable, inhospitable and unaccomodating of the human race.

We go by some carriage from this Town to Neufchatel because I have strained my leg, and am unable to walk. I hope to be

than forty-eight hours, having resolved to return home by water. Taking advantage of the Reuss and the Rhine, they could reach England without travelling a league on land. This they made a brave attempt to do, travelling through Germany and Holland, although sometimes they found it necessary to take a land conveyance. Rotterdam was at length reached, and from that place they sailed on September 8, arriving in London on September 13, and three days later they had taken lodgings at 56 Margaret Street, Cavendish Square. Professor Dowden says: "Shelley's relations with Harriet, though at times they wore a friendly appearance, could hardly be sound or happy at heart. From the Continent he had written to her as though each of the now-divided pair might be sincerely regardful of the other's interests; and, if we may trust Miss Clairmont, he had sent from Calais or Paris, through Harriet, directions to his bankers to honour her calls for money as far as his account permitted. On landing penniless from Rotterdam, Shelley drove to his bankers, and ascertained that all his money had been drawn. Failing elsewhere to procure the means of paying for his passage and the smaller charges of waterman and coachman, he applied, says Miss Clairmont, to Harriet, and not without success, although to the twenty pounds which she handed to him were added the reproaches of an injured wife." (*Life*, Vol. I, pp. 463–4.) Shelley and Mary kept a journal from the day of their union until Shelley's death. Some extracts from Mary's journal were afterwards published in 1817 together with a few of Shelley's letters belonging to the year 1816, and an account of his visit to the Continent for that year, etc., as *History of a Six Weeks' Tour, Through a Part of France, Switzerland, Germany and Holland.* . . . Professor Dowden has given a charming account of this tour in his *Life of Shelley*, Vol. I, pp. 439–460, with extracts from *Shelley's Journal;* the episode reads like a passage from Rousseau's *Confessions*.

recovered by that time; but on our last day's journey I was perfectly unable to walk, and Mary resigned the mule to me. Our walk has excepting this been sufficiently agreeable. We have met none of the robbers they prophesied at Paris. You shall know our adventures more detailed if I do not hear at Neufchatel, that I am soon to have the pleasure of communicating to you in person, and of welcoming you to some sweet retreat I will procure for you among the mountains.

I have written to Peacock to superintend money affairs. He is expensive, inconsiderate and cold but surely not utterly perfidious and unfriendly and unmindful of our kindness to him. Besides interest will secure his attention to these things.

I wish you to bring with you the two deeds which Tahourdin has to prepare for you, as also a copy of the settlement.

Do not part with any of your money. But what shall be done about the books. You can consult on the spot. With love to my sweet little Ianthe.

Ever most affectionately yours

S.

I write in great haste. We depart directly.

CCXXXVIII
TO MARY WOLLSTONECRAFT GODWIN

[*London,*
Monday, October 24, 1814.]

Staples Inn is within the jurisdiction of Middlesex. You may meet me with perfect safety at Adams's. No. 60 Fleet Street; I shall be in the shop precisely at 12 o'clock.

This separation is a calamity not to be endured patiently; I cannot support your absence. I thought that it would be less painful to me. But I feel a solitariness and a desolation of heart where you have been accustomed to be. But my beloved this will not last. Prudence and self denial will discomfit our enemies. We must be circumspect and active. I shall meet you soon. Be punctual. Bring the letter.[1]

---

[1] The period between Shelley's return from France in September, 1814, and January, 1815, when the death of Sir Bysshe took place, was one of dire poverty and privation

97

LETTERS

CCXXXIX
TO MARY WOLLSTONECRAFT GODWIN

[*London,*
Afternoon of Monday, October 24, 1814.]

I could not meet you at Adams'; I was unable to come before *one :* and of course missed you.

My own beloved girl we shall soon be restored to each other. The wretchedness of our separation I am convinced will endow me with eloquence and energies adequate to the peril. I am mournful and dejected *now*, but it is exquisite pleasure that I feel compared with the happiest moments of former times. Yes; a few days, perhaps a few hours, and the most inveterate of our enemies cannot deprive us of each other.

I have spent the day at Ballacheys.[1] I have been indefatigable in painting to him [the] horrible aspect of my affairs. He is indolent and listless but not like the Hookhams a cool villain. He sent for a friend of his, Mr. Watts a stock broker. Mr. Watts is an old, somewhat benevolent looking bald headed man. He said he would perhaps lend me 400£. He will give his answer on Thursday [October 27]. He seemed touched by my misfortunes, and indignant at the treachery of the Hookhams. I have reason to think that if he lends me this money on Post Obit: I may place the action to the credit of human nature.

My imagination is confounded by the uniform prospect of the perfidy and wickedness and hard heartedness of mankind. Mary for Shelley and Mary. Professor Dowden says that "the days of sorest trial, including those of severance [of Mary] from Shelley, lay between October 23rd and November 9th." On Saturday evening, October 22, a letter, addressed to Shelley, was handed into his lodgings in St. Pancras. The letter was from Fanny Godwin, who warned Shelley, it would seem, of some design against his personal liberty, in which directly or indirectly the Hookham brothers were believed to be concerned. The debt was apparently one of Harriet's, for which, of course, Shelley was responsible, and perhaps Hookham had informed the creditor—Charters—of Shelley's address. He endeavoured to raise £100 towards Charters's debt, but Harriet promised to raise the money herself. Shelley, however, had to leave the St. Pancras lodgings for fear of arrest for debt. (Dowden's *Shelley*, Vol. I, pp. 488–490.) In a letter dated August 31, 1844, Thomas Charters applied to Peacock in his capacity as executor, for the payment of Shelley's debt for coachmaker's work done for him up to November, 1815, amounting to £532 11s. 6d., for which he stated he held Shelley's Bill of Exchange drawn at four years after date with judgment entered up to secure payment. (Ingpen's *Shelley in England*, p. 638.)

[1] A member of the firm of Ballachey and Bridges.

most amply redeems their blackest crimes. But I confess to you that I have been shocked and staggered by Godwin's cold injustice. The places where I have seen that mans fine countenance bring bitterness home to my heart to think of his cutting cruelty.

I care not for the Hookhams. I'll tear their hearts out by the roots with irony and sarcasm if I find that they have dared to lift a thought against me. But in my absence from you, O light of my life, my very spirit of hope, I have at moments almost felt despair to think how cold and worldly Godwin has become.

When, where shall I meet you. I am at the London Coffee House. Write to me. But do not send a porter. Send Peacock or come yourself. ουκ εχω αργυριον.

I send you the Times newspaper. See where I have marked with ink and stifle your horror and indignation until we meet.[2]

I so passionately love my own Mary that we must not be absent long.

Give my love to Jane. I think that she has a sincere affection for you.

$$E\mu o\nu \ \kappa\rho\iota\tau\epsilon\rho\iota o\nu \ \tau\omega\nu \ \alpha\gamma\alpha\theta\omega\nu \ \tau o\delta\epsilon.^3$$

[Addressed]
    [MRS. SHELLEY *deleted*] MARY,
      2 *or* 5 *Church Terrace*,
      Pancrass

MARY TO SHELLEY

[*London*,
Tuesday, October 25, 1814.]

For what a minute did I see you yesterday. Is this the way my beloved, we are to live till the 6th. In the morning I look for you and when I awake I turn to look on you. Dearest Shelley, you are solitary and uncomfortable. Why cannot I be with you, to cheer you and to press you to my heart? Oh my love, you have no friends; why then should you be torn from the only one who has affection for you? But I shall see you tonight, and that is the hope that I shall live on through the day. Be happy, dear Shelley, and think of me! Why do I say this, dearest, and only one. I know how tenderly you love me and how you repine at this absence from me. When shall we be free from fear of treachery? I send you the letter I told you of from Harriet, and a letter we received yesterday from Fanny(¹). The history of this interview I will tell you when I come,

---

[2] In the *Times* for Saturday, October 22, 1814, there is a long letter on the Abolition of the Slave Trade, describing the horrors of the slavers' caravans, chiefly drawn from Mungo Park's *Travels*, a book from which Shelley read aloud to Mary in December, 1814.

[3] "This is my test of people that are good."

(¹) This letter made appointments for a meeting between Fanny and Clare.

but perhaps as it is so rainy a day Fanny will not be allowed to come at all. My love my own one be happy. I was so dreadfully tired yesterday that I was obliged to take a coach home. Forgive this extravagance, but I am so very weak at present, and I had been so agitated through the day, that I was not able to stand; a morning's rest, however, will set me quite right again and I shall be quite well when I meet you this evening. Will you be at the door of the Coffee House at five o'clock, as it is disagreeable to go into those places and I shall be there exactly at that time, and we will go into St. Paul's, where we can sit down.

I send you "Diogenes,"(¹) as you have no books. Hookham was so ill-tempered as not to send the book I asked for.

CCXL

TO MARY WOLLSTONECRAFT GODWIN

[? *Same day as last, October* 25, 1814.]

I have written an extremely urgent letter to Harriet to induce he[r] to send money. I have written also to Hookham, who did not call on Peacock. I have told Harriet that I shall be at Pancras when her answer arrives. I shall see you to-night, My beloved Mary fear not. Have confidence in the fortunate issue of our distresses. I am desolate and wretched in your absence; I feel disturbed and wild even to conceive that we should be separated. But this is most necessary, nor must we omit caution even on our unfrequent meetings. Recollect that I am lost if the people can have watched you to me. I wander restlessly about; I cannot read or even write. But this will soon pass. I should not infect my own Mary with my dejection; she has sufficient cause for disturbance to need consolation from me. Well, we shall meet to-day. I cannot write. But I love you with so unalterable love that the contemplation of me will serve for a letter. If you see Hookham, do not insult him openly; I have still hopes. We must not resign an inch of hope. I will make this remorseless villain loathe his own flesh in good time. He shall be cut down in his season. His pride shall be trampled into atoms; I will wither up his selfish soul by peacemeal.

Your only love

Σμερδναισι γαμφηλαισι συριζων φονον.¹

[Addressed]
MARY

(¹) Probably a translation of Wieland's *Diogenes*.
¹ "Hissing forth murder with awful jaws." (Æschylus, *Prometheus*, 355.)

LETTERS

[? *Thursday Morning, October* 27, 1814.]

I write to tell you when you come to bring the £5 with you. Perhaps it were as well to bring the pistols to Davidson's.[1] All is yet confused and undecided. I write this at Ballachy's. Do not on any account call at Peacock's or write to him again. I will explain at three o'clock. I am full of business and of hopes. Watch if you are followed. My dearest, best Mary, let me see your sweet eyes full of happiness when we meet; all will be well. I hope to have deserved many kisses.

[Addressed] MARY. In great haste. [And in capital letters] CERTAINLY.

MARY TO SHELLEY

[*Thursday Morning, October* 27, 1814, *in reply to the last.*]

MY OWN LOVE,
    I do not know by what compulsion I am to answer you, but your porter says I must; so I do.
    By a miracle I saved your £5 and I will bring it. I hope, indeed, oh my loved Shelley, we shall indeed be happy.
    I meet you at three and bring heaps of Skinner Street news. Heaven bless my love and take care of him.

HIS OWN MARY.

[*Night of October* 27, 1814.]

Oh! my dearest love, why are our pleasures so short and so interrupted? How long is this to last?

Know you, my best Mary, that I feel myself, in your absence, almost degraded to the level of the vulgar and impure. I feel their vacant, stiff eyeballs fixed upon me, until I seem to have been in-

---

[1] Shelley had parted with his solar microscope for £5 to Davidson, a pawnbroker, of Skinner Street: see Letter No. 188.

fected with th[eir] loathsome meaning—to inhale a sickness that sub-
dues me to languor. Oh! those redeeming eyes of Mary, that they
might beam upon me before I sleep! Praise my forbearance—oh!
beloved one—that I do not rashly fly to you, and at least secure a
moments bliss. Wherefore should I delay; do you not long to meet
me? All that is exalted and buoyant in my nature urges me towards
you, reproaches me with the cold delay, laughs at all fear and
spurns to dream of prudence. Why am I not with you? Alas!
we must not meet.

I have written a long letter to Jane, though in no mood for writing; I have directed it in a feigned hand to surprise her.

I did not, for I could not, express to you my admiration of your
letter to Fanny. The simple and impressive language in whch you
clothed your argument, the full weight you gave to every part, the
complete picture you exhibited of what you intended to describe,
was more than I expected.

How hard and stubborn must be the spirit that does not confess
you to be the subtlest and most exquisitely fashioned intelligence;
that among women there is no equal mind to yours! And I possess
this treasure! How beyond all estimate is my felicity! Yes; I am
encouraged—I care not what happens; I am most happy.

Meet me to-morrow at three o'clock in St. Paul's, if you do not
hear before.

Adieu; remember love at vespers before sleep. I do not omit *my*
prayers.

[Addressed]
MARY

CCXLIII
TO MARY WOLLSTONECRAFT GODWIN

[*Friday Night, October* 28, 1814.]

My beloved Mary, I know not whether these transient meetings produce not as much pain as pleasure. What have I said? I
do not mean it. I will not forget the sweet moments when I saw your
eyes—the divine rapture of the few and fleeting kisses. Yet, indeed,

this must cease; indeed we must not part thus wretchedly to meet amid the comfortless tumult of business; to part, I know not how.

Well, dearest love. Tomorrow—tomorrow night! That eternal clock! oh, that I could "fright the steeds of lazy paced time!" I do not think that I am less impatient now than formerly to repossess to entirely engross my own treasured love—It seems so unworthy a cause for the slightest separation! I could reconcile it to my own feelings to go to Prison if they would cease to persecute us with interruptions. Would it not be better my heavenly love to creep into the loathliest cave so that we might be together?

Mary, love, we must be united. I will not part from you again after Saturday night. We must devise some scheme. I must return. Your thoughts alone can waken mine to energy; [my mind] without yours is dead and cold as the dark midnight river when the moon is down. It seems as if you alone could shield me from impurity and vice. If I were absent from you long I should shudder with horror at myself. My understanding becomes undisciplined without you. I believe I must become in Mary's hands what Harriet was in mine. Yet how differently disposed how devoted and affectionate; how beyond measure reverencing and adoring the intelligence that governs me—I repent me of this simile it is unjust— it is false. Nor do I mean that I consider you much my superior, evidently as you surpass me in originality and simplicity of mind.— How divinely sweet a task it is to imitate each others excellences, and each moment to become wiser in this surpassing love so that, constituting but one being, all real knowledge may be comprised with the maxim γνωθι σεαυτον (know thyself) with infinitely more justice than in its narrow and common application!

I enclose you Hookhams note; wh[at do you] think of it?

My head aches. I am not well. I am tired with this comfortless estrangement from all that is dear to me.

My own dearest love Goodnight.

I meet you in Staples Inn at 12 tomorrow . . 1/2 before twelve.

I have written to Hooper and Sir J. Shelley.

[Addressed]
MARY

LETTERS

[A FRAGMENT]

[*Friday Night,
Oct. 28, 1814.*]

    So this is the end of my letter—dearest love—What do they mean—(¹) I detest Mrs. G[odwin]; she plagues my father out of his life and then—Well, no matter—Why will Godwin not follow the obvious bent of his affections and be reconciled to us—No; his prejudices, the world, and *she*—do you not hate her my love—all these forbid it—What am I to do?—trust to time of course, for what else can I do Good-night my love—to-morrow I will seal this blessing on your lips—dear, good creature, press me to you, and hug your own Mary to your heart. perhaps she will one day have a father till then be everything to me love—and indeed I will be a good girl and never vex you any more. I will learn Greek and—but when shall we meet when I may tell you all this, and you will so sweetly reward me—Oh we must meet soon, for this is a dreary life I am weary of it—a poor widowed deserted thing no one cares for her—but ah—love is not that enough—indeed I have a very sincere affection for my own Shelley.

    But Good night I am woefully tired and so sleepy. I shall dream of you, ten to one, when you, naughty one, have quite forgotten me.

    Take me—one kiss—well, that is enough. to-morrow!

CCXLIV
TO MARY WOLLSTONECRAFT GODWIN

[? *November* 1, 1814.]

    When will you meet me to-morrow? At *one* I must be on Change. [*Deletion* Meet me at 1/2 past 11] I think it best that you should obtain from Hookham all the information you can get, and then write to me and appoint a meeting at some hour which you think best.

    Adieu, my beloved. [*Deletion* forget me not] a thousand of the sweetest kisses live in memory. Adieu. I go to sleep.

    If you are inclined to work over any Latin, read Cicero's Paradoxa, one particularly concerning Regulus.

    Adieu, my own beloved, my Mary.

    Good-night.

[Addressed]
MARY

(¹) Referring to Mrs. Godwin's letter.—Note by Professor Dowden.

LETTERS

TO MARY WOLLSTONECRAFT GODWIN

[*Wednesday Morning, November 2, 1814.*]

MY BELOVED GIRL,

I think it dangerous that you should see me to-day; or at least until evening. I suspect that your or Jane's coming here might afford an occasion of discovery against which it would be impossible to provide by any foresight. I consent to resign this exquisite pleasure only because it is so clearly apparent to me that the most horrid consequences might ensue.

I think that you had better continue to send to the Hookham's in the course of the day to learn the course of Mrs. Stewart's affair.[1] It is this of course which I dread. How lonely and desolate are these solitary nights! This wretched and comfortless waking I cannot contemplate without a feeling that approaches to despair the continuance of this isolation. How terrible if month after month should pass without you, or only to see you by snatches and moments. All now depends on avoiding Mrs. Stewart. I shall not remain at Peacock's, I will not incur the least risk. A few days, perhaps a few hours will terminate our difficulties.

Love me my dearest best Mary, love me in confidence and security; do not think of me as one in danger, or even in sorrow— the remembrance and expectation of such sweet moments as we experienced last night consoles, strengthens, and redeems me from despondency. *There is eternity in these moments;* they contain the true elixir of immortal life. My best love, adieu.

[Addressed]
    MARY

---

[1] Mrs. Stewart was one of the creditors.

LETTERS

TO MARY WOLLSTONECRAFT GODWIN

Thursday Evening [*November* 3, 1814.]

I received both your letters this evening: they were apparently written at different times. The Post is too uncertain and dilatory to be endured.

The threatened arrest of Godwin on Thursday, I have not heard of before this moment. So soon as I have finished this letter I shall seek for Lambert.[1] If my interference would ever have been effectual it may still be so; as I learn that three days are always allowed before any procedure is commenced. I should have delayed writing until after this visit, if I did not fear to lose the 8-o'clock delivery.

I have seen the Farmer.[2] He requires that some responsible person should guarantee the payment of the money. I shall offer Hookham an indemnity to perform this piece of service. I suspect that these are very powerfully persuasive reasons that will assist my plea. In case of success his bill, will be paid.

Of course I have yet heard no more of Ballachy. I am full of confidence and hope on this affair. I hardly doubt the event. Unless I were thus fully confident I would not venture to excite your expectations. But tomorrow at 3—*at three* you will meet me at Gray's Inn Gardens and the result will then be known!

My own beloved Mary do I not love you? Is not your image the only consolation to my lonely and benighted condition? Do I not love you with a most inextinguishable love . . a feeling that well compensates for the altered looks of those who love none but themselves. What sentiment but disgust and indignation is excited by the desertion of those who fly because they think constancy *imprudent*. The feeling is sweet, most ennobling, and producing a celestial calm, with which thy sick and weary spirit reposes upon one who may not be doubted; to whom the slightest taint of suspicion is death irrevocable annihilation—Tomorrow blest creature I shall clasp you again—*for ever*. Shall it be so?

[1] Godwin's creditor. A letter of Shelley (the present whereabouts of which I cannot trace) to Mr. Lambert, asking for financial assistance, was sold as Lot 394 at Puttick & Simpson's sale, July 12, 1878.
[2] Probably William Bryant, of Worth Rectory, East Grinstead.

LETTERS

Shall it be so? This is the ancient language, that love can alone translate.

Best, dearest, adieu—one kiss.

I have most hopes of the Sussex Farmer.

[Addressed]
MARY

MARY TO SHELLEY

[*Thursday Night, November* 3, 1814.]

DEAREST LOVE,—I am so out of spirits I feel so lonely but we shall meet to-morrow so I will try to be happy—Gray's inn Gardens is, I fear, a dangerous place yet can you think of any other? I received your letter to-night. I wanted one, for I had [not] received one for nearly two days but do not think I mean anything by this my love(¹)—I know you took a long, long walk yesterday, so you could not write; but I who am at home who do not walk out I could write to you all day love. Another circumstance has made me feel more solitary that letter I received to-day—(²) Dear Shelley, you will say I was deceived—I know I am not. I know her unexampled frankness and sweetness of character; but what must that character be who resists opinions preach—Oh dear! what am I writing? I am indeed disappointed. I did think Isabel perfectly unprejudiced. She adores the shade of my mother. But then a married man—it is impossible to knock into some peoples heads that Harriet is selfish and unfeeling and that my father might be happy if he chose. By that cant concerning *selling his daughter* I should half suspect that there has been some communication between the Skinner St[reet] folks and them. Heigho, love, such is the world. How you reason and philosophize about love—do you know, if I had been asked I could not have given one reason in its favour, yet I have as great opinion as you concerning its exalted-ness and love very tenderly to prove my theory—adieu for the present; it has struck eight, and in an hour or two I will wish you good-night. Well, so now I am to write a good-night, with the old story of I wish I could say it to you. Yes, my love, it has indeed become an old story, but I hope the last chapter is come. I shall meet you to-morrow, love; if you do but get money love which indeed you must, we will defy our enemies and our friends (for aught I see they are all as bad as one another) and we will not part again. Is not that a delightful word it shall cheer my dreams.

No answer from Hooper—I wish he would write. Oh how I long to be at our dear home, where nothing can trouble us, neither friends or enemies! Don't be angry at this you know my love that they are all a bad set; but Nantgwillt—do you not wish to be settled there in a house you know love with your own Mary—nothing to disturb you, studying, walking and other such like amusements—oh its much better, believe, not to be able to see the light of the sun for the mountains than for houses.

You do not say a word in your letter, you naughty love, to ease one of my anxieties— not a word of Lambert, of Harriet, of Mrs. Stewart, of money, or anything—but all

(¹) Shelley's letter of Wednesday morning, directed "Mary," had been delivered early by hand.—Note by Professor Dowden.
(²) A letter bringing to a close Mary's relations with her girl-friend in Dundee, Isabel Baxter. The letter was written by Mr. David Booth, a man remarkable for his talents and force of character, of whom we shall hear again. Miss Isabel Baxter was engaged to be married (if she was not already married) to Mr. Booth. Journal, November 3: "Received a letter from Mr. Booth; so all my hopes are over then. Ah! Isabel, I did not think you would act thus."—Note by Professor Dowden.

the reasonings you used to persuade Mr. Peacock love was a good thing. Now you know I did not want converting; but my love, do not be displeased at my chattering in this way, for you know that the expectation of a letter from you when absent always makes my heart jump, so do you think it says nothing when one actually arrives?

Your own MARY, who loves you so tenderly.

CCXLVII

TO MARY WOLLSTONECRAFT GODWIN

[*Friday, Nov.* 4, 1814.]

So my beloved boasts that she is more perfect in the practise than I in the theory of love. Is it thus? No sweet Mary, you only meant that you loved me *more* than you could express, that reasoning was too cold and slow for the rapid fervour of your conceptions. Perhaps in truth Peacock had infected me; my disquisitions were cold, my subtleties unmeaningly refined. And I am a harp responsive to every wind. The scented gale of summer can wake it to sweet melody, but rough cold blasts draw forth discordances and jarring sounds.

My own love did I not appear happy to-day.[1] For a few moments I was entranced in most delicious pleasure. Yet I was absent and dejected. I knew not when we might meet again, when I might hold you in my arms, and gaze on your dear eyes at will, and snatch momentary kisses in the midst of our happy hours, and sport in security with my entire and unbroken bliss. I was about to return—whither? oh! I knew not, nor was it matter of concern. from *you*, from our delightful peace, to the simple expectation of felicity. I *shall be happy* is not so divine as I *am*. To be content to let "I dare not wait upon I would, like the poor cat i' the adage" to those that love is feverish agitation and sickening disquietude. And my poor Mary that loves me with such tenderness and truth, is her loneliness no pain to me? But to-morrow night at 1/2 past 12.[2]

I called on Lambert at 5, when we parted. He was absent from town. I am to meet him tomorrow morning. I called on Pike . . he proposes £12000 ready money for the reversion of Goring Castle. Before I conclude anything it shall be fairly valued. I should think

[1] Mary and Clare had met Shelley in Gray's Inn Gardens. Clare was perhaps in the way, for she enters in her Journal, "I am much disappointed in Shelley to-day. I thought him uniformly kind and considerate, but I find him act as weakly as other people."
[2] The second Saturday night, when the bailiffs lost their power for twenty-four hours.

108

myself fortunate to get this price: although the expense of the Building was so immense. Hookham has been with me. I do not despair of arranging something with Chartres, so that £100 may be placed at my disposal. Hookham is to meet me with C. on 'change to-morrow, I shall previously have disposed of Ballachy to my purpose, and entertain some confidence of success.[3] H. seems interested in the affair. Mrs. P. will go to the L[ondon] Coffee H[ouse] to-morrow and call for my letters. I hope to hear from Sir John [Shelley-Sidney.] Mrs. Stewarts affair, which I have most of all at heart—that relentless enemy of all comfort remains as it did. H. urges Tahourdin to complete it, but she will not at present. I expect to hear from Hooper to-morrow. Thus it is—my letters are full of money, whilst my being overflows with unbounded love, and elevated thoughts. How little philosophy and affection consort with this turbid scene . . . this dark scheme of things finishing in unfruitful death! There are moments in your absence my own love, when the bitterness with which I regret the unrecoverable time wasted in unprofitable solitude and worldly cares is a most painful weight. You alone reconcile me to myself and to my beloved hopes.

Good-night my excellent love,

my own Mary.

[Addressed]
MARY

CCXLVIII
TO G. B. BALLACHEY

DEAR SIR,

Will you have the goodness to send to Mr. Thomas Hookham Junr., No. 15 Old Bond Street, £100 and the bill for £100 drawn in favour of Charters. Charters has made some objections, but I doubt not that Mr. H. calling on him with the money would effectually overrule them.

Dear Sir, your obliged Servant,

P. B. SHELLEY.

[Addressed]
G. B. BALLACHEY, Esq.

[3] The Journal tells us (October 31) of Ballachey's "rascally proposition for £300 a year till his [Shelley's] father's death for £15,000 of *post-obit*."

LETTERS

TO MARY WOLLSTONECRAFT GODWIN

1814.
[Date uncertain.[1]*]*

Meet me at *one* and not at 3, at St. Paul's. I will be there at *one*.

Your good-night, my own love, came most welcomly. I did not forget to kiss you εἰδῶλον Κἐνον before I slept. And I slept last night thanks to your sweet goodnight. I think we had better immediately get other lodgings: as now all danger but from Mrs. Stewart is over. What think you of Pimlico or Sloane Street? Talk of this with Jane before you come.

CCL
TO MARY WOLLSTONECRAFT GODWIN

[Tuesday, Nov. 8, 1814.]

Call on me at 4 o'clock.

I have heard nothing. I have sent to Hookham's his answer is that he will call in the course of the day.

I shall now go out and seek Lodgings. I shall not decide on them until I have H's answer.

I saw Hogg last night I am disappointed in him though my expectations were very moderate.

I cannot write.

My dearest, best love only one more day, and we meet. Your affection is my only and sufficient consolation. I find that I have no personal interest in any human being but you, and you I love with my whole nature.

[Addressed]
    MRS. SHELLEY
        2 *or* 5 *Church Terrace*,
            Pancras
    M. W. G.

---

[1] I find it difficult to assign this letter to November 7 or 8, yet it is more difficult to place it elsewhere.—Note by Professor Dowden.

LETTERS

CCLI
TO R. HAYWARD

41 *Hans Place, [London]*,[1]
Jan. 17, 1815.

Sir,

I very much regret that I am unable to call on you so early as eleven to-morrow. I fear it will not be possible for me to be with you until between twelve and one, when as the affair is so vitally important to me I shall depend on you.—If possible let it be more than £100.

Your very obliged Sert.,

PERCY BYSSHE SHELLEY.

Enclosed in envelope addressed
HAYWARD, Esq.
    Solicitor,
        Tookes Court,
            Chancery Lane
[Postmark]
    12 *o'clock*
    18 *Ja*
    1815 *Noon*

---

[1] This letter is in the Pierpont Morgan Library.

Shelley was in London on January 3, 1815, when he signed an order to "Pay Mr. Brown or bearer Thirty Pounds." On January 6, 1815, Sir Bysshe Shelley died, and his son Timothy, Shelley's father, succeeded to the baronetcy. Shelley went to Field Place, but by his father's orders he was refused admittance. By June Sir Timothy agreed to an arrangement by which Shelley was to receive an income of £1,000 a year. He at once sent Harriet £200 to pay her debts, and he arranged for a sum of £200 a year to be paid to her in quarterly instalments. With the annuity of £200 which Mr. Westbrook allowed his daughter, she was provided with an income of £400 a year. Shelley probably remained in London until June. Mrs. Shelley says that in the summer of 1815 he made a tour along the coast of Devonshire; on June 22, as we see from his letter to Williams, he was at Torquay, and on July 27 Mary dates a letter to Shelley, who was looking for a house, from Clifton. In August the Shelleys settled in a house at Bishopgate.

III

LETTERS

CCLII
TO R. HAYWARD

13 *Arabella Road,*
Pimlico, [London],
April 7, 1815.

DEAR SIR,

I wish you would as soon as convenient inform me of the terms on which the security granted to Mr. Billing would be cancelled. It is important to me that you should allow no further delay to take place in this communication.

I think the lease of the House ought to be advertised for auction without delay.

Your obliged, etc., servant,

P. B. SHELLEY.

CCLIII
TO JOHN WILLIAMS

At Mrs. Wadling's,
Torquay, Devonshire,
June 22, 1815.

DEAR WILLIAMS,

I have some idea of visiting Merionethshire again, particularly if I should hear of any house which would afford any probability of suiting me. I write to you, therefore, to inquire whether there is in any remote and solitary situation a house to *let* for a time, with the prospect of purchase when my affairs will permit. I did not ask Mr. Nanney the terms of Dolmgleneyx; perhaps you can inform me of them. I assure you that it was not without much inconvenience that I paid the bond of £100. I would, if possible, have relieved you from the whole, but I have no hesitation in promising a final arrangement in the autumn. It will not suit me to purchase any house at present, but should the solitude and beauty of any place you can recommend or obtain for me induce me to wish to make it my permanent residence, I should have the command of money in the winter sufficient to enable me to possess it; still it best accords with my purpose to try at first.

Yours truly,

P. B. SHELLEY.

X

AUGUST, 1815, TO APRIL 24, 1816

BISHOPGATE—"ALASTOR"

CCLIV
TO THOMAS JEFFERSON HOGG

Bishopgate,[1]
August, 1815.

My dear Friend,

I am glad to hear of your safe arrival and the innocent symptoms of diseased action which you detail. My life has been very regular and undisturbed by new occurrences since your departure. My health has been considerably improved under Lawrence's care; and I am so much more free from the continual irritation under which I lived, as to devote myself with more effect and consistency to study. I have read some of the Orations of Cicero—That against

[1] Peacock says (*Fraser's Magazine*, January, 1860, p. 97), "In the summer of 1815, Shelley took a furnished house at Bishopgate, the eastern entrance of Windsor Park, where he resided till the summer of 1816. . . . I was then living at Marlow, and frequently walked over to pass a few days with him. At the end of August, 1815, we made an excursion on the Thames to Lechlade, in Gloucestershire, and as much higher as there was water to float our skiff. It was a dry season, and we did not get much beyond Inglesham. . . . We started from, and returned to Old Windsor, and our excursion occupied about ten days. This was, I think, the origin of Shelley's taste for boating, which he retained to the end of his life." Besides Shelley and Peacock, Mary and Charles Clairmont were of the party. Shelley's letter to Hogg, referred to in the next, describing the excursion is not forthcoming, but a letter dated September 16, 1815, from Charles Clairmont to his sister Jane (self-named, and henceforth known, as Clare or Claire), gives an account of the water-party. At Oxford they stayed from seven in the evening till four o'clock the next afternoon. After seeing the Bodleian Library and the Clarendon Press, they "visited the very rooms where the two noted infidels, Shelley and Hogg (now, happily, excluded the society of the present residents), pored, with the incessant and unwearied application of the alchymist, over the certified and natural boundaries of human knowledge." When they reached Lechlade, and could proceed no further on account of the water-weeds, Shelley wanted to go on, and to traverse various rivers and canals until they reached the Falls of the Clyde, a distance of two thousand miles. The idea was abandoned when it was ascertained that the Commissioners required £20 for the privilege of passing the Severn Canal. Clairmont adds, "We have all felt the good effects of this jaunt, but in Shelley the change is quite remarkable; he has now the ruddy, healthy complexion of the autumn upon his countenance, and he is twice as fat as he used to be." Peacock states that Shelley resided at Bishopgate till the summer of 1816, but the poet started for his second visit to the Continent at the beginning of the May of that year. The last letter that I have been able to find dated from Bishopgate is that of February 26, 1816, to William Godwin.

Verres contains some passages of wonderful power, although on the whole I consider them inferior in the interest they produced to those of his metaphysical essays which I have read. This must surely spring from their intrinsic inferiority, for it is unusual that an address to the passions should awaken less interest than an appeal to reason. I have begun also the *Pharsalia*. My opinion on the relative merits of Lucan and Virgil is no less unpopular than some of the others I entertain.

It excites my wonder to consider the perverted energies of the human mind. That so much benevolence and talent, as the missionary who travelled with you seemed to possess, should be wasted in such profitless endeavours, nor serve to any other end than to expose its possessor to perpetual disappointments. Yet who is there that will not pursue phantoms, spend his choicest hours in hunting after dreams, and wake only to perceive his error and regret that Death is so near? One man there is, and he is a cold and calculating man, who knows better than to waste life; but who alas! cannot enjoy it. Even the men who hold dominion over nations fatigue themselves by the interminable pursuit of emptiest visions; the honour and power which they seek is enjoyed neither in acquirement, possession or retrospect; for what is the fame that attends the most skilful deceiver or destroyer? What the power which awakens not in its progression more wants than it can supply?

You will see in the papers the continuance of that same system which the Allies had begun to pursue; and a most spirited remonstrance of the King of France's ministers against the enormities of their troops. In considering the political events of the day, I endeavour to divest my mind of temporary sensations, to consider them as already historical. This is difficult. Spite of ourselves the human beings which surround us infect us with their opinions; so much as to forbid us to be dispassionate observers of the questions arising out of the events of the age.

It is already the end of August. Those leaves have lost their summer glossiness which, when I see you again, will be fluttering in the wind of autumn. Such is mortal life.

Your affectionate friend,
P. B. S.

LETTERS

TO LACKINGTON, ALLEN & CO.
London

Bishopgate,
September 10, 1815.

GENTLEMEN,

I should have applied to your letter before, but was absent from home. On my return I do not delay to enclose you a list of the books which I wish to be provided with, and to answer the questions you propose on the subject.

Where I have omitted to specify in the list the edition which I prefer, I beg to leave the choice to your discretion. I am also indifferent in most instances whether or no the books be bound. Modern English books with the exception of Shakespeare I wish to be unbound.

I have the 2nd Volume of the 21st Edition of Locke's Essay on the Human Understanding. I should be obliged to you if you could procure me the 1st vol. which is deficient.

I remain, Gentlemen,
Your very obt. sert.
PERCY B. SHELLEY.

[Addressed]
MESSRS. LACKINGTON, ALLEN & CO.,
1 *Finsbury Sqa...re,*
London
[Postmark]
STAINES
[and]
D
11 *Sep* 11
1815

LETTERS

Bishopgate Heath
Sept. 16. 1815

MY DEAR SIR

On my return from a journey I am much gratified by the receipt of your letter. I rejoice to hear that you are in London, and hope that your intended stay has not so far elapsed but that I may have the pleasure of seeing you. It would I assure you afford me sincere satisfaction to welcome you to Bishopgate, where I have taken a house, and continue to employ myself in the cultivation of philosophic truth. Do you go to the Continent alone or accompanied by your friends? and when may your English friends expect your return? If during your absence you can in any manner employ me in a manner beneficial to yourself I hope that you will not hesitate to command my services.

Always your sincere friend

P. B. SHELLEY.

[Addressed]
A. B. PERIERA Esqre
29 *St. Swithin's Lane*
Lombard Street
London
[Postmark]
18 Se 1815

CCLVII
TO THOMAS JEFFERSON HOGG

Bishopgate,
September, 1815.

MY DEAR FRIEND,

Your letter has lain by me for the last week, reproaching me every day. I found it on my return from a water excursion on the Thames, the particulars of which will have been recounted in another letter. The exercise and dissipation of mind attached to

[1] Printed by permission from the original in Balliol College, Oxford. Dr. Peck suggests that possibly this correspondent may have been Baptista, the young Brazilian whom Shelley met at Edinburgh in 1813, and who praised *Queen Mab* so enthusiastically.

118

such an expedition have produced so favourable an effect on my health, that my habitual dejection and irritability have almost deserted me, and I can devote six hours in the day to study without difficulty. I have been engaged lately in the commencement of several literary plans, which, if my present temper of mind endures, I shall probably complete in the winter. I have consequently deserted Cicero, or proceed but slowly with his philosophic dialogues. I have read the Oration for the poet Archias, and am only disappointed with its brevity.

I have been induced by one of the subjects which I am now pursuing to consult Bayle. I think he betrays great obliquity of understanding and coarseness of feeling. I have also read the four first books of Lucan's "Pharsalia"—a poem, as it appears to me, of wonderful genius and transcending "Virgil." Mary has finished the fifth book of the "Æneid," and her progress in Latin is such as to satisfy my best expectations.

The East wind—the wind of autumn—is abroad, and even now the leaves of the forest are shattered at every gust. When may we expect you? September is almost past, and October, the month of your promised return, is at hand, when we shall be happy to welcome you again to our fireside.

No events, as you know, disturb our tranquillity. Adieu.

Ever affectionately yours,

PERCY B. SHELLEY.[1]

---

[1] Corrected from a transcript by Mary Shelley in the Henry E. Huntington Memorial Library and Art Gallery, California.

LETTERS

CCLVIII
TO WILLIAM LAING
Edinburgh

London,
September 27, 1815.

SIR,

On unpacking the books which arrived from Edinburgh, I discovered the following have been omitted, doubtless thro' mistake:

Drummond's "Academical Questions."
Euripides' "Hippolytus" (Marsh).
Euripides' "Heraclidæ" (Elmsley).
Hoogeveen's "De Particulis."

I should feel myself obliged if you would send these books, which have undoubtedly been mislaid and confounded with yours— addressed to me at Mr. Hookham, Old Bond Street.

Your obedient servt.,

P. B. SHELLEY.

[Addressed]
MR. WILLIAM LAING,
Bookseller,
Edinburgh

CCLIX
TO BROOKES & CO.
London

Bishopgate Heath,
Oct. 9, 1815.

GENTLEMEN,

I have to request that you would be so obliging as to remit and place to my account *ten pounds:* directed to "Miss Clairmont, Post Office, Enniscorthy, Wexford, Ireland."

Your obliged Sert.

PERCY BYSSHE SHELLEY.

[Addressed]
MESSRS. BROOKES & CO.,
Bankers,
Chancery Lane, London

LETTERS

Bishopgate,
October 19, 1815.

DEAR SIR,

If I do not mistake you are Mr. Godwin's legal adviser in a suit proceeding against him from Mr. Hogan. The debt I imagine is £200 or £250. The object of my letter is to learn (if you think yourself justified in favouring me with the information) Mr. Godwin's precise situation with respect to this suit. I have heard that it must arrive at its conclusion next term, that there are no means of delay. I am anxious to know how far that statement is correct. If, however, it is impossible to prolong it beyond the beginning of next month, I wish to enquire whether Mr. Hogan is absolutely determined not to accommodate the affair in any manner short of the actual payment of the debt and costs, or whether Mr. Godwin has offered no security which he considers safe. In the latter case I imagine that I could suggest thro' my own liability a means of relieving Mr. Godwin from the action. You would oblige me by not informing Mr. Godwin of my application, until it shall appear that it is likely to be attended with some favourable issue.

Your very obedient servant,

PERCY B. SHELLEY.

—. HAYWARD, Esq.,
Took's Court,
London

LETTERS

CCLXI
TO LACKINGTON, ALLEN & CO.

Bishopgate,
Nov. 9, 1815.

GENTLEMEN,

Will you have the goodness to send me as soon as possible, the two following books.—"Memoirs of Prince Alexy Haimatoff" published by Hookham & Co. and an Italian poem by Manno called *Adone.*

I expect every day to receive from you the remainder of the books I ordered. I wish however that these two books should be sent without waiting for the completion of what remained on the former list.

Your very obed. sert.

PERCY B. SHELLEY.

[Addressed]
MESSRS. LACKINGTON, ALLEN & CO.,
Finsbury,
London

CCLXII
TO LACKINGTON, ALLEN & CO.
London

Bishopgate,
Dec. 17, 1815.

GENTLEMEN,

The parcel arrived safe containing most of the books of the original order.

I wish any edition of Quintus Curtius, which is not extremely dear, and which contains the supplements of Freinhemius, to be sent as early as convenient.

Your obedient sert,

P. B. SHELLEY.

[Addressed]
MESSRS. LACKINGTON & CO.,
Finsbury Square,
London
[Postmark]
Dec. 18, 1815

LETTERS

Bishopgate Heath,
Dec. 24, 1815.

GENTLEMEN,

In the course of this week, Mr. Joseph Hume of Somerset House, will present a check of £200, which I would be obliged to you to pay on receiving a promissory note for the amount payable at a month's date or under. I should also feel obliged if you would trouble yourselves to present the note when due and to receive the money.

Your obliged and obedient St.

P. B. SHELLEY.

[Addressed]
MESSRS. BROOKES & Co.,.
Bankers,
Chancery Lane, London
[Postmark]
25 *Dec.,* 1815,
Staines

CCLXIV
TO WILLIAM GODWIN
London

Bishopgate,
January 7,[1] 1815, [for 1816.]

SIR,

I will endeavour to give you, as clear as possible a history of the proceedings between myself and my father.

A small portion of the estates to which I am entitled in reversion were comprehended in the will of Mr. John Shelley, my great-

[1] Shelley probably came to London during the ensuing week, as he addressed the following note to his banker from Hanover Square, on "January 11, 1816. Mr. Shelley presents his compliments to Messrs. Brookes and Co., and requests the favour of their taking a receipt from Mr. John Billing, of Quality Court, when they pay a check which he will present for £13 2s. 6d.—Messrs. Brooks & Co., Bankers, 25 Chancery Lane."

123

uncle, and devised to the same uses as the larger portion which was settled on my father's marriage jointly by my grandfather and father. This portion was valued at £18,000, which my father purchased of me with an equivalent of £11,000. I signed on this occasion two deeds; the one was to empower my attorney to suffer what is called a recovery, the other a counterpart of the deed of conveyance.

Before these transactions, however, and at the very commencement of our negotiations, I signed a deed which was the preliminary and the basis of the whole business. My grandfather had left me the option of recovering a life estate in some very large sum (I think £140,000) on condition that I would prolong the entail, so as to possess only a life estate in my original patrimony. These conditions I never intended to accept, although Longdill considered them very favourable to me, and urged me by all means to grasp at the offer. It was my father's interest and wish that I should refuse the conditions, because my younger brother would inherit, in default of my compliance with them, this life estate. Longdil and Whitton[2] therefore made an agreement that I should resign my rights to this property, and that my father, in exchange for this concession, should give me the full price for my reversion. In compliance with the terms of this agreement, I signed a deed importing that I disclaimed my grandfather's property. My father did not sign his part of the agreement, because he could not do so without forfeiting the new entail (which says that whoever in whatsoever manner endeavours to break thro the intentions of the testator shall not enjoy the fortune), but Mr. Whitton engaged tacitly to Longdill that my father would buy the reversion on the terms already settled.

Now, Whitton professes my father's willingness to proceed, but urges every consideration calculated to delay the progress of the affair. Longdill told me that he saw Whitton wished to procure as much delay as possible, but that he still thought it was their intention not entirely to give up the negotiation. Whether both Whitton and Longdill are not quietly making their advantage out

[2] Longdill and Whitton were the attorneys of Shelley and Sir Timothy Shelley respectively.

of the inexperience and credulity of myself and my father is a doubt that has crossed my mind.

You say that you will receive no more than £1,250 for the payment of those encumbrances from which you think I may be considered as *specially* bound to relieve you. I would not desire to persuade you to sell the approbation of your friends for the difference between this sum, and that which your necessities actually require, but the mention of your friends has suggested a plan to my mind which possibly you may be able to execute. You have undoubtedly some well-wishers who, although they would refuse to give you so large a sum as £1,200, might not refuse to lend it you on security which they might consider unexceptionable. I think you could lay before any rich friend such a statement of your case, as that, if he could refuse to lend £1,200 on my security his desire of benefiting you must be exceedingly slight. There is every probability in favour of the arrangement with my father being completed within the year. I can give evidence of the existence of the negotiation between us.

If this prospect should fail, I still remain heir to property of £6,000 or £7,000 a year. Why not ask Grattan or Mackintosh, or Lord Holland, whom I have heard named as your. . . . [*The rest of this letter is wanting.*]

CCLXV
TO JOHN MURRAY
London

Bishopgate, near Egham,
Jan. 16, 1816.

SIR,

I take the liberty of sending you a copy of all the sheets, but the last, of a vol. of poems[1] which it is my intention to publish. I send them for the purpose of enabling you to judge whether you would become the publisher and on what terms.

[1] The little volume was "Alastor;/or,/The Spirit of Solitude:/and other Poems. By/ Percy Bysshe Shelley./London:/Printed for Baldwin, Craddock, and Joy, Pater-/noster

LETTERS

I should certainly prefer to sell the copyright. But I am aware that an Author cannot expect much encouragement for his first poetical production before the public shall have passed their judgment on its merits. I have therefore printed 250 copies with the view of offering it to publication so as to meet the opinions of the publisher as to its probability of success.

I have written to Mr. Hamilton, the printer, to send you the sheet which is deficient, title-page, etc.

I beg to apologize for addressing you as a total stranger.

Your obedient servant,

PERCY BYSSHE SHELLEY.

[Addressed]
MR. MURRAY, *Bookseller*

Row; and Carpenter and Son,/Old Bond-Street:/By S. Hamilton, Weybridge, Surrey./1816." The other poems in the volume are the verses (1) "O! there are spirits of the air," supposed to have been addressed to Coleridge; (2) "Stanzas—April, 1814"; (3) "Mutability"; (4) "The pale, the cold, and the moony smile"; (5) "A summer-evening churchyard"; (6) "To Wordsworth"; (7) "Feelings of a Republican on the Fall of Bonaparte"; (8) "Superstition"; (9) "Sonnet. From the Italian of Dante"; (10) "Translated from the Greek of Moschus"; (11) "The Dæmon of the World. A Fragment" from *Queen Mab*. In Mrs. Shelley's note on *Alastor* she says, "In the summer of 1815, after a tour along the southern coast of Devonshire and a visit to Clifton, he [Shelley] rented a house on Bishopgate Heath, on the borders of Windsor Forest, where he enjoyed several months of comparative health and tranquil happiness. The later summer months were warm and dry. Accompanied by a few friends, he visited the source of the Thames, making the voyage in a wherry from Windsor to Cricklade. His beautiful stanzas (5) in the churchyard at Lechlade were written on that occasion. *Alastor* was composed on his return. He spent his days under the oak-shades of Windsor Great Park; and the magnificent woodland was a fitting study to inspire the various descriptions of forest scenery we find in the poem." Peacock says that when Shelley was at a loss for a title for his poem, "I proposed that which he adopted. The Greek word Ἀλάστωρ is an evil genius, κακυδαίμων, though the sense of the two words is somewhat different as in the Φανεὶς Ἀλάστωρ ἢ κακὸς δαίμων ποδέν, of Æschylus. The poem treated the Spirit of Solitude as a spirit of evil. I mention the true meaning of the word, because many have supposed 'Alastor' to be the name of the hero of the poem."

LETTERS

Bishopgate,
Jan. 18, 1816.

SIR,
     I consent to sell an annuity which shall produce enough to cover Hogan's demand, on these conditions:—

That you should agree to pay the interest, until I am able to discharge the principal. I shall take your word for the fulfilment of this part of the contract.

That entire secrecy should be observed. It will be necessary that the solicitor who engages in the management of the affair should defer registering the annuity for judgment for the period of a year.

Do you know the quarter whence the money can be procured? I would prefer any other than Hayward for reasons which I could enumerate if it were necessary. The person who proposed to lend £1,000, would probably lend a quarter of that sum. You had better apply to him in the first instance and enquire whether he will do so. I, not residing in London, am obviously incompetent to conduct the affair.

Clairmont informs me that in a former instance he explained with you on the subject of the claim which you urge to be repaid the £200 subtracted by me from the £1,200 of nominal debt which he agreed to state on your part for the purpose of putting me in possession of the £200. He told you that he believed you to be mistaken in your construction of my message, and on explaining with me I confirmed his remembrance of the real state of the arrangement.

Perhaps it is well that you should be informed that I consider your last letter to be written in a certain style of haughtiness and incroachment which neither awes nor imposes on me. But I have no desire to transgress the limits which you place to our intercourse, nor in any future instance will I make any remarks but such as arise from the strict question in discussion.

Perhaps you do well to consider every word irrelevant to that question which does not regard your personal advantage.

P. B. SHELLEY.

LETTERS

I forgot to inform you that no paper has been signed by my father which regards the affair of the estates.

The general intention and fundamental basis of the business have been st[ated] and admitted in many instances by W[hit]ton in writing, tho' I should conceive not in a manner which constitutes a legal objection.

[Addressed]
W. GODWIN, Esq.,
41 *Skinner Street,*
Snow Hill,
London

CCLXVII
TO WILLIAM GODWIN
London

Bishopgate,
January 21, 1816.

SIR,

It is impossible to procure any letter from Whitton, or any evidence of the affair with my father. Any attempt to possess myself of such a document would risk an entire destruction of my prospects in that quarter. But I apprehend that a reference to my banker would answer the same end. It would prove to the inquirer that I am in the regular receipt of £800 per an. I should conceive that a person who had an opportunity of making 15 per cent. of so small a sum as £200 or £300 would consider this fact a sufficient assurance of the safety of his loan.

Particularly when he reflects in addition upon the strong presumption which he can deduce from various circumstances of the approaching settlement of my affairs.

If the person who applied to you is, contrary to my expectation, disposed to think differently of the matter, then let Hayward be applied to.

There are some objections to Hayward, some of which incite me to require caution in treating with him, some demand explanation, and are only worth considering as they impede the loan.

1st. Secrecy is to be secured, which is somewhat difficult, unless his own interest is implicated.

2nd. This real or pretended want of confidence in my representations is to be overcome.

When I applied to him for the purpose of borrowing money for my own wants he inquired whether by the late arrangement with my father all incumbrances on the estate were cancelled. I replied in the affirmative since, although I did not know that Nash had been actually paid, yet an offer being then pending by which he was to receive £4,500 for what he purchased from me the year before at £2,600, I did not doubt, nor did Longdill doubt, but that he would resign on these terms his claim on the estate.

I spoke, therefore, according to my belief, according to the real fact, and according to the purpose for which alone it imported him to know when I replied that the estate was no longer incumbered. But, indeed, I know not whether Hayward would presume to make this accusation to anyone, whom he knew had direct communication with me, or concerning whom it might not reasonably be doubted whether the misrepresentations did not as probably originate with any informer or with himself. Hayward is to be applied to, if your person fails. But I hope the necessity will not arise. If you clearly perceive that there is no other mode of raising the money, I do not require a day's delay. You can either apply to Hayward, or I will write him, as you choose.

If Hayward refuses, and we can raise money on my security in no manner, did it never suggest itself to you, that your signature joined with mine might effect what neither would effect singly?

With respect to the question which you asked on the subject of the £200, I certainly never gave Clairmont the smallest ground for the representation on which your mistake rests. I accept, and thank you for your explanation. If you really think me vicious, such haughtiness as I imputed to you is perhaps to be excused. But I, who do not agree with you in that opinion, cannot be expected to endure it without remonstrance. I can easily imagine how difficult it must be, in addressing a person whom we despise or dislike, to abstain from phrases, the turn of which is peculiar to the sentiments with which we cannot avoid regarding such a person. Perhaps I did wrong to feel so deeply or notice so readily a spirit of which you seem to have been unconscious.

P. B. SHELLEY.

[Addressed]
    W. GODWIN, Esq.,
        41 *Skinner Street,*
            Snow Hill, London

CCLXVIII
TO WILLIAM GODWIN
London

Bishopgate,
January 23,[1] 1816.

SIR,

I fear that [it] is quite impossible to procure any documents from Longdill. I do not mean to say that if the loan cannot be procured without it, I will refuse to attempt to procure them. But Longdill is now out of town, and the few days that will pass during his absence may be employed in discovering whether we can do without him.

Hayward, it seems, must be applied to. Let this be done without delay. I should conceive that the same advantages which made it appear probable that the person you mentioned would find the money, would operate with greater force on Hayward.

I told Hayward that I did not know when the affair with my father would terminate, or even whether it might not be entirely abandoned.

I conceive that he relied in reality far more on my present income than my future expectations, and that if he declines to procure any additional loan, it will spring not from any doubt of the

---

[1] On the day following, January 24, William, the son of Shelley and Mary Godwin, was born; he was named after his grandfather, William Godwin, baptised on March 9, 1818, died at Rome, June 7, 1819, and was buried, like his father, in the Protestant Cemetery at Rome.

validity of my security, but because some object which he might have contemplated in his former services was not attained.

As soon as we have procured Hayward's answer, we shall either be certain that he will advance the money, or that he will not.

If he decides in the negative, I will lose no time in taking whatever measures may appear good to you for procuring it from some other quarter.

I am most undoubtedly in earnest, as much so as I should have been last November, had such explanations been made as I have since received, and the same spirit of promptitude shewn to share with me the burthens incident to the pecuniary difficulties with which I have been so long surrounded.

I hope that you will not refrain from applying to Hayward on the ground that these letters from Whitton may possibly be procured. I have not myself even seen them that I recollect; and it is most likely that they would be found to express only a general intention on my father's part to divide the estates, a fact of which Hayward certainly entertains no doubt. I am, indeed, earnest that you should not defer to put the question to Hayward.

I am sorry that I cannot appeal to my memory for the precise words of the message which you received with the £1,000 in the spring. I am certain only that it was not, because I am aware of arrangements made in my own mind, by which it could not be such as you represent Clairmont to have delivered it. My meaning was that you should receive no more than that £1,000 until the second settlement with my father, which was then expected in November: and I consider that giving in your debt at [£]1,200, as an accommodation to me, enabling me to procure, as I did, [£]200, which I should not otherwise have received. My message certainly in some manner expressed this view of the subject to Clairmont, and no other.[2]

P. B. SHELLEY.

[Addressed]
    W. GODWIN, Esq.,
    41 *Skinner Street*,
        Snow Hill, London

[2] The £1,200 which Shelley had promised to procure for Godwin had been included by Sir Timothy in reckoning his son's debts.

LETTERS

Bishopgate,
January 25, 1816.

SIR,

Longdill told me a week ago that he was then going into the country for ten days. Relying on your information, however, I have written to him, requesting that he will immediately see Whitton, inform him of my dissatisfaction on the subject of his delay, and extort some satisfactory answer. This he was to have done ten days ago. At least until the result of this measure is known to me, I am unwilling to excite suspicions in Longdill that I am in treaty for borrowing money on annuity. The mode of address which you suggest would undoubtedly appear unnatural to me. I might destroy L.'s confidence in the regularity and prudence of my conduct at a time when perhaps the whole success of the affair with my father depends on its preservation.

Hayward, in November, was profuse in his professions both of willingness and ability to procure me money on annuity. If I wanted £1,000 he said that he could readily procure the sum. He knew at that period the uncertainty [of] the negotiations with my father. Perhaps he may believe that the chances are now multiplied against the probability of its accomplishment. At least, it appears to me, that the additional security which he would feel from your assertions that the interest was safe, may be considered sufficient to overbalance these contingencies. I feel unwilling, until you should have urged him on to this point, and extorted from him a declaration whether in the last resort he would refuse to serve you by negotiating the loan, to accede to the doubtful and difficult measure of obtaining the letters to which I have alluded, from Longdill. Add to which, it is very doubtful if they would, when procured, be serviceable or satisfactory.

A Mr. Bryan[t], a Sussex man, has written to me to know whether I would sell the reversion of a small estate in that country, on terms of 5 per cent. I have replied, that I cannot do so, being under engagement to sell the whole estate to my father; but if this engagement should be annulled, I should be glad to listen to his proposal.

He writes in answer, that "he could find me purchasers at a fair price for sev[era]l things." He says he dines every day, during term, at Anderton's Coffee House, Fleet Street. If you entertain any doubt of Hayward, perhaps you had better see this Bryant, or I will do so, or write to him as appears good to you. But I am certainly anxious that you should urge Hayward to a decisive and immediate reply. I will spare no pains, or any danger which it is not evident ruin to incur, but that you shall have the money in March. If Hayward fails, do not fear an ultimate failure. I am persuaded that my situation is now widely different, and far more commanding and respectable than when I with difficulty procured money to live.

You seem strangely to have misunderstood the affair in April. Certainly I did fix on [£]1,200 as your contingent from the sum then raised, on purpose to apply [£]200 to my own demands; which I should have been unable so to apply without your co-operation, unless, indeed, instead of £1,000 I had given you only £800, which your refusal to have co-operated in this manner would have compelled me, in self defence, however reluctantly, to do. I thought you understood and acquiesced in this arrangement. There is nothing remarkable in this foolish mistake but the unskilfulness or unfaithfulness of our interpreters, and it is well that such imperfect intercourse did not, as in many instances it might, have produced more serious errors.

I should come to town willingly on the business of this loan, when it appears that my presence is required. If Hayward eventually refuses to negotiate it for us, then I certainly think some personal discussion is needed. I could perhaps then make clear to you the reasonableness of my reluctance to apply to Longdill. But I shall leave this subject henceforth entirely to your own feelings. Probably my feelings on such an occasion would not be less distressing than your own. So far as those feelings are concerned, I should certainly reluctantly entertain the idea of such an interview. But I would not sacrifice anything essential to the raising of this money to exempt myself from the sensations, however painful, which could not fail to arise on meeting a man, who having been once my friend, would receive me with cold looks and haughty words.

Fanny and Mrs. Godwin will probably be glad to hear that Mary has safely recovered from a very favourable confinement, and that her child is well.

P. B. SHELLEY.

[Addressed]
W. GODWIN, Esq.,
41 *Skinner Street,*
Snow Hill, London

CCLXX
TO WILLIAM GODWIN
London

Bishopgate,
January 28, 1816.

SIR,

A letter which I received from Longdill by yesterday's post decides, I fear, the question of applying to him for the letters of Whitton. I will briefly recapitulate the contents. It says that in compliance with my requests he has applied to Whitton. He tells me that W. has by no means been idle in the affair. My father wishes to bring the matter to bear, but he judges it necessary previously to ask the Lord Chancellor's advice. This Longdill also considers essential even to my interest. The bill to be given in is now before counsel. Longdill's expression is, that this will cause considerable delay. It is evident now that my father's intentions are sincere. What time the Chancery affair will take we cannot know.

This much, however, is certain, that my Father desires to settle the thing, however awkward and long are the measures he takes for that settlement.

The arrangement in the spring could not be completed without a Chancery suit, though it is certain that there is not the smallest ground for a similar proceeding in the present instance. In all probability it is of a much simpler nature. I cannot obviously now procure Whitton's former letters. But surely Hayward can substantiate if he would take the trouble to inquire in an underhand and professional manner the facts which I now relate. These facts I imagine are sufficient to satisfy him if he only requires such satisfaction as he was contented with last autumn.

I forgot to answer one question. Nash's suit is nominally instituted by me, but really by my father, and for his interests and at his expense.

P. B. SHELLEY.

Since I wrote the former page, I have discovered Longdill's letter, which I thought I had mislaid. I enclose it for you to read and if you please to use.

Of course if you show it to Longdill you will use due caution about the last paragraph of it.

[Addressed]
  W. GODWIN, Esq.,
    41 *Skinner Street,*
      Snow Hill, London

CCLXXI
TO CARPENTER & SON
Old Bond Street, London

Bishopgate, near Egham,
Feby. 6, 1816.

GENTLEMEN,

In consequence of the advice with which you were so kind as to favour my friend Mr. Scharper, I have made arrangements with Messrs. Baldwin & Co. for the publication of the small Vol. of Poems[1] left for your inspection a week or two ago. I expect they will be ready for publication in the course of a few days, at which time Messrs. B. & Co. have my directions to furnish you with copies. As your names appear in the title Page and advertisements,

---

[1] *Alastor.*

135

applications for the work at the west end of the Town will, of course, be made at your house, and I doubt not you will use your utmost exertions for its success.

Gentlemen, I remain,

Your obliged and faithful Ser.

PERCY B. SHELLEY.

[Addressed]
MESSRS. CARPENTER & SON,
    13 *Old Bond Street,*
        London
[Postmark]
STAINES
    D
  7 F. 7
  1816

CCLXXII
TO WILLIAM GODWIN
London

6 *Garden Court, Temple* [*London*],[1]
Friday night, February 16, 1816.

SIR,

In the course of a few weeks I shall certainly leave the neighbourhood of London, and possibly even execute my design of settling in Italy. I have felt it necessary to decide on some such measure in consequence of an event which I fear will make even a more calamitous change in your prospects.

It is the opinion of the lawyers that my father ought not to complete the intended affair with me and that he cannot arrange any other. If you do not feel it necessary to explain with me in person on this subject, I can state the detail in a letter. Such, however, is the bare fact. The impossibility of effecting anything by *post-obit* or sale of reversion has been already adverted to by me. I am far from retracting any engagement made for your benefit, but I cannot refrain from suspecting under these new circumstances how

----

[1] This letter was written at Hogg's chambers.

far I am justified, even by my sincere zeal for your interests, in signing the deed which, Hayward informs me, is in progress. You will believe that I am the more disinterested in what I say when I inform you that my own difficulties suspended by the intended settlement now come upon me with tenfold weight, so that I have every prospect of wanting money for my domestic expenditure.

I intended to have left town at two o'clock to-morrow; I will not do so, if you wish to see me. In that latter case, send a letter *by a porter* to Mr. Hogg's, of Garden Court, Temple, making your own appointment.

Yet I do not know that it is best for you to see me. On me it would inflict deep dejection. But I would not refuse anything which I can do, so that I may benefit a man whom, in spite of his wrongs to me, I respect and love.

Besides I shall certainly not delay to depart from the haunts of men. Your interests may suffer from your own fastidiousness; they shall not be injured by my wayward hopes and disappointments.

Jane,[2] of course, is with you. She is uninformed as to the latest and most decisive particulars relating to the overthrow of my hopes.

I shall write to you by Sunday's post if I receive no answer to this letter.

P. B. SHELLEY.

[Addressed]
WILLIAM GODWIN, Esq.,
  41 *Skinner Street,*
   Snow Hill

---

[2] Clare or Claire Clairmont, who was known in her family as Jane.

137

LETTERS

CCLXXIII
TO WILLIAM GODWIN
London

London,
February 17, 1816.[1]

SIR,

I hasten to relieve your anxiety. I have seen Hayward and arranged with him to sign the deed at twelve o'clock next Monday week. In what I have said to him, as you will discover, I have taken every imaginable precaution that you should not be disappointed.

P. B. S.

[Addressed]
WILLIAM GODWIN, Esq.,
41 *Skinner Street,*
Snow Hill

CCLXXIV
TO WILLIAM GODWIN
London

Bishopgate,
February 18, 1816.

SIR,

You will have received my letter in answer to yours sent to Garden Court in the course of Saturday evening. This will entirely satisfy you as to my intentions about the deed. I promised you further details by this post on the subject of the affair with my father. It is the opinion of the most eminent lawyers that my father cannot become a party to the projected arrangements without forfeiting the property devised by my grandfather's will. In consequence of this opinion, and for the purpose of ascertaining

---

[1] This letter is endorsed (at the head) by Charles Clairmont, as follows :—
"The date of this letter is written in Godwin's handwriting—Most probably to remember by the date when the deed would be signed.—CH. CLAIRMONT."

138

some other point not necessarily connected with my immediate interest, they recommend a suit in Chancery. They are desirous that their own opinion, however well founded, should be confronted with the Lord Chancellor's. It is, moreover, the duty of one of the Counsel, Mr. Butler, as trustee, to be extremely cautious in his conduct. Longdill entertains no doubt that the issue of this appeal will be unfavourable to my views. He considers the question indeed as already decided, and the proceedings in Chancery, so far at least as they regard that part of the affair, entirely superfluous.

I understand that the existence of two or three words in the will occasions this most unexpected change. The words are these:— "For the time being"—the application of those words to the present case is explained to be, that in case my father should survive myself and my infant son, my younger brother, at the expiration of his minority, might require my father to fulfil those conditions of the will which he would incapacitate himself from fulfilling by cutting off the entail. It is altogether a most complex affair, the words of the will being equivocal to a singular degree. A new difficulty arises also from the import of my signature to the Deed of Disclaimer, as it is called, given in the presumption of the completion of this settlement. One thing alone is certain, that until my father's death I shall receive no portion of the estate.

How does this information affect your prospects? Does anything remain to be done by me? You have entire knowledge of my resources, my situation, and my disposition towards you; what do you think I can do, or I ought to do, to set you free?

I informed you that I should be in town on Monday week, at twelve o'clock, to sign the deed at Hayward's. My letter of Friday night asserts that I should not be in town again before I left the neighbourhood; but I did not foresee that the deed would not be ready at Hayward's or that there would be so much difficulty and expense in conveying it to Bishopgate.

P. B. Shelley.

LETTERS

Bishopgate,
February 21, 1816.

SIR,

I saw Turner yesterday, who engaged to convey to you by that night's post a reassurance on the points which he called on me to ascertain. I should have written to you myself if I had not returned too late from a long walk with Turner, in which I endeavoured to make him understand as clearly as possible the present state of my affairs and my dispositions towards you.

I shall certainly not leave this country, or even remove to a greater distance from the neighbourhood of London, until the unfavourable aspect assumed by my affairs shall appear to be unalterable; or until all has been done by me which it is possible for me to do for the relief of yours. This was my intention from the moment that I first received an intimation of the change. I wrote to you for the purpose of giving you an opportunity of making my assistance as available to you as possible before I departed.

When I wrote to you from London I certainly was more firmly persuaded than now of the inefficacy of any further attempt for the settlement of my affairs. You have suggested a view of the question that makes me pause. At all events I shall remain here, or in this neighbourhood, for the present, and hold myself in readiness to do my utmost towards advancing you the money.

You are perhaps aware that one of the chief motives which strongly urges me either to desert my native country, dear to me from many considerations, or resort to its most distant and solitary regions, is the perpetual experience of neglect or enmity from almost every one but those who are supported by my resources. I shall cling, perhaps, during the infancy of my children to all the prepossessions attached to the country of my birth, hiding myself and Mary from that contempt which we so unjustly endure. I think, therefore, at present of only settling in Cumberland, or Scotland. In the event, the evils which will flow to my children from our desolate and solitary situation here point out an exile as the only resource to them against that injustice which we can easily despise. You will observe that the mere circumstance of our departing to the North of England and not immediately putting into effect our Italian scheme, it is strictly within the limits of the most formal intercourse that you should know. I might have misunderstood Turner, for I did not urge him to explain or literally repeat expressions, but it appeared to me from his conversation that you had communicated with him on the subject of our ancient intimacy, and of the occasion of its close, in a manner that expressed to a certain degree of interest in my future prospects. I determined on that account to present to you a real picture of my feelings, inasmuch as they would influence my plan of residence. If this exposure should be indifferent to you, *silence* will afford an obvious protection against additional mistake.

P. B. SHELLEY.

I expect anxiously the plan to which you allude as an infallible expedient for my father to adopt that he might settle with me.

I confess my hopes on that subject are very faint.

Hayward wrote to-day to say that he had everything ready for Monday, twelve o'clock. I shall be punctual.

[Addressed]
  W. GODWIN, Esq.,
    41 *Skinner Street*,
      Snow Hill, London

LETTERS

Bishopgate,
February 26, 1816. *Monday night.*

I wish to God Turner's delusion had assumed any other shape, or that the painful task of destroying its flattering effects was reserved for someone less interested in your concerns than myself. He has entirely misapprehended the whole case. But I will endeavour to state it clearly.

I possessed in January, 1815, a reversion expectant on the death of the survivor of my grandfather and father, approaching so nearly to the nature of an absolute reversion, that by a few ceremonies I could, on these contingencies failing, possess myself of the fee-simple and alienate the whole.

My grandfather had exerted the utmost power with which the law invested him to prevent this ultimate alienation, but his power terminated in my person, and was exercised only to the restraint of my father. The estate of which I now speak is that which is the subject of the settlement of 1792.

My grandfather's will was dictated by the same spirit which had produced the settlement. He desired to perpetuate a large mass of property. He therefore left the moiety of about £240,000 to be disposed of in the following manner. My father was to enjoy the interest of it *during his life. After my father's death* I was to enjoy the interest *alone* in like manner, conditionally on my having previously deprived myself of the absolute power which I now possess over the settled estates of 1792; and so reduce myself to the reversion of a life annuity of £12,000 or £14,000 per an. in exchange for a *reversion* of landed property of 6, 7, or 8,000 per an. All was *reversion.* I was entitled, in no view of the case, to any *immediate* advantage.

My grandfather's will limited my option of accepting these conditions to one year from the date of his death. But I did not hesitate a moment to refuse them, nor, until Longdill informed me that it was my father's desire and interest that I should act as I intended to act, did I see any necessity of making a secret of my

142

resolution. I allowed Longdill, however, to manage these affairs in his own way; and he agreed with Whitton that I should refuse to accept my grandfather's legacy and that my father should purchase of me my interest in the settled estates at a fair price. The project of this arrangement was very satisfactory to me, as I saw myself about to realize the very scheme best suited to the uncertainty of my health and the peculiarity of my views and situation, by the sacrifice of that which I never intended to accept.

I signed the deed of disclaimer for the purpose of making my father certain of my intentions, so that our operations need not wait for the expiration of the year appointed by my grandfather's will. If, as Turner says, I have the power to stand in the same situation with respect to my grandfather's will, now, as on the day of his death, that power is entirely worthless, and must, as you see, be placed out of our consideration.

Now, lawyers say, that my father dares not buy my interest in the settled estates of 1792, because such an act might induce a forfeiture of the additional income he derives from concurring with the intentions of the will.

After this clear recapitulation of facts with which I had imagined you to be fully acquainted, I entreat you not to adopt Turner's delusive inference that because "I am ready and desirous to fulfil my engagements, your difficulties are therefore at an end."

Your letter of this morning, indeed, throws a new light on Turner's intervention, at least as I regard it. The mistake, the vital mistake he has made appears to me by no means consistent with the legal acuteness you describe him to possess. I cannot help thinking that you transfer your just appreciation of his taste and his wit to a subject on which the very subtlety essential to these qualifications leads him astray. Or perhaps you are right in this judgment, and he is not enough interested for you, not enough your friend to force his attention to the point. If he would think or act for your or my interests as for his own then possibly he might deserve your opinion.

If after this explanation you continue to think that his suggestions would be available, I will contrive to see him without delay.

But without rejecting whatever Turner's kindness or experience could afford, are there no means of arriving at the same end? You do not understand the state of my affairs so exactly as a lawyer could explain them to you. You believe that I, from ignorance of law, and the usages of the world, let pass opportunities of settling with my father. Cannot you explain the exact situation in which you, stand with me to Sir James Mackintosh? He, I am informed, really desires to serve you but is unable. If he knew how much of your future comfort depends on your having a true conception of the state of my affairs, surely he would with pleasure enter into such explanations with me, as would make him master of the subject. His various life makes his experience far more valuable than that of Turner, even if you should judge that this latter surpassed him in intrinsic mental worth.

I will not add to the length of this letter by explaining a circumstance of little moment but which asks a good many words; I shall so soon see either Turner or some other interlocutor on your part.

I trust to your kindness that you will forbear shewing this letter to Turner. I have spoken my real doubts of his efficiency which, should an occasion require I would not shrink to repeat in his presence. But he is apt to take offence, and I am too generally hated not to feel that [the] smallest kindness from an old acquaintance is valuable.

P. B. SHELLEY.

I open this letter to mention that for some days I shall be quite incapable of active exertion. I was seized last night with symptoms of irritable fever, and my state requires rest to prevent serious effects.

[Addressed]
WILLIAM GODWIN, Esq.,
41 *Skinner Street,*
Snow Hill, London

LETTERS

CCLXXVII
TO WILLIAM GODWIN
London

13 *Norfolk Street, London,*
March 6, 1816.

SIR,

The first part of your letter alludes to a subject in which my feelings are most deeply interested, and on which I could wish to receive an entire explanation. I confess that I do not understand how the pecuniary engagements subsisting between us in any degree impose restrictions on your conduct towards me. They did not, at least to your knowledge or with your consent, exist at the period of my return from France, and yet your conduct towards me and your daughter was then precisely such as it is at present. Perhaps I ought to except the tone which you assumed in conversation with Turner respecting me, which, for anything that I learn from you, I know not how favourably he may not have perverted. In my judgment, neither I, nor your daughter, nor her offspring, ought to receive the treatment which we encounter on every side. It has perpetually appeared to me to have been your especial duty to see that, so far as mankind value your good opinion, we were dealt justly by, and that a young family, innocent and benevolent and united, should not be confounded with prostitutes and seducers. My astonishment, and I will confess when I have been treated with most harshness and cruelty by you, my indignation has been extreme, that, knowing as you do my nature, any considerations should have prevailed on you to have been thus harsh and cruel. I lamented also over my ruined hopes, hopes of all that your genius once taught me to expect from your virtue, when I found that for yourself, your family, and your creditors, you would submit to that communication with me which you once rejected and abhorred, and which no pity for my poverty or sufferings, assumed willingly for you, could avail to extort. Do not talk of *forgiveness* again to me, for my blood boils in my veins, and my gall rises against all that bears the human form, when I think of what I, their benefactor and ardent lover, have endured of enmity and contempt from you and from all mankind.

145

I cannot mix the feelings to which you have given birth with details in answer to your views of my affairs. I can only say that I think you are too sanguine, but that I will do all that I can not to disappoint you. I see much difficulty and some danger, but I [am] in no temper to overrate my own inconveniences. I shall certainly remain in London some days, perhaps longer, as affairs appear to require. Meanwhile, oblige me by referring to the letter in which I mention Bryant, and enclose me his direction as soon as possible. I have left his letter at Bishopgate. I will take an early opportunity of replying to your letter at length, if no other mode of explanation suggests itself.

[Addressed]
W. GODWIN, Esq.,
41 *Skinner Street,*
Snow Hill

CCLXXVIII
TO ROBERT SOUTHEY

Messrs. Longdill & Co.,
5 *Gray's Inn Square,* [*London*],
March 7, 1816.

MY DEAR SIR,

I cannot refrain from presenting you with a little poem,[1] the product of a few serene hours of the last beautiful autumn. I shall never forget the pleasure which I derived from your conversation, or the kindness with which I was received in your hospitable circle during the short period of my stay in Cumberland some years ago. The disappointment of some youthful hopes, and subsequent misfortunes of a heavier nature, are all that I can plead as my excuse for neglecting to write to you, as I had promised from Ireland. The true weight of this apology you cannot know. Let it be sufficient that, regarding you with admiration as a poet, and with respect as a man, I send you, as an intimation of those sentiments, my first serious attempt to interest the best feelings of the human heart, believing that you have so much general charity

[1] *Alastor,* etc. See note to Shelley's letter to Murray, January 16, 1816.

146

as to forget, like me, how widely in moral and political opinions we disagree, and to attribute that difference to better motives than the multitude are disposed to allege as the cause of dissent from their institutions.

Very sincerely yours,

PERCY B. SHELLEY.

CCLXXIX
TO WILLIAM GODWIN
London

13 *Norfolk Street*, [*London*],
March 7, 1816.

SIR,

The hopes which I had concieved of recieving from you the treatment and consideration which I esteem to be justly due to me were destroyed by your letter dated the 5th.—The feelings occasioned by this discovery were so bitter and so excruciating that I am resolved for the future to stifle all those expectations which my sanguine temper too readily erects on the slightest relaxation of the contempt and the neglect in the midst of which I live. I must appear the reverse of what I really am, haughty and hard, if I am not to see myself and all that I love trampled upon and outraged. Pardon me I do entreat you, if pursued by the conviction that where my true character is most entirely known, I there meet with the most systematic injustice, I have expressed myself with violence.—Overlook a fault caused by your own equivocal politeness, and I will offend no more.

We will confine our communication to business.

I have left a note at Anderton's Coffee House appointing an interview with Bryant.[1] If I have a *fair offer* on the subject of rever-

[1] At the sale of Shelley's letters to Bryant there was a note dated March 7, 1816, Norfolk Street, Strand, in which Shelley expressed "a wish to see Mr. Bryant on the subject which was mentioned a fortnight since." Mr. S. de Ricci suggests that this may be the document, owned by the late Charles W. Frederickson, in the third person, from the same place and with the same date, which is described in the catalogue of his sale as " 'Mr. Percy Shelley presents his compliments &c.' making an appointment."

sion, there is at once an end to the objections which I should be inclined to make to any other arrangement from the supposition of my father's settling in some manner on the basis of the original proposal. If Bryant is in earnest I will make Longdill treat with him. Longdill will not consent to treat with him unless his terms approach to reasonableness. I do not scruple to promise you the advance if it can be managed thus.—I have a vital objection to auction, or any enquiries among professed money-lenders. I should suffer more in my negociation with my father from such measures which would probably be unsuccessful, than from a fair bargain which might be carried into effect.

The affair with Nash has a tendency the opposite to that which you attribute to it. It is now in Chancery, "tho' from what fund it is to be paid no one knows," and will infallibly be decided in my favour. It will be decided that he is to receive his capital and 5 per cent., and no more. This proves that the bond is good property, but that all speculations by which more than 5 per cent. is to be made (and no one will advance money without larger profit) will be annulled by the Chancellor.

I entirely agree with you on the subject of raising money by annuity.

I plainly see how necessary immediate advances are to your concerns, and will take care that I shall fail in nothing which I can do to procure them.

I shall remain in Town at least another week, that I may give every possible attention to this subject.—My own concerns are decided, I fear, already.

P. B. SHELLEY.

[Addressed]
W. GODWIN, Esq.,
41 *Skinner Street*,
Snow Hill
[Postmark]
7 o'clock
7 MR
1816 NT

LETTERS

London
March 9, 1816.

SIR,

I have made an appointment with Bryant which he has not kept, probably because he has not called at the coffee house yet. I do not regret this neglect as I think, under the circumstances I am about to mention, that a negotiation with him would be safest postponed.

Since Wednesday I have been daily expecting a message from Longdill to require my signature for the answer in Chancery. Not having heard from him I called this morning—the answer was ready. In the progress of conversation I asked Longdill how soon he thought Whitton would be ready. He replied coldly, he supposed in a month or two, that he scarcely knew the mode which Whitton designed to adopt, but that it ought to be very indifferent to me, since it would certainly be decided that we must not touch the estates. It happened at this period of the conversation that Whitton came in. His manner and tone on the subject were the very reverse of Longdill's. He blamed Longdill for having neglected to send for me to sign the answer yesterday, which delay he observed would prevent our cause from being heard on Wednesday, the day which he had provided. He seemed to regret that *one day* had been lost, he said that the production of the infant had already procrastinated the proceedings much to the displeasure of Sir Timothy. He expressed on my father's account the greatest anxiety for the approaching decision, and that in a manner that makes me hope that it is possible that Mr. Hart and Butler and Sir T. Romilly should be in the wrong. Whitton expresses much confidence in the expectation that the decision will enable me and my father to divide the whole estates.—It is advisable under these circumstances to suspend all other negotiations. The cause must be heard some day next week.

[Addressed]
W. GODWIN, Esq.,
41 *Skinner Street,*
Snow Hill

LETTERS

CCLXXXI
TO WILLIAM GODWIN
London

13 Norfolk Street, London,
March 16, 1816.

SIR,

Turner has been with you, and he will have informed you that I have been active in the endeavour to raise money. I have seen Dawe, and attempted by every possible inducement to urge him to make the advance. He has not refused, and even has promised that if he can procure any money he would willing[ly] lend it.

I have seen Bryant also, but nothing can be done with him until the question between my father and myself is disposed of. This cause is to come on and to receive judgment next Tuesday.

[Addressed]
W. GODWIN, Esq.,
41 *Skinner Street*

CCLXXXII
TO WILLIAM BRYANT

33 Howard Street, Strand,[1]
Monday, Ma[rch] 18, 1816.

Mr. Shelley presents his complts. to Mr. Bryant, and is exceedingly obliged to him for the loan of the MSS. which shall be taken care of and returned at an early opportunity. Mr. S. would, *if possible,* be at Mr. Bryant's at 12 o'Clock. He fears that an engagement will detain him beyond that hour. He hopes that it would equally suit Dr. Bethune to change the appointment to 2 o'Clock when Mr. S. will not fail—

---

[1] Shelley wrote to Bryant from 13 Norfolk Street on March 20, 1816, stating that he had changed his address and that he need not mention the origin of their correspondence. On the day following, March 21, 1816, he wrote as follows from "Marchmont Street, London. Mr. Shelley made a mistake [in his address] and has to request therefore that Mr. Bryant will favour him by transmitting whatever communication he has in his power to make here, and not to Craven Street."

LETTERS

13 *Norfolk Street, London,*
March 21, 1816.

SIR,

I have not been unemployed in attempting to raise money, though I fear ineffectually. I have seen Bryant [1] twice, and I fear that nothing favourable will result from my negotiation with him; he has promised, however, to write if he should be able to do anything. My principal hope is Dawe, from whom I think money might be obtained if Turner would undertake to persuade him. Can you suggest any other means than those in which I have engaged?

The decision in Chancery is postponed until to-morrow (Thursday). I shall inform you of the event immediately.

P. B. SHELLEY.

[Addressed]
W. GODWIN, Esq.,
41 *Skinner Street,*
Snow Hill

[26] *Marchmont Street,* [*London*],
March 29, 1816.

I had a long and most painful conversation with Turner last night on the subject of your pecuniary distress.—I am not, as he, I fear, leaves you to infer, unwilling to do my utmost, nor does my disposition in the least depend on the question of your demonstrating personal kindness to myself or Mary.—I see that, if anything is to be done, it must be done instantly. You know

1 Shelley wrote from 26 Marchmont Street, London, on March 26, 1816, requesting Mr. Bryant to put an end to the state of painful uncertainty arising out of the expectations excited by his last conversation.

my habitual, my constitutional inability to deal with monied men. I have no friend who will supply my deficiencies,—none who interest themselves in my own, much less in your concerns, which I have, as much as one man can make those of another, made my own. Can you not yourself see these money-lenders? Hayward's partner was in Chancery yesterday when he heard my title to the reversion admitted to be excellent, and my powers, over that which I pretend to, unimpeached.—Would H[ayward] advance money on *post-obit* bond or deferred annuity? Can you not see him?

I shall be absent from town to-day, to-morrow, and a part of the following day. Fanny can communicate, should anything important occur, with Mary on the subject. Her sentiments in all respects coincide with mine; her interest is perhaps greater; her judgment, from what she knows of our situation, of what ought or can be done, is probably more calm and firm.—

Chancery, as you have heard, has given a doubtful and hesitating opinion. Whatever is to be done for me will be reluctantly done.

P. B. SHELLEY.

[Addressed]
W. GODWIN, Esq.,
41 *Skinner Street,*
Snow Hill

CCLXXXV
TO WILLIAM BRYANT

26 *Marchmont Street,*
Brunswick Square [*London*],
April 8, 1816.

DEAR SIR,

I request that if any enquiries are made respecting the negotiation in which we are at present engaged, you take every possible care to give no information to the enquirer, or allow it to be suspected that any negotiation at all is pending.—My father has been made acquainted with the application for the register of my birth at Warnham, and has been informed of the address to which it was sent. It is of great importance to me, as I am to be saved from additional domestic dissensions, to allow the real fact not to transpire, at least, until the business is concluded.

Your obed. sert.

P. B. SHELLEY.

I hope speedily to hear from you.

[Addressed]
— BRYANT, Esq.,
West Place,
West Square, St. George's Fields

CCLXXXVI
TO WILLIAM BRYANT

26 Marchmont Street, [London],
April 14, 1815. [? 1816.]

DEAR SIR,
Do not trouble yourself about my interest in the timber— my father can only cut under the restraint of an injunction from Chancery, and is bound by that injunction to bring the money into court to await the decision of the case. You misunderstood me—I only said that Mr. Whitton had informed me that it was not my father's intention to touch the timbers which Dr. Bethune considers ornamental. I was led to interest myself in this by understanding from you that Dr. Bethune would lend me £500. I have indeed the most urgent necessity for the advance of such a sum. Do you think any friends of yours at Worth, do you think Dr. Bethune would lend it to me on my bond at a year or eighteen months? I should assuredly be able to pay it when due, since the affair with my father would either have gone off altogether, and then I could make a security on the estate, or we should have agreed on terms, and I should be in immediate possession of my share of the reversion. I am in awkward circumstances for want

of £500, and if you stand my friend in procuring it for me, you may depend upon my showing myself a friend to you.

Dear Sir,
Your obliged serv't.
PERCY B. SHELLEY.[1]

W. BRYANT, Esq.,
Worth Rectory,
East Grinstead, Sussex

CCLXXXVII
TO WILLIAM BRYANT

26 *Marchmont Street,*
Brunswick Square [*London*],
April 24, 1816.

DEAR SIR,

In reply to the proposal made by you some months since to me on the part of Dr. Bethune, I wrote the other day to say that I would sell him the reversion at a fair price. In answer to your request as to the nature of the title I can convey (?) accept the following statement. The estates, of which this of Dr. Bethune is a part, are given, by settlements dated August, 1791, to my father for life, to me in remainder. On my father's death by recovery I obtain the fee of these estates. I can make a deed which shall be binding upon myself in case I survive my father, and which shall be binding upon my infant son if I do not survive my father, either to alienate any particular estate, or to pay a certain sum of money. I have levied a fine and acquired this power, which I believe is called a *base fee*, which as I have before stated I am fully competent to convey. If I and my infant son should die before my father the security falls to the ground. But Dr. B. or any person might insure my life against my father's to

---

[1] Apparently Bryant did not reply to this letter by April 20, 1816, as Shelley wrote to him on that date, from 26 Marchmont Street, and said, "Pray be so kind as to answer it immediately and relieve me from the suspense which the reliance on your exertions for my accomodation has produced."

154

whatever amount he should be beneficially interested. He need sustain no *loss in any case;* and would only fail in his object of obtaining possession of the farm in question, if, what is very improbable, my father should survive not only me, but both myself and my infant son.

Dear Sir,
Your very obedient servant,

PERCY B. SHELLEY.

CCLXXXVIII
TO ———

26 *Marchmont Street,*
Saturday.

MY DEAR SIR,
I very much regret that I am engaged to-morrow at the hour you appoint, but I will call on Monday morning at your Chambers.

Your very obliged sert.

P. B. SHELLEY.

CCLXXXIX
TO WILLIAM BRYANT

Marchmont St.,
Thursday Mor. [? *April* 1816].

Mr. Shelley is suddenly obliged to leave town for a week or a fortnight. Mr. Bryant will have the goodness to address his communications to No. 26, Marchmont Street, whence they will be forwarded immediately.—Mr. S. is obliged by the loan of the books &c. which he returns.

XI

MAY 3 TO AUGUST 2, 1816

SECOND VISIT TO THE CONTINENT

CCXC
TO WILLIAM GODWIN
London

Dover,[1]
May 3, 1816.

No doubt you are anxious to hear the state of my concerns. I wish that it was in my power to give you a more favourable view of them than such as I am compelled to present. The limited condition of my fortune is regretted by me, as I imagine you will know, because among other designs of a similar nature I cannot at once put you in possession of all that would be sufficient for the comfort and independence which it is so unjust that you should not have already received from society.

Chancery has decided that I and my father may not touch the estates. It has decided also that all the timber, worth it is said £60,000, must be cut and sold, and the money paid into court to abide *whatever equities* may hereafter arise. This you already know from Fanny—

All this reduces me very nearly to the situation I described to you in March, so far as relates to your share in the question. I shall receive nothing from my father except in the way of charity. *Post-obit* concerns are very doubtful, and annuity transactions are confined within an obvious and very narrow limit.

My father is to advance me, a sum to meet as I have alleged,

---

[1] Peacock says, "In the early summer of 1816, the spirit of restlessness again came over him [Shelley], and resulted in a second visit to the Continent." Shelley remained for some days in London awaiting the decision of Chancery. Besides Shelley, Mary and their little boy, William, Clare Clairmont was of the party. Paris was reached on May 8. The journey lay over the same ground that they had traversed on foot nearly two years before, in 1814, through Troyes, and as far as Neufchâtel. Here they took another road, through Dijon, Dôle, Poligny, Champagnolles, Les Rousses, to Geneva, where they put up at the Hôtel de Sécheron.

engagements contracted during the dependence of the late negotiation. This sum is extremely small, and is swallowed up, almost, in
such of my debts and the liquidation of such securities as I have
been compelled to state in order to obtain the money at all. A few
hundred pounds will remain; you shall have £300 from this source
in the course of the summer. I am to give a *post-obit* security for
this sum, and the affair at present stands that the deeds are to be
drawn in the course of 6 weeks or 2 months, and that I am to return
for their signature and to receive the money. There can be no doubt
that, if my applications in other quarters should not be discovered
by my father, the money will be in readiness for you by the time
that Kingdoms's discounts recur.

I am afraid nothing can be done with Bryant.—He promised to
lend me £500 on *my mere bond;* of course he failed, and this failure
presents no good augury of his future performances. Still the
negotiation is open, and I cannot but think that the only, or at
least the best chance for success would be your interference. Perhaps you would dislike to be mistaken for my personal friend
which it would be necessary you should appear, provided you ac-
quiesce in this suggestion. I am confident that it would be a most
favourable circumstance. It is necessary, I must remark, that
secrecy should at present be observed—

Hayward has also an affair in hand. He says he thinks he can get
me £300 on Post Obit.

Neither Bryant nor Hayward know that I have left England, and
as I must in all probability, nay certainly return in a few weeks to
sign these deeds if the people should agree, or at least to get the
money from my father, I thought it might relax their exertions to
know that I was abroad. I informed them that I was gone for a
fortnight or three weeks into the country. I have not even disengaged my lodgings in Marchmont Street.

The motives which determined me to leave England and which
I stated to you in a former letter have continued since that period
to press on me with accumulated force. Continually detained in a
situation where what I esteem a prejudice does not permit me to
live on equal terms with my fellow-beings I resolved to commit
myself to a decided step. I therefore take Mary to Geneva, where I

shall devise some plan of settlement and only leave her to return to London, and exclusively devote myself to business.

I leave England—I know not, perhaps for ever. I return, alone, to see no friend, to do no office of friendship, to engage in nothing that can soothe the sentiments of regret almost like remorse which under such circumstances every one feels who quits his native land. I respect you, I think well of you, better perhaps than of any other person whom England contains; you were the philosopher who first awakened, and who still as a philosopher to a very great degree regulate my understanding. It is unfortunate for me that the part of your character which is least excellent should have been met by my convictions of what was right to do. But I have been too indignant, I have been unjust to you.—Forgive me.—Burn those letters which contain the records of my violence, and believe that however what you erroneously call fame and honour separate us, I shall always feel towards you as the most affectionate of friends.—

P. B. SHELLEY.

Address—Poste Restante, Geneve.

I have written in great haste, expecting every moment to hear that the Pacquet sails.

[Addressed]
— GODWIN, Esq.,
41 *Skinner Street,*
London

CCXCI
TO THOMAS LOVE PEACOCK

Hotel de Sécheron,[1] *Geneva*
May 15, 1816

After a journey of ten days, we arrived at Geneva. The journey, like that of life, was variegated with intermingled rain and sunshine, though these many showers were to me, as you know,

[1] Shelley and his little party moved by the end of May from the hotel to a cottage known as Campagne Chapuis, or Campagne Mont Algère, about two miles from Geneva, near Coligny, on the opposite side of the Lake. The cottage, separated from the water's edge only by a small garden, stood five or eight minutes' walk below the

LETTERS

April showers, quickly passing away, and foretelling the calm brightness of summer.

The journey was in some respects exceedingly delightful, but the prudential considerations arising out of the necessity of preventing delay, and the continual attention to pecuniary disbursements, detract terribly from the pleasure of all travelling schemes.

. . . .

You live by the shores of a tranquil stream, among low and woody hills. You live in a free country, where you may act without restraint, and possess that which you possess in security; and so long as the name of country and the selfish conceptions it includes shall subsist, England, I am persuaded, is the most free and the most refined.

Perhaps you have chosen wisely, but if I return and follow your example, it will be no subject of regret to me that I have seen other things. Surely there is much of bad and much of good, there is much to disgust, and much to elevate, which he cannot have felt or known who has never passed the limits of his native land.

So long as man is such as he now is, the experience of which I speak will never teach him to despise the country of his birth—far otherwise, like Wordsworth, he will never know what love subsists between that and him until absence shall have made its beauty more heartfelt; our poets and our philosophers, our mountains and our lakes, the rural lanes and fields which are so especially our own, are ties which, until I become utterly senseless, can never be broken asunder.

These, and the memory of them, if I never should return, these and the affections of the mind, with which, having been once united, they are inseparable, will make the name of England dear to me for ever, even if I should permanently return to it no more.

But I suppose you did not pay the postage of this, expecting nothing but sentimental gossip, and I fear it will be long before I play the tourist properly, I will, however, tell you that to come to Geneva we crossed the Jura branch of the Alps.

Villa Diodati, where Milton, returning from Italy in 1639, had visited his friend, Dr. John Diodati, the Genevan professor of theology. A vineyard lay between Shelley's cottage and the villa, where, haunted by the British tourist and gossip-monger, Byron took refuge on June 10.—Professor Dowden's *Life of Shelley*, Vol. II, p. 14.

The mere difficulties of horses, high bills, postillions. and cheating, lying *aubergistes*, you can easily conceive; fill up that part of the picture according to your own experience, and it cannot fail to resemble.

The mountains of Jura exhibit scenery of wonderful sublimity. Pine forests of impenetrable thickness, and untrodden, nay, inaccessible expanse, spreading on every side. Sometimes descending, they follow the route into the valleys, clothing the precipitous rocks, and struggling with knotted roots between the most barren clefts. Sometimes the road winds high into the regions of frost, and there these forests become scattered, and loaded with snow.

The trees in these regions are incredibly large, and stand in scattered clumps over the white wilderness. Never was scene more awfully desolate than that which we passed on the evening of our last day's journey.

The natural silence of that uninhabited desert contrasted strangely with the voices of the people who conducted us, for it was necessary in this part of the mountain to take a number of persons, who should assist the horses to force the chaise through the snow, and prevent it from falling down the precipice.

We are now at Geneva, where, or in the neighbourhood, we shall remain probably until the autumn. I may return in a fortnight or three weeks, to attend to the last exertions which L[ongdill] is to make for the settlement of my affairs; of course I shall then see you; in the meantime it will interest me to hear all that you have to tell of yourself.

.   .   .   .

P. B. SHELLEY.

LETTERS

MESSRS. BROOKES, DIXON & SON
London

Geneva,
June, 21, 1816.

GENTLEMEN,

You would oblige me by sending on my account five pounds to T. Peacock Esqr. Great Marlow, Bucks.—I should be glad also to receive a statement of the present situation of my accounts with you, addressed " Poste Restante, Geneva," and have the honor to be,

Gentlemen,
Your obliged hm. Svt.

PERCY BYSSHE SHELLEY.

[Addressed]
MESSRS. BROOKES, DIXON & SON,
25, *Chancery Lane,*
London, Angleterre

CCXCIII
TO WILLIAM GODWIN
London

Evian, Savoie,
June 23, 1816.
[*Sunday.*]

SIR,

Your letter reached me the moment before I set off on a little tour of the borders of the lake. I write therefore from the first post town I arrive at.

You know that we are not on those intimate terms as to permit that I should have minutely explained to you the motives which determined my departure, or that, if explained, you would have judged them with the judgment of a friend. I can easily imagine that you were disquieted by it. But I have ever been most unwillingly the cause of disquiet to you, meaning you all possible good.

I entirely approve of your seeing Bryant,[1] and I think, if no unappreciated circumstances render the farm in question more valuable than he states, that the terms his client offers are unusually favourable. But I think if you undertake the business, you ought to ascertain this. The property need not actually be valued, as the expense of valuation is proportionately immense, but a clearer conception of its value than the purchaser's assertion or even the rental affords, might, I should conceive, be obtained by one so clear-sighted and experienced in these affairs as yourself. But perhaps I am unjust to you to suppose that you would not in all these respects consider my property as my own.

There is a copy of the settlement, as I imagine, at Jew King's,[2] which he said he would sell for ten pounds. Enclosed is a note, which, as probably it is inconvenient to you to pay this sum, directs my bankers to give as much to Mr. Martin.[3] I have put this name, supposing that you would not like your own to be stated.

I dare say you can get the settlement for £5, if, as I strongly believe, it is yet in King's possession. If it is not, I can think of no other resource than Longdill, from whom I conceive that a copy might be obtained on the ground of your having on a former occasion lent me a copy, and my not having returned it, and his having collected all the copies belonging to me, and the person to whom

[1] Bryant's offer to purchase from Shelley a farm for seventeen hundred pounds made it necessary for a copy of the settlement of 1791 to be obtained in order to proceed with the negotiations. Godwin complained of Shelley's "unfortunate absence," which rendered it impossible for the document to be procured.

[2] Probably John King, who is described, in the *Biographical Dictionary of Living Authors*, 1816, as "a well-known character in London of the Jewish persuasion, and bred to the law, which profession he quitted, long since, to follow another nearly connected with it, that of lending money to the embarrassed. He has had recourse to many ingenious speculations, and has always contrived to live in a style of fashion, though generally involved in law-suits, and sometimes living within the rules of a prison. The history of this extraordinary personage would occupy a volume, and doubtless will be exhibited hereafter for the benefit of the next generation." He is credited with the authorship of three publications. King is said to have been the father of "Rosa Matilda," otherwise Charlotte Dacre, whose romances, *Zofloyo, or the Moor*, and others delighted Shelley in his youth. See Byron's *English Bards and Scotch Reviewers*, note to line 740, and *The Modern Dunciad*, 1814, by G. Daniel, p. 8.

[3] Shelley addressed the following letter to Brookes & Co.:

Geneva, June 23, 1816.

" Gentlemen, oblige by paying Mr. Martin, the bearer of this note, ten pounds, and by placing it to my account. I have the honour to be, Gentlemen, your obed. Svt.
PERCY BYSSHE SHELLEY.
By favour of Mr. Martin."

this copy belongs having a right to it. You remember that you borrowed what I now speak of from a law student, that you lent it to me, and that it was never returned. In the present state of the negotiations with Bryant the utmost care must be taken that no circumstances relating to it transpires. I hope that you were impressed with the necessity of secrecy on this point. Nothing but my persuasion that you will act as if you were, engages my consent to the negotiations.

May I request that if you obtain the settlement that you will cause a copy to be made and keep it for me?

The style of this letter, I fear, will appear to you unusual. The truth is that I feel the unbounded difficulty of making myself understood on the commonest topic, and I am obliged to adopt for that purpose a cold and stiff set of phrases. No person can feel deeper interest for another or venerate their character and talents more sincerely, or regret more incessantly his own impotent loneliness, than I for you and yours.

Remember me kindly to Fanny both for her own and for her sister's sake.

P. B. SHELLEY.

Address still Geneva. I shall have returned in a few days from this date.

[Addressed]
WILLIAM GODWIN, Esq.,
41 *Skinner Street,*
Snow Hill, London,
Angleterre

CCXCIV
TO R. HAYWARD
[Extract]

Geneva,
June 24, 1816.

Your letter has been forwarded to me here . . . I am surprised to hear that your client, Mr. Billing, declines an additional advance, having always found that his annuity was regularly paid, and knowing the security to be unexceptional. But I suppose that

166

he has taken something into his head about that Chancery affair, and I cannot be persuaded that my situation is the same now as before the questions between my father and myself was . . .[1]

CCXCV
TO THOMAS LOVE PEACOCK

Montalegre, near Coligni, Geneva,[1]
July 12 [1816].

It is nearly a fortnight since I have returned from Vevai. This journey has been on every account delightful, but most especially, because then I first knew the divine beauty of Rousseau's imagination, as it exhibits itself in " Julie." It is inconceivable what an enchantment the scene itself lends to those delineations, from which its own most touching charm arises. But I will give you an abstract of our voyage, which lasted eight days, and if you have a map of Switzerland, you can follow me.

We left Montalegre at half-past two on the 23rd of June. The lake was calm, and after three hours of rowing we arrived at Hermance, a beautiful little village, containing a ruined tower, built, the villagers say, by Julius Cæsar. There were three other towers similar to it, which the Genevese destroyed for their own fortifications in 1560. We got into the tower by a kind of window. The walls are immensely solid, and the stone of which it is built so hard, that it yet retained the mark of chisels. The boatman said that this tower was once three times higher than it is now. There are two staircases in the thickness of the walls, one of which is entirely

---

[1] The word here has been almost blotted out. In this letter (now in Mr. Carl H. Pforzheimer's collection, New York) Shelley encloses the draft of a will.

[1] "During his [Shelley's] stay in Switzerland he became acquainted with Lord Byron. They made an excursion round the Lake of Geneva, of which he sent me the detail in a diary. This diary was published by Mrs. Shelley [*History of a Six Weeks' Tour*, 1817], but without introducing the name of Lord Byron, who is throughout called ' my companion.' The diary was first published during Lord Byron's life, but why his name was concealed I do not know. Though the changes are not many, yet the association of the two names gives it great additional interest."—Peacock's note.

demolished, and the other half-ruined, and only accessible by a ladder. The town itself, now an inconsiderable village inhabited by a few fishermen, was built by a Queen of Burgundy, and reduced to its present state by the inhabitants of Berne, who burnt and ravaged everything they could find.

Leaving Hermance, we arrived at sunset at the village of Nerni-[er]. After looking at our lodgings, which were gloomy and dirty, we walked out by the side of the lake. It was beautiful to see the vast expanse of these purple and misty waters broken by the craggy islets near to its slant and "beached margin." There were many fish sporting in the lake, and multitudes were collected close to the rocks to catch the flies which inhabited them.

On returning to the village, we sat on a wall beside the lake, looking at some children who were playing at a game like ninepins. The children here appeared in an extraordinary way deformed and diseased. Most of them were crooked, and with enlarged throats; but one little boy had such exquisite grace in his mien and motions, as I never before saw equalled in a child. His countenance was beautiful for the expression with which it overflowed. There was a mixture of pride and gentleness in his eyes and lips, the indications of sensibility, which his education will probably pervert to misery or seduce to crime; but there was more of gentleness than of pride, and it seemed that the pride was tamed from its original wildness by the habitual exercise of milder feelings. My companion gave him a piece of money, which he took without speaking, with a sweet smile of easy thankfulness, and then with an unembarrassed air turned to his play. All this might scarcely be; but the imagination surely could not forebear to breathe into the most inanimate forms, some likeness of its own visions, on such a serene and glowing evening in this remote and romantic village, beside the calm lake that bore us hither.

On returning to our inn, we found that the servant had arranged our rooms, and deprived them of the greater portion of their former disconsolate appearance. They reminded my companion of Greece; it was five years, he said, since he had slept in such beds. The influence of the recollections excited by this circumstance on our conversation gradually faded, and I retired to rest with no unpleasant sensations, thinking of our journey to-morrow, and of the pleasure of recounting the little adventures of it when we return.

The next morning we passed Yvoire, a scattered village with an ancient castle, whose houses are interspersed with trees, and which stands at a little distance from Nerni, on the promontory which bounds a deep bay, some miles in extent. So soon as we arrived at this promontory, the lake began to assume an aspect of wilder magnificence. The mountains of Savoy, whose summits were bright with snow, descended in broken slopes to the lake: on high the rocks were dark with pine forests, which become deeper and more immense, until the ice and snow mingle with the points of naked rock that pierce the blue air; but below, groves of walnut, chestnut, and oak, with openings of lawny fields, attested the milder climate.

As soon as we had passed the opposite promontory, we saw the river Drance, which descends from between a chasm in the mountains, and makes a plain near the lake, intersected by its divided streams. Thousands of *besolets*, beautiful water-birds, like sea-gulls, but smaller, with purple on their backs, take their station on the shallows where its waters mingle with the lake. As we approached Evian, the mountains descended more precipitously to the lake, and masses of intermingled wood and rock overhung its shining spire.

We arrived at this town about seven o'clock, after a day which involved more rapid changes of atmosphere than I ever recollect to have observed before. The morning was cold and wet; then an easterly wind, and the clouds hard and high; then thunder showers and wind shifting to every quarter; then a war blast from the south, and summer clouds hanging over the peaks, with bright blue sky between. About half-an-hour after we had arrived at Evian, a few flashes of lightning came from a dark cloud, directly overhead, and continued after the cloud had dispersed. "Diespiter, per pura tonantes egit equos:" a phenomenon which certainly had no influence on me, corresponding with that which it produced on Horace.

The appearance of the inhabitants of Evian is more wretched, diseased, and poor, than I ever recollect to have seen. The contrast indeed between the subjects of the King of Sardinia and the citizens

LETTERS

of the independent republics of Switzerland, affords a powerful illustration of the blighting mischiefs of despotism, within the space of a few miles. They have mineral waters here, *eaux savonneuses* they call them. In the evening we had some difficulty about our passports, but so soon as the syndic heard my companion's rank and name, he apologised for the circumstance. The inn was good. During our voyage, on the distant height of a hill, covered with pine-forests, we saw a ruined castle, which reminded me of those on the Rhine.

We left Evian on the following morning, with a wind of such violence as to permit but one sail to be carried. The waves also were exceedingly high, and our boat so heavily laden, that there appeared to be some danger. We arrived, however, safe at Meillerie,[2] after passing with great speed mighty forests which overhung the lake, and lawns of exquisite verdure, and mountains with bare and icy points, which rose immediately from the summit of the rocks, whose bases were echoing to the waves.

We here heard that the Empress Maria Louisa had slept at Meillerie before the present inn was built, and when the accommodations were those of the most wretched village in remembrance of St. Preux. How beautiful it is to find that the common sentiments of human nature can attach themselves to those who are the most removed from its duties and its enjoyments, when Genius pleads for their admission at the gate of Power. To own them was becoming in the Empress, and confirms the affectionate praise contained in the regret of a great and enlightened nation. A Bourbon dared not even to have remembered Rousseau. She owed this power to that democracy which her husband's dynasty outraged, and of which it was however, in some sort, the representative among the nations of the earth. This little incident shows at once how unfit and how impossible it is for the ancient system of opinions, or for any power built upon a conspiracy to revive them, permanently to subsist among mankind. We dined there, and had some honey, the best I have ever tasted, the very essence of the mountain flowers, and as fragrant. Probably the village derives its name from this

[2] Shelley spells the name of this place throughout this letter, Mellerie, in *History of a Three Weeks' Tour*.

production. Meillerie is the well-known scene of St. Preux's visionary exile; but Meillerie is indeed enchanted ground, were Rousseau no magician. Groves of pine, chestnut, and walnut overshadow it; magnificent and unbounded forests to which England
affords no parallel. In the midst of these woods are dells of lawny
expanse, inconceivably verdant, adorned with a thousand of the
rarest flowers, and odorous with thyme.

The lake appeared somewhat calmer as we left Meillerie, sailing
close to the banks, whose magnificence augmented with the turn
of every promontory. But we congratulated ourselves too soon; the
wind gradually increased in violence, until it blew tremendously;
and, as it came from the remotest extremity of the lake, produced
waves of a frightful height, and covered the whole surface with a
chaos of foam. One of our boatmen, who was a dreadfully stupid
fellow, persisted in holding the sail at a time when the boat was on
the point of being driven under water by the hurricane. On discovering his error, he let it entirely go, and the boat for a moment
refused to obey the helm; in addition, the rudder was so broken
as to render the management of it very difficult; one wave fell in,
and then another. My companion, an excellent swimmer, took off
his coat, I did the same, and we sat with our arms crossed, every
instant expecting to be swamped. The sail was however again held,
the boat obeyed the helm, and still in imminent peril from the immensity of the waves, we arrived in a few minutes at a sheltered
port, in the village of St. Gingoux.

I felt in this near prospect of death a mixture of sensations,
among which terror entered, though but subordinately. My feelings would have been less painful had I been alone; but I knew
that my companion would have attempted to save me, and I was
overcome with humiliation, when I thought that his life might
have been risked to preserve mine. When we arrived at St. Gingoux, the inhabitants, who stood on the shore, unaccustomed to see
a vessel as frail as ours, and fearing to venture at all on such a sea,
exchanged looks of wonder and congratulation with our boatmen,
who, as well as ourselves, were well pleased to set foot on shore.[3]

[3] "I have traversed all Rousseau's ground with the 'Héloïse' before me; and am struck
to a degree that I cannot express, with the force and accuracy of his descriptions and

St. Gingoux is even more beautiful than Meillerie; the mountains are higher, and their loftiest points of elevation descend more abruptly to the lake. On high, the aerial summits still cherish great depths of snow in their ravines, and in the paths of their unseen torrents. One of the highest of these is called Roche de St. Julien, beneath whose pinnacles the forests became deeper and more extensive; the chestnut gives a peculiarity to the scene, which is most beautiful, and will make a picture in my memory, distinct from all other mountain scenes which I have ever before visited.

As we arrived here early, we took a *voiture* to visit the mouth of the Rhone. We went between the mountains and the lake, under groves of mighty chestnut trees, beside perpetual streams, which are nourished by the snows above, and form stalactites on the rocks, over which they fall. We saw an immense chestnut tree, which had been overthrown by the hurricane of the morning. The place where the Rhone joins the lake was marked by a line of tremendous breakers; the river is as rapid as when it leaves the lake, but is muddy and dark. We went about a league farther on the road to La Valais, and stopped at a castle called La Tour de Bouverie, which seems to be the frontier of Switzerland and Savoy, as we were asked for our passports, on the supposition of our proceeding to Italy.

On one side of the road was the immense Roche de St. Julien, which overhung it; through the gateway of the castle we saw the snowy mountains of La Valais, clothed in clouds, and, on the other side, was the willowy plain of the Rhone, in a character of striking

the beauty of their reality: Meillerie, Clarens, and Nevy, and the Château de Chillon are places of which I shall say little, because all I could say must fall short of the impressions they stamp. Three days ago, we were most nearly wrecked in a squall off Meillerie, and driven to shore. I ran no risk, being so near the rocks, and a good swimmer; but our party were wet and incommoded a good deal. The wind was strong enough to blow down some trees, as we found on landing; however, all is righted, and right." (Byron to John Murray, June 27, 1816.) Moore also alludes to the adventure on the Lake: "Towards the end of June, Lord Byron, accompanied by his friend Shelley, made a tour in his boat round the Lake. In the squall off Meillerie, which he [Byron] mentions, their danger was considerable. In the expectation, every moment, of being obliged to swim for his life, Lord Byron had already thrown off his coat, and, as Shelley was no swimmer, insisted upon endeavouring, by some means, to save him. This offer, however, Shelley positively refused; and seating himself quietly upon a locker, and grasping the rings at each end firmly in his hands, declared his determination to go down in that position, without a struggle."—Moore's *Life of Byron*, 1844, p. 320.

contrast with the rest of the scene, bounded by the dark mountains that overhang Clarens, Vevai, and the lake that rolls between. In the midst of the plain rises a little isolated hill, on which the white spire of a church peeps from among the tufted chestnut woods. We returned to St. Gingoux before sunset, and I passed the evening in reading " Julie."

As my companion rises late, I had time before breakfast, on the ensuing morning, to hunt the waterfalls [4] of the river that fall into the lake at St. Gingoux. The stream is, indeed, from the declivity over which it falls, only a succession of waterfalls, which roar over the rocks with a perpetual sound, and suspend their unceasing spray on the leaves and flowers that overhang and adorn its savage banks. The path that conducted along this river sometimes avoided the precipices of its shores, by leading through meadows; sometimes threaded the base of the perpendicular and caverned rocks. I gathered in these meadows a nosegay of such flowers as I never saw in England, and which I thought more beautiful for that rarity.

On my return, after breakfast, we sailed for Clarens, determining first to see the three mouths of the Rhone, and then the castle of Chillon; the day was fine, and the water calm. We passed from the blue waters of the lake over the stream of the Rhone, which is rapid even at a great distance from its confluence with the lake; the turbid waters mixed with those of the lake, but mixed with them unwillingly. (See "Nouvelle Héloïse," Lettre 17, Part 4.) I read "Julie" all day; an overflowing, as it now seems, surrounded by the scenes which it has so wonderfully peopled, of sublimest genius, and more than human sensibility. Meillerie, the castle of Chillon, Clarens, the mountains of La Valais and Savoy, present themselves to the imagination as monuments of things that were once familiar, and of beings that were once dear to it. They were created indeed by one mind, but a mind so powerfully bright as to cast a shade of falsehood on the records that are called reality.

> [4] "Take all that's mine ' beneath the moon,'
> If I with her but half a noon
> May sit beneath the walls
> Of some old cave, and mossy nook,
> When up she winds along the brook
> To hunt the waterfalls."

Wordsworth's "Louisa, after accompanying her on a mountain excursion."

We passed on to the castle of Chillon, and visited its dungeons and towers. These prisons are excavated below the lake; the principal dungeon is supported by seven columns, whose branching capitals support the roof. Close to the very walls, the lake is eight hundred feet deep; iron rings are fastened to these columns, and on them were engraven a multitude of names, partly those of visitors, and partly doubtless of the prisoners, of whom now no memory remains, and who thus beguiled a solitude which they have long ceased to feel. One date was as ancient as 1670. At the commencement of the Reformation, and indeed long after that period, this dungeon was the receptacle of those who shook, or who denied the system of idolatry, from the effects of which mankind is even now slowly emerging.

Close to this long and lofty dungeon was a narrow cell, and beyond it one larger and far more lofty and dark, supported upon two unornamented arches. Across one of these arches was a beam, now black and rotten, on which prisoners were hung in secret. I never saw a monument more terrible of that cold and inhuman tyranny, which it had been the delight of man to exercise over man. It was indeed one of those many tremendous fulfilments which render the "pernicies humani generis" of the great Tacitus so solemn and irrefragable a prophecy. The gendarme, who conducted us over this castle, told us that there was an opening to the lake, by means of a secret spring, connected with which the whole dungeon might be filled with water before the prisoners could possibly escape!

We proceeded with a contrary wind to Clarens against a heavy swell. I never felt more strongly than on landing at Clarens, that the spirit of old times had deserted its once cherished habitation. A thousand times, thought I, have Julia and St. Preux walked on this terraced road, looking towards these mountains which I now behold; nay, treading on the ground where I now tread. From the window of our lodging our landlady pointed out "le bosquet de Julie." At least the inhabitants of this village are impressed with an idea that the persons of that romance had actual existence. In the evening we walked thither. It is indeed Julia's wood. The hay was making under the trees; the trees themselves were aged, but vigorous and interspersed with younger ones, which are destined to be their successors, and in future years, when we are dead, to afford a shade to future worshippers of nature, who love the memory of that tenderness and peace of which this was the imaginary abode. We walked forward among the vineyards, whose narrow terraces overlook this affecting scene. Why did the cold maxims of the world compel me at this moment to repress the tears of melancholy transport which it would have been so sweet to indulge, immeasurably, even until the darkness of night had swallowed up the objects which excited them.

I forgot to remark, what indeed my companion remarked to me, that our danger from the storm took place precisely in the spot where Julie and her lover were nearly overset, and where St. Preux was tempted to plunge with her into the lake.

On the following day we went to see the castle of Clarens, a square strong house, with very few windows, surrounded by a double terrace that overlooks the valley, or rather the plain of Clarens. The road which conducted to it wound up the steep ascent through woods of walnut and chestnut. We gathered roses on the terrace, in the feeling that they might be the posterity of some planted by Julie's hand. We sent their dead and withered leaves to the absent.

We went again to "the bosquet de Julie," and found that the precise spot was now utterly obliterated, and a heap of stones marked the place where the little chapel had once stood. Whilst we were execrating the author of this brutal folly, our guide informed us that the land belonged to the convent of St. Bernard, and that this outrage had been committed by their orders. I knew before, that if avarice could harden the hearts of men, a system of prescriptive religion has an influence far more inimical to natural sensibility. I know that an isolated man is sometimes restrained by shame from outraging the venerable feelings arising out of the memory of genius, which once made nature even lovelier than itself; but associated man holds it as the very sacrament of his union to forswear all delicacy, all benevolence, all remorse; all that is true, or tender, or sublime.

We sailed from Clarens to Vevai. Vevai is a town more beautiful in its simplicity than any I have ever seen. Its market-place, a spacious square interspersed with trees, looks directly upon the mountains of Savoy and La Valais, the lake, and the valley of the Rhone. It was at Vevai that Rousseau conceived the design of "Julie."

From Vevai we came to Ouchy, a village near Lausanne. The coasts of the Pays de Vaud, though full of villages and vineyards, present an aspect of tranquillity and peculiar beauty which well compensates for the solitude which I am accustomed to admire. The hills are very high and rocky, crowned and interspersed with woods. Waterfalls echo from the cliffs, and shine afar. In one place we saw the traces of two rocks of immense size, which had fallen from the mountain behind. One of these lodged in a room where a young woman was sleeping, without injuring her. The vineyards were utterly destroyed in its path, and the earth torn up.

The rain detained us two days at Ouchy. We, however, visited Lausanne, and saw Gibbon's house. We were shown the decayed summer-house where he finished his History, and the old acacias on the terrace, from which he saw Mont Blanc, after having written the last sentence. There is something grand and even touching in the regret which he expresses at the completion of his task. It was conceived amid the ruins of the Capitol. The sudden departure of his cherished and accustomed toil must have left him, like the death of a dear friend, sad and solitary.

My companion gathered some acacia leaves to preserve in remembrance of him. I refrained from doing so, fearing to outrage the greater and more sacred name of Rousseau; the contemplation of whose imperishable creations had left no vacancy in my heart for mortal things. Gibbon had a cold and unimpassioned spirit. I never felt more inclination to rail at the prejudices which cling to such a thing, than now that "Julie" and Clarens, Lausanne and the "Roman Empire," compelled me to contrast between Rousseau and Gibbon.[5]

[5] Byron mentions the acacia leaves in his letter to John Murray: "Ouchy, near Lausanne, June 27, 1816. I am thus far (kept back by stress of weather) on my way back to Diodati (near Geneva) from a voyage in my boat round the Lake; and I enclose you a sprig of *Gibbon's acacia* and some rose-leaves from his garden, which

LETTERS

When we returned, in the only interval of sunshine during the day, I walked on the pier which the lake was lashing with its waves. A rainbow spanned the lake, or rather rested one extremity of its arch upon the water, and the other at the foot of the mountains of Savoy. Some white houses, I know not if they were those of Meillerie, shone through the yellow fire.

On Saturday, the 29th of June, we quitted Ouchy, and after two days of pleasant sailing arrived on Sunday evening at Montalegre.

CCXCVI
TO WILLIAM GODWIN
London

Geneva,
July 17, 1816.

SIR,

I write by this post to Mr. Hume, giving the authority which you request. Before this letter arrives you will, however, have received another from me affording a solution of the questions contained in your last, and rendering that request superfluous. The delay which has occurred in writing to Mr. Hume and to you arose simply from my expecting by every post an acknowledgment of the letters to which you allude. I need not again assert that I think Mr. Turner neither a good man nor a good judge of men. He

with part of his house I have just seen. You will find honourable mention in his *Life* made of this 'acacia,' when he walked out on the night of concluding his history. The garden and *summer-house*, where he composed, are neglected, and the last utterly decayed; but they still show it as his 'cabinet,' and seem perfectly aware of his memory." The following is the memorable passage in Gibbon's *Life* to which Byron and Shelley allude: "It was on the day, or rather night, of the 27th of June, 1787, between the hours of eleven and twelve, that I wrote the last lines of the last page, in a summer-house in my garden. After laying down my pen, I took several turns in a *berceau* or covered walk of acacias, which commands a prospect of the country, the lake and the mountains. The air was temperate, the sky was serene, the silver orb of the moon was reflected from the waters, and all nature was silent. I will not dissemble the first emotions of joy on the recovery of my freedom, and perhaps the establishment of my fame. But my pride was soon humbled, and a sober melancholy was spread over my mind, by the idea that I had taken an everlasting leave of an old and agreeable companion, and that whatsoever might be the future date of my History, the life of the historian must be short and precarious."

177

acted in your affairs with duplicity, and accused me indirectly of the duplicity which he was conscious attached to his own conduct.

Mr. Turner was, in the instance which you state, and will be in every instance, deceived in his judgment of me, for no other reason than because he suspects me to be like himself.

I recommend to you caution in ascertaining the value of the estates before you allow the deeds to be drawn, as of course, although the business is nominally confided to Mr. Hume, you are really the agent.

I suppose it will be necessary to despatch the deeds hither for signature; a power of attorney, I fear, would not suffice. However that may be, let us choose first the easiest and the quietest, next, the securest plan. I shall not remain longer at Geneva than affairs require, and hope to have the earliest and minutest intelligence from you on a question so important to us both.

PERCY B. SHELLEY.

[Addressed]
  W. GODWIN, Esq.,
    41 *Skinner Street,*
      Snow Hill, London,
      Angleterre

CCXCVII
TO THOMAS LOVE PEACOCK

Geneva,
July 17, 1816.

My opinion of turning to one spot of earth and calling it our home, and of the excellences and usefulness of the sentiments arising out of this attachment, has at length produced in me the resolution of acquiring this possession.

You are the only man who has sufficient regard for me to take an interest in the fulfilment of this design, and whose tastes conform sufficiently to mine to engage me to confide the execution of it to your discretion.

178

I do not trouble you with apologies for giving you this commission; some slight negotiations about the letting of a house—the superintendence of a disorderly garden, some palings to be mended, some books to be removed and set up. I require only rural exertion, walks, and circuitous wanderings.

I wish you would get all my books and all my furniture from Bishopgate,and all other effects appertaining to me. I have written to —— to secure all that belongs to me there to you. I have written also to L[ongdill] to give up possession of the house on the 3rd of August.

When you have possessed yourself of all my affairs. I wish you to look out for a home for me and Mary and William, and the kitten, who is now *en pension*. I wish you to get an unfurnished house, with as good a garden as may be, near Windsor Forest, and take a lease of it for fourteen or twenty-one years. The house must not be too small. I wish the situation to resemble as nearly as possible that of Bishopgate, and should think that Sunning Hill, or Winkfield Plain, or the neighbourhood of Virginia Water, would afford some possibilities.

Houses are now exceedingly cheap and plentiful; but I entrust the whole of this affair entirely to your own discretion.

I shall hear from you, of course, as to what you have done on this subject, and shall not delay to remit you whatever expenses you may find it necessary to incur. Perhaps, however, you had better sell the useless part of the Bishopgate furniture—I mean those odious curtains, etc.

Will you write to L[ongdill] to tell him that you are authorized on my part to go over the inventory with Lady L——'s [1] people on the third of August, if they please, and to make whatever arrangements may be requisite. I should be content with the Bishopgate house, dear as it is, if Lady L—— would make the sale of it a post-obit transaction. I merely suggest this, that if you see any possibility of proposing such an arrangement with effect, you might do it.

My present intention is to return to England, and to make that most excellent of nations my perpetual resting place. I think it is

[1] Probably Lady Longford.

extremely probable that we shall return next spring—perhaps before, perhaps after, but certainly we shall return.

On the motives and on the consequences of this journey, I reserve much explanation for some future winter walk or summer expedition. This much alone is certain, that before we return we shall have seen, and felt, and heard, a multiplicity of things which will haunt our talk and make us a little better worth knowing than we were before our departure.

If possible, we think of descending the Danube in a boat, of visiting Constantinople and Athens, then Rome and the Tuscan cities, and returning by the south of France, always following great rivers. The Danube, the Po, the Rhone, and the Garonne; rivers are not like roads, the work of the hands of man; they imitate mind,which wanders at will over pathless deserts,and flows through nature's loveliest recesses, which are inaccessible to anything besides. They have the viler advantage also of affording a cheaper mode of conveyance.

This eastern scheme is one which has just seized on our imaginations. I fear that the detail of execution will destroy it, as all other wild and beautiful visions; but at all events you will hear from us wherever we are, and to whatever adventures destiny enforces us.

Tell me in return all English news. What has become of my poem?[2] I hope it has already sheltered itself in the bosom of its mother, Oblivion, from whose embraces no one could have been so barbarous as to tear it except me.

Tell me of the political state of England—its literature, of which when I speak Coleridge is in my thoughts;—yourself, lastly your own employments, your historical labours.

I had written thus far when your letter to Mary dated the 8th arrived. What you say of Bishopgate of course modifies that part of this letter which relates to it. I confess I did not learn the destined ruin without some pain, but it is well for me perhaps that a situation requiring so large an expense should be placed beyond our hopes.

You must shelter my roofless Penates, dedicate some new temple to them, and perform the functions of a priest in my absence. They

[2] *Alastor, or the Spirit of Solitude, and other Poems*, 1816.

are innocent deities, and their worship neither sanguinary nor absurd.

Leave Mammon and Jehovah to those who delight in wickedness and slavery—their altars are stained with blood or polluted with gold, the price of blood. But the shrines of the Penates are good wood fires, or window frames intertwined with creeping plants; their hymns are the purring of kittens, the hissing of kettles; the long talks over the past and dead, the laugh of children, the warm wind of summer filling the quiet house, and the pelting storm of winter struggling in vain for entrance. In talking of the Penates, will you not liken me to Julius Cæsar dedicating a temple to Liberty?

As I have said in the former part of my letter, I trust entirely to your discretion on the subject of a house. Certainly the Forest engages my preference, because of the sylvan nature of the place, and the beasts with which it is filled. But I am not insensible to the beauties of the Thames, and any extraordinary eligibility of situation you mention in your letter would overwhelm our habitual affection for the neighbourhood of Bishopgate.

Its proximity to the spot you have chosen[3] is an argument with us in favour of the Thames. Recollect, however, we are now choosing a fixed, settled, eternal home, and as such its internal qualities will affect us more constantly than those which consist in the surrounding scenery, which whatever it may be at first, will shortly be no more than the colours with which our own habits shall invest it.

I am glad that circumstances do not permit the choice to be my own. I shall abide by yours as others abide by the necessity of their birth.

Lord Byron is an exceedingly interesting person, and as such is it not to be regretted that he is a slave to the vilest and most vulgar prejudices, and as mad as the winds.

P. B. S.

Peacock was living at Great Marlow, in Buckinghamshire.

LETTERS

CCXCVIII
TO THOMAS LOVE PEACOCK[1]

Hotel de Londres,
Chamounix,
July 22, 1816.

MY DEAR PEACOCK,

Whilst you are engaged in securing a home for us, we are wandering in search of recollections to embellish it. I do not err in conceiving that you are interested in details of all that is majestic or beautiful in nature. But how shall I describe to you the scenes by which I am now surrounded? To exhaust epithets which express the astonishment and the admiration—the very excess of satisfied expectation, where expectation scarcely acknowledged any boundary—is this to impress upon your mind the images which fill mine now, even until it overflows? I too have read before now the raptures of travellers. I will be warned by their example. I will simply detail to you, all that I can relate, or all that if related I could enable you to conceive of what we have done or seen since the morning of the 20th when we left Geneva—

The plains which surround Geneva, and intervene between that city and the Alps are interesting and pretty. After four hours travelling we arrive at Bonneville, a little town situated on the Arve which here runs through a valley enclosed between two lofty mountains clothed with wild forests of pine and chestnut. Proceeding from Bonneville the road winds along the foot of the mountains, thro' the woods. In three hours more we arrived at Cluses, and suddenly turning to the right enter a narrow pass where the Arve appears to have forced its way and to have left on each side in ruins, the perpendicular mountains. The scene resembles that of Matlock differing only in the immensity of its proportions. From Cluses to St. Martin, in the map it is called Sallanches, the character of the scenery continues the same, the mountains perpetually

[1] This letter, in an altered form, was included with another letter to Peacock, that of July 12, in Mrs. Shelley's *History of a Six Weeks' Tour*, 1817. The letter was first printed in full in a privately issued pamphlet of 85 copies at the Essex House Press, August 1901, under the care of Mr. C. R. Ashbee for the then owner, Mr. Wilfrid Buckley. The original is in the Pierpont Morgan Library, New York, and is now printed by permission. The altered form of the letter will be found in the *History of a Six Weeks' Tour*—Prose Works.

becoming more elevated, and exhibiting at every turn of the road more craggy summits, loftier waterfalls, wider extent of forests, darker and more deep recesses. At St. Martin we sleep. From St. Martin we ascend on mules to Chamounix accompanied by two guides who held the mules on which Mary and Clare rode. For an hour, we proceed along the valley of the Arve—a valley surrounded on all sides by immense mountains whose jagged precipices were intermixed on high with dazzling snow. After having visited a waterfall which was very fine we turned to the left and still following the valley, or now rather the vast ravine which is the couch and the creation of the terrible Arve, approached Chamounix. We ascended winding between mountains whose immensity staggers the imagination. We crossed the path of a torrent which three days since had descended from the snow and torn the road away. We dined at Servoz, a little village where there are lead and copper mines, and where we saw a cabinet like those of Keswick and Bethgelart. We saw in this cabinet some chamois horns, and the horns of an exceedingly rare animal called the Bauctin.[1] This animal inhabits the deserts of snow which lie to the south of Mont Blanc. It is an animal of the goat kind but considerably larger, the horns weigh at least 25 English pounds, it is inconceivable how so small an animal should support so inordinate a weight. These horns are of a very peculiar formation, being broad, massy and pointed at the end, and surrounded with a number of rings which are supposed to afford an indication of its age. There were seventeen of these rings on the largest horns.

From Servox, three leagues remain to Chamounix. Mont Blanc was before us. The Alps with their innumerable glaciers on high, all around; closing in the complicated windings of the single vale: —forests inexpressibly beautiful—but majestic in their beauty—interwoven beech and pine and oak overshadowed our road or receded, whilst lawns of such verdure as I have never seen before, occupied these openings, and extending gradually becoming darker with their recesses. Mont Blanc was before us but was covered with cloud, and its base furrowed with dreadful gaps was seen alone. Pinnacles of snow, intolerably bright, part of the chain connected

[1] Probably the Ibex or Bouquetin.

183

with Mont Blanc shone thro' the clouds at intervals on high. I never knew, I never imagined what mountains were before. The immensity of these aerial summits excited, when they suddenly burst upon the sight, a sentiment of extatic wonder, not unallied to madness—And remember this was all one scene. It all pressed home to our regard and to our imagination. Though it embraced a great number of miles the snowy pyramids which shot into the bright blue sky seemed to over hang our path—the ravine, clothed with gigantic pines and black with its depth below—so deep that the very roaring of the untameable Arve which rolled through it could not be heard above—was close to our very footsteps. All was as much our own as if we had been the creators of such impressions in the minds of others, as now occupied our own. Nature was the poet whose harmony held our spirits more breathless than that of the divinest.

As we entered the valley of Chamounix, which in fact may be considered as a continuation of those which we have followed from Bonneville and Cluses, clouds hung upon the mountains, at the distance perhaps of 6000 feet from the earth, but so as effectually to conceal not only Mont Blanc, but the other 'aiguilles' as they call them here, attached and subordinate to it. We were travelling along the valley, when suddenly we heard a sound as of a burst of smothered thunder rolling above. Yet there was something earthly in the sound that told us it could not be thunder. Our guide hastily pointed out to us a part of the mountain opposite from whence the sound came. It was an avalanche. We saw the smoke of its path among the rocks and continued to hear at intervals the bursting of its fall. It fell on the bed of a torrent which it displaced and presently we saw the torrent also spread itself over the ravine which was its couch. We arrived at Chamounix at 6 o'clock. We did not, as we had designed, visit the glacier de Boisson today, altho' it comes within a few minutes walk of the road, wishing to survey it at leisure when unfatigued. We saw this glacier which comes close to the fertile plain. Its surface is irregularly broken into a thousand unaccountable figures. Conical and pyramidal crystallizations more than 50 feet in height rise from its surface, and precipices of ice of a dazzling splendour overhang the woods and meadows of the vale. This glacier winds from the valley until it joins the masses of frost from which it was produced above, winding thro' its own ravine like a bright belt flung over the black region of pines. There is more in all these scenes than mere magnitude of proportion—there is a majesty of outline, there is an awful grace in the very colour which invest these wonderful shapes—a charm which is peculiar to them, quite distinct even from the reality of their unutterable greatness.

Chamounix, 24th [July].

Yesterday morning we went to the source of the Arveiron. It is about a league from the village. The river rolls impetuously, from an arch of ice, and spreads itself in many streams over a vast space of the valley ravaged and laid bare by its inundations. The glacier by which its waters are nourished overhang this cavern and the plain and the forests of pines which surrounds it with terrible precipices of solid ice. On the other side rises the immense glacier of Montanvert, 50 miles in extent, occupying a chasm among mountains of inconceivable height and of forms so pointed and abrupt that they seem to pierce the sky. From this glacier we saw as we sat on a rock close to one of the streams of the Arveiron, masses of ice detach themselves from on high, and fall with a loud dull noise into the vale. The violence of their fall turned them into powder which flowed over the rocks in imitation of the waterfalls whose ravines they usurped and filled. In the evening I went with Ducrée my guide, the only tolerable person I have seen in this country, to visit the glacier of Boisson. This glacier like that of Montanvert comes close to the vale, overhanging the green meadows and the dark woods with the dazzling whiteness of its precipices and pinnacles. These glaciers flow perpetually into the valley, ravaging in their slow but irresistible progress the pastures and the forests which surround them, and performing a work of desolation in ages which a river of lava might accomplish in an hour, but far more irretrievably—for where the ice has once been the hardiest plant refuses to grow—if even, as in some extraordinary instances, it should recede after its progression has once commenced. The glaciers perpetually move onwards at the rate of a foot each day

185

with a motion which commences at the spot where on the boundaries of perpetual congelation they are produced by the freezing of the waters which arise from the partial melting of the eternal snows. They drag with them from the regions whence they derive their origin all the ruins of the mountain, enormous rocks and immense accumulations of sand and stones. These are driven onwards by the irresistible progress of the stream of solid ice and when they arrive at a declivity of the mountain sufficiently rapid, roll down scattering ruin. I saw one of these rocks which had descended in the spring—winter here is the season of silence and safety—which measured 40 feet in every direction. The verge of a glacier, like that of Boisson, presents the most vivid image of desolation that it is possible to conceive. No one dares to approach it, for the enormous pinnacles of ice perpetually fall and are perpetually reproduced. The pines of the forest which bounds it at one extremity are overthrown and shattered:—there is something inexpressibly dreadful in the aspect of the few branchless trunks which nearest to the ice rifts still stand in the unprooted soil. The meadows perish overwhelmed with sand and stones. Within this last year the glaciers have advanced three hundred feet into the valley. Saussure, the naturalist, says that they have their periods of increase and decay—the people of the country hold an opinion entirely different, but, as I judge, more probable. It is agreed by all that the snows on the summit of Mont Blanc and the neighbouring mountains perpetually augment, and that ice in the form of glacier subsists without melting in the valley of Chamounix during its transient and variable summer. If the snow which produces the glaciers must augment and the heat of the valley is no obstacle to the perpetual subsistence of such masses of ice as have already descended into it, the consequence is obvious: The glaciers must augment and will subsist at least until they have overflowed this vale. I will not pursue Buffon's sublime but gloomy theory, that this earth which we inhabit will at some future period be changed into a mass of frost. Do you who assert the supremacy of Ahriman imagine him throned among these desolating snows, among the palaces of death and frost, sculptured in this their terrible magnificence by the unsparing hand of necessity, and that he casts around him at the first essays of his final usurpation avalanches, torrents, rocks and thunders . . . and above all, these deadly glaciers at once the proofs and the symbols of his reign. Add to this the degradation of the human species, who in these regions are half deformed or idiotic and all of whom are deprived of anything that can excite interest and admiration. This is a part of the subject more mournful and less sublime:—but such as neither the poet nor the philosopher should disdain. It presents views development of which I reserve for conversation.

Today, we departed on the promise of a fine day to visit the glacier of Montanvert in that part where it fills a flat valley, and is called the sea of ice. This valley is 950 toises, or 7600 feet, above the level of the sea. We had not proceeded far before the rain began to fall, but we persisted until we had accomplished more than half our journey, when we returned wet through.

Chamounix, July 25.

We have returned from visiting this glacier: a scene in truth of dizzying wonder. The path that winds to it along the side of a mountain now clothed with pines, now intersected with snowy hollows, is wide and steep. The cabin of Montanvert is 3 leagues from Chamounix, half of which distance is performed on mules, not so surefooted but that the first day the one which I rode fell, in what the guides call a 'mauvais pas,' so that I narrowly escaped being precipitated down the mountain. The guide continually held that which Mary rode. . . . We passed over a hollow covered with snow down which vast stones detached from the rock above are accustomed to roll. One had fallen the preceding day a little time after we had returned. The guides desired us to pass quickly, for it is said that sometimes the least sound will accelerate their fall. We arrived at Montanvert, however, safe. On all sides precipitous mountains the abodes of unrelenting frost surround this vale. Their sides are banked up with ice and snow broken and heaped up and exhibiting terrific chasms. The summits are sharp and naked pinnacles whose overhanging steepness will not even permit snow to rest there. They pierce the clouds like things not belonging to this earth. The vale itself is filled with a mass of undulating ice, and

187

has an ascent sufficiently gradual even to the remotest abysses of these horrible deserts. It is only half a league, about 2 miles, in breadth and seems much less. It exhibits an appearance as if frost had suddenly bound up the waves and whirlpools of a mighty torrent. We walked to some distance upon its surface—the waves are elevated about 12 or 15 feet from the surface of the mass, which is intersected with long gaps of unfathomable depth, the ice of whose sides is more beautifully azure than the sky. In these regions everything changes and is in motion. This vast mass of ice has one general progress which ceases neither day nor night. It breaks and bursts forever; its undulations sink whilst others rise. From the precipices which surround it the echo of rocks which fall from their aerial summits, or of the ice and snow scarcely ceases for one moment. One would think that Mont Blanc was a living being and that the frozen blood forever circulated through his stony veins.

We dined—Mary, Clare and me—on the grass in the open air surrounded by this scene. The air is piercing and clear. We met, I lament to say, some English people here; I will not detail to you the melancholy exhibitions of tourism, which altho' they emanate from the snobisms and exigences of these vulgar great, corrupt the manners of the people, and make this place another Keswick. But the inhabitants of Cumberland are not for a moment to be compared with these people, on whose stupidity, avarice and imposture engenders a mixture of [?] horrible and disgusting. In the evening we returned to Chamounix. The next morning we returned thro' the rain to St. Martin. The scenery had lost something of its immensity, thick clouds hanging over the highest mountains; but visitings of sunset intervened between the showers and blue sky between the accumulated clouds of snowy whiteness which brought them; and all the charm of its grandeur remains. We repassed 'Pont Pelissier,' a wooden bridge over the Arve and the ravine of the Arve. We repassed the pine forests which overhang the defile, the château of Saint Michel, a haunted ruin built on the edge of a precipice and shadowed over by the eternal forest. We repassed the vale of Servoz, a vale more beautiful because more luxuriant than that of Chamounix:—Mont Blanc forms one of the sides of this vale also, and the other is enclosed by an irregular

amphitheatre of enormous mountains, one of which is in ruins and
fell 50 years ago into the higher part of the valley: the smoke of its
fall was seen in Piedmont and the people went from Turin to in-
vestigate whether a volcano had not burst forth among the Alps.
It continued falling for many days, spreading with the shock and
the thunder of its ruin consternation thro' the neighbouring vales
and destroying many persons. In the evening we arrived at St.
Martin. The next day we wound through the valley which I have
described before and arrived in the evening at our home.

We have bought some specimens of minerals and plants and two
or three crystal seals at Mont Blanc, to preserve the remembrance
of having approached it. There is a Cabinet d'Histoire Naturelle
at Chamounix, just as at Matlock and Keswick and Clifton: the
proprietor of which is the very vilest specimen of that vile species of
quack that together with the whole army of aubergistes and guides
and indeed the entire mass of the population subsist on the weakness and credulity of travellers as leeches subsist on the blood of the
rich. The most interesting of my purchases is a large collection of
the seeds of rare Alpine plants, with their names written upon the
outside of the papers which contain them. These I mean to colo-
nize in my garden in England: and to permit you to make what
choice you please of them. They are companions which the celandine, the classic celandine, need not despise. They are as wild and
more daring than he, and will tell him tales of things even as touching and as sublime as the gaze of a vernal poet.

Did I tell you that there are troops of wolves among these mountains? In the winter they descend into the vallies which the snow
occupies six months of the year, and devour everything they find
outside of the doors. A wolf is more powerful than the fiercest and
strongest dog. There no bears in these regions,—we heard when
we were at Lucerne that they were occasionally found in the
forests which surround that lake.

We returned from St. Martin to our temporary home thro' the
vale of the Arve.

August 2, 1816.

I have kept this letter some days that you might derive at least
the advantage from its magnitude of not receiving another on

business. But not having heard from you in the meantime I send it now. I write to Hookham by this post to inform him that I am to receive money, and that I mean to pay him. I write also to St. Croix. Be so kind as to write for me to Furnival[1] to say that it entirely arose from an omission that his bill was not paid and that you will speedily settle it for me. The coal man to whom I owe £18 may wait, but it would be as well to speak to him or write to him to assure him of payment. In giving you these commissions I am using the privilege of a friend, a privilege which the interest I know you take in my concerns, and so far as I care for it myself, my reputation will engage you to allow me. They will instruct you also in the continuance of my determination to return to England, and domesticate myself in the home which I hope you are preparing. I enclose you a draft for £25, having heard from Longdill that the sale of my things at Bishopgate was done by his order and that I should receive very little from it. Receive it on my account and disburse it at your own discretion. You had better send the draft to the bankers in a letter signed with your name as I have omitted to insert the word 'bearer' lest it might be lost. If Hookham is anxious about me you may show him this letter. I am glad to hear from your account that he does not withhold from me the justice which I am conscious I deserve.

Always yours faithfully,

PERCY B. SHELLEY.

---

[1] Mr. George Frederick Furnivall was a surgeon at Egham who attended Mary (in the absence of Dr. Pope, of Staines) at the birth of her second child. Shelley had great confidence in Furnivall, who would sometimes ride from Egham to Marlow, a distance of seventeen miles, to visit the poet. His son, Dr. Frederick James Furnivall, told me that it was the habit of his father to destroy all correspondence, and that he found none of Shelley's letters among his papers. One of the last notes that Mr. Furnivall received from Shelley was from Italy respecting Mary Shelley's health. On examining his father's consultation books Dr. Furnivall discovered Shelley's name not in the book devoted to the richer folk, but in a small book recording visits to his poorer patients, and against the poet's account of some seven guineas, the doctor had noted the receipt of one guinea. This story, however, is difficult to reconcile with the fact that among the cheques formerly in Mr. W. T. Spencer's possession was one for £10 payable to Mr. Furnival or bearer, dated January 28, 1816, and another for £13 15s. payable to G. Furnival, Esq. or bearer, dated July 30, 1817.

LETTERS

TO LORD BYRON

Chamouni, Hôtel de Ville de Londres,
July 22, 1816.

My DEAR LORD BYRON,
We have this moment arrived at Chamouni—the evening of
the day after our departure. An opportunity chances to offer itself
of sending a letter. I shall not attempt to describe to you the scenes
through which we have passed. I hope soon to see in poetry the
feelings with which they will inspire you. The Valley of the Arve
(strictly speaking it extends to that of Chamouni) gradually increases in magnificence and beauty, until, at a place called Servoz,
where Mont Blanc and its connected mountains limit one side of
the valley, it exceeds and renders insignificant all that I had before
seen, or imagined. It is not alone that these mountains are immense in size, that their forests are of so immeasurable an extent;
there is grandeur in the very shapes and colours which could not
fail to impress, even on a smaller scale. I write in the hope—may I
say so?—that we possibly shall see you here before our return. No
sooner had we entered this magnificent valley than we decided to
remain several days. An avalanche fell as we entered it. We
heard the thunder of its fall, and in a few minutes more the smoke
of its path was visible, and a torrent which it had forced from its
bed overflowed the ravine which enclosed it. I wish the wonders
and graces of these " palaces of Nature " would induce you to visit
them whilst we, who so much value your society, remain yet near
them.
How is our little William? [1] Is he well?
Clare sends her love to you, and Mary desires to be kindly remembered.

Yours faithfully,

P. B. SHELLEY.

P.S. The roads are excellent, and every facility is accumulated for
the traveller. You can go as far as Sallanches in a carriage, after

[1] William Shelley.

191

LETTERS

which, although it is possible to accomplish the rest of the journey in a *char du pays*, I would advise you, as we have done, to hire mules. A guide is not absolutely necessary, although we took one; for the road, with one insignificant exception, is perfectly plain and good. There is apparently a very trifling ascent from Geneva to Chamouni.

CCC

TO BROOKES SON AND DIXON

London

Geneva:[1] *August 2, 1816.*

GENTLEMEN,

I have sent a draft to T. L. Peacock Esqr. of Great Marlow, payable to him alone, which I request you would have the goodness to honour.—I know not whether I have fulfilled the requisite forms in sending such a draft from Geneva as I should have written in London—if that should be the case, I should be obliged by your considering this letter as a sufficient authority.—The draft is for £25.

Gentlemen, I have the honour to be

Your obliged Servant,

PERCY BYSSHE SHELLEY.

[Addressed]
MESSRS. BROOKES SON & DIXON,
    25 *Chancery Lane,*
    London,
    Angleterre
[Postmark]
SUISSE PAR,
BEFFORT

---

[1] From Geneva Shelley uttered the following promissory note:—
" Genève le 5 Août, 1816. A dix jours de datte payer par cette premier de change a l'ordre de Messieurs H. Hentsch &c. la somme de Cent Vignt cinq livres Sterlings, valeur reçue comptant que passerez sans aucun autre avis de : Messrs. Brookes & Son, 25, Chancery Lane, London.
PERCY BYSSHE SHELLEY."

XII

SEPTEMBER 8, 1816, TO SEPTEMBER 22, 1817

MARLOW

CCCI
TO LORD BYRON

Portsmouth,
September 8, 1816.

MY DEAR LORD BYRON,
Nine days of tedious voyaging over land and sea have brought us hither. We had some pleasant moments in our journey through France, visitings of sunshine in stormy weather. We passed, not through Paris, but by a shorter route through Versailles, and Fontainebleau, and stayed to visit those famous Palaces, which, as I will hereafter tell you, are well worth visiting as monuments of human power; grand, yet somewhat faded; the latter is the scene of some of the most interesting events of what may be called the master theme of the epoch in which we live—the French Revolution. Our passage from Havre hither was wretched—26 hours. We have just dined after our arrival, and I learn that the post departs in a few minutes—but I am anxious to give you the earliest intelligence of the safe arrival of the Childe.[1] His only adventure since he quitted the paternal roof has been inglorious. He was taken for a smuggler, and turned over and over by a greasy Custom-house officer, to see if lace, &c., were hidden within. He is now quite safe, and locked in my portmanteau.

You shall hear from me again in three days. Adieu—take care of your health—tranquilise yourself—and be persuaded with Coleridge that "hope is a most awful duty, the nurse of all other virtues." I assure you that it will not depart, if it be not rudely banished, from such a one as you.

[1] *Childe Harold*, Canto III.

LETTERS

Mary unites with me in sincerest wishes for your happiness. Clare is about to enjoin me some messages which are better conceived than expressed.

Your sincere friend,

P. B. SHELLEY.

Make my remembrances to Hobhouse[2]—as also to Mr. Davies.[3] I hope that the former has destroyed whatever scruples you might have felt, in dismissing Polidori.[4] The anecdote which he recounted to me the evening before I left Geneva made my blood run cold.

CCCII
TO LORD BYRON

London,
26, *Marchmont Street,*
September 11, 1816.

MY DEAR LORD BYRON,

I have just seen Murray and delivered the poem to him. He was exceedingly polite to me; and expressed the greatest eagerness to see the Poem. He had already heard that it was considered to surpass all your other productions, and that this was Madame de Staël's opinion. I shall call on Mr. Kinnaird to-morrow. Murray tells me that Lady Byron is in London, and that her health has materially improved. Her very change of residence confirms this statement.

Mary and Clare left me at Portsmouth, for Bath. I arrive here —at my antient lodgings; dreadfully vacant and lonely. No companions but the ghosts of old remembrances, all of whom contrive to make some reproach to which there is no reply. My lawyer is, I find, at Lancaster. I have written to him to return hither; but his delay will add to the time that I must inevitably waste in this peopled desert. Fanny Godwin came last night and talked to me

[2] John Cam Hobhouse, afterwards Lord Broughton.
[3] Scrope Beardmore Davies.
[4] John William Polidori, Physician to Byron, who dismissed him at Diodati.

196

of her father's affairs, to which there is fortunately now assistance near. She told me that he had made great progress in his novel.[1] She told me, too, that Northcote the painter, who is an ardent admirer of all your compositions, had recommended Godwin to read "Glenarvon,"[2] affirming that many parts of it exhibited extraordinary talent.

The harvest is not yet cut. There are, however, as yet no very glaring symptoms of disaffection, though the distress is said to be severe. But winter is the season when the burthen will be felt. Most earnestly do I hope that despair will not drive the people to premature and useless struggles.

I shall write to you again soon—at this moment I am suffering under a spasmodic headache that does not allow me to connect two ideas. Let me hear from you, and let me hear good news of you. The deep interest that I feel in everything that concerns you leads me to expect with eagerness the most minute details.

My dear Lord Byron,
Yours sincere friend,
P. B. SHELLEY.

CCCIII
TO LORD BYRON

Bath,
September 29, 1816.

MY DEAR LORD BYRON,

You have heard from Kinnaird the arrangement which has been made about "Childe Harold."[1] You are to receive 2,000 guineas. There was no objection made on Murray's, though there was a trifling mistake arising from his believing that he could get

[1] *Mandeville*, published in 1817.
[2] By Lady Caroline Lamb.

[1] In a letter from Byron to Murray, from Diodati, Geneva, September 29, 1816, he says: "with regard to the price, [for *Childe Harold*] *I* have fixed *none*, but left it to Mr. Kinnaird, Mr. Shelley and yourself to arrange. Of course, they would do their best; and as to yourself, I knew you would make no difficulties."

197

it for 1,200, which was no sooner made than obviated. I hope soon to inform you that I have received the first proof. I saw Kinnaird, and had a long conversation with him. He informed me that Lady Byron was now in perfect health—that she was living with your sister. I felt great pleasure from this intelligence. I consider the latter part of it as affording a decisive contradiction to the only important calumny that ever was advanced against you. On this ground at least it will become the world hereafter to be silent. Kinnaird spoke of some reports which he says Caroline Lamb industriously propagates against you. I cannot look on these calumnies in the serious light which others do. They appear to be innocent from their very extravagance, if they were not still more so from their silliness. They are the sparks of a straw fire, that vanish when their fuel fails. You are destined, believe me, to assume a rank in the estimation of mankind where such puerile hostilities cannot reach. There wants nothing but that you should clearly feel, and not disdain to pursue this destination, to deliver you at once from all these inquietudes which the opinion of the fickle multitude delights to inflict upon too sensitive minds. You are now in Italy—you have, perhaps, forgotten all that my unwelcome anxiety reminds you of. You contemplate objects that elevate, inspire, tranquilise. You communicate the feelings, which arise out of that contemplation, to mankind; perhaps to the men of distant ages. Is there nothing in the hope of being the parent of greatness, and of goodness, which is destined, perhaps, to expand indefinitely? Is there nothing in making yourself a fountain from which the thoughts of other men shall draw strength and beauty, to excite the ambition of a mind that can despise all other ambition? You have already given evidence of very uncommon powers. Having produced thus much, with effort, as you are aware, very disproportionate to the result; what are you not further capable of effecting? What would the human race have been if Homer, or Shakespeare, had never written? or if any false modesty, or mistake of their own powers, had withheld them from consummating those unequalled achievements of mind by which we are so deeply benefited? I do not compare you with these. I do not know how great an intellectual compass you are destined to fill. I only know that your powers are astonishingly great, and that they ought to be exerted to their full extent.

It is not that I should counsel you to aspire to fame. The motive to your labours ought to be more pure, and simple. You ought to desire no more than to express your own thoughts; to address yourself to the sympathy of those who might think with you. Fame will follow those whom it is unworthy to lead. I would not that you should immediately apply yourself to the composition of an Epic Poem; or to whatever other work you should collect all your being to consummate. I would not that the natural train of your progress should be interrupted; or any step of it anticipated. I delight in much of what you have already done. I hope for much more, in the same careless spirit of ardent sentiment. I hope for no more than that you should, from some moment when the clearness of your own mind makes evident to you the "truth of things," feel that you are chosen out from all other men to some greater enterprise of thought; and that all your studies should, from that moment, tend towards that enterprise alone: that your affections, that all worldly hopes this world may have left you, should link themselves to this design. *What* it should be, I am not qualified to say. In a more presumptuous mood, I recommend the Revolution of France as a theme involving pictures of all that is best qualified to interest and to instruct mankind. But it is inconsistent with the spirit in which you ought to devote yourself to so great a destiny, that you should make use of any understanding but your own—much less mine.

Shall we see you in the spring? How do your affairs go on? May I hear from you respecting these? Though anxious to know how your estates go on, I have not called on Hanson, overcome by my fear of the awkwardness of such a visit. We are now all at Bath, well and content. Clare is writing to you at this instant. Mary is reading over the fire; our cat and kitten are sleeping under the sofa; and little Willy is just gone to sleep. We are looking out for a house in some lone place; and one chief pleasure which we shall expect then, will be a visit from you. You will destroy all our rural arrangements if you fail in this promise. You will do more. You will strike a link out of the chain of life which, esteeming you, and cherishing your society as we do, we cannot easily spare. Adieu.

Your sincere friend,

P. B. SHELLEY.

CCCIV
TO WILLIAM GODWIN
London

5 *Abbey Church Yard, Bath,*
October 2, 1816.

I am exceedingly sorry to disappoint you again. I cannot send you £300 because I have not £300 to send. I enclose within a few pounds the wrecks of my late negotiation with my father.[1]

In truth I see no hope of my attaining speedily to such a situation of affairs as should enable me to discharge my engagements towards you. My father's main design, in all the transactions which I have had with him, has gone to tie me up from all such irregular applications of my fortune. In this he might have failed had he not been seconded by Longdill, and between them both I have been encompassed with such toils as were impossible to be evaded. When I look back I do not see what else I could

[1] Shelley had promised to send Godwin £300 on the expectation of receiving a considerable sum from his father to pay certain debts contracted on the faith of a successful issue of his negotiations of the spring. But these expectations were not realised, and Shelley was therefore unable to fulfil his promise to Godwin, who was sorely disappointed, having given a bill on demand for that amount to an exacting creditor. Godwin's novel, *Mandeville*, was progressing favourably, but everything depended on his tranquillity of mind. He had told Shelley in August that the book would be better than *St. Leon*, and would take place, next after Caleb Williams. "I am in good tone and anxious to proceed. The tone I must confess is kept up with considerable effort, and is only preserved by a faith that relates to you, and a confident hope that the relief so long expected from your quarter will at length be fully realized. If I am disappointed in this, if my affairs in the meantime go to a wreck that can no longer be resisted, then the novel will never be finished." Such an appeal as this was particularly moving to Shelley, who prized inordinately Godwin's imaginative work; but to fulfil his engagements was not in his power. Such money as he had, however, he sent without delay."—Professor Dowden's *Life of Shelley*, Vol. II, p. 46.

have done than submit: what is called firmness would have, I sincerely believe left me in total poverty.

In the present instance I expected to have saved 5 or £600; 300 of which, as I informed you, were devoted to you. I have saved only 248; my father having made an indispensable condition that all my debts should be paid. I do not think that any thing can be done with Bryant. Turner had he chosen might have managed the affair with Dawe. But nothing is more evident than that this person has some malignant passions which he seeks to gratify at my expense and at yours.—I do not indeed know what can be done, except thro' private confidence.

Shall I conclude this unwelcome letter by assuring you of the continuance of those dispositions concerning your welfare [*sic*] which I have so often expressed? Shall I say that I am ready to co-operate in whatever plan may be devised for your benefit?

P. B. SHELLEY.

[Addressed]
  WILLIAM GODWIN, Esq.,
    41 *Skinner Street*,
      Snow Hill,
        London
[Postmark]
  Bath Oct. 2, 1816

CCCV
TO JOHN MURRAY
London

No. 5 *Abbey Churchyard, Bath*,
Oct. 2, 1816.

MY DEAR SIR,
    Be so kind as to address the proofs of " Childe Harold," when you print it, to me according to the above address. I shall remain here probably during the whole winter, and you may depend on no attention being spared on my part to render the proofs as correct as possible.

201

LETTERS

I imagine that Lord Byron is anxious that the poem should be committed to the press as soon as possible; the time of publication of course depends upon your own discretion. For myself, I cannot but confess the anxiety I feel that the public should have an early opportunity of confirming—I will not say by a more extensive, but by a profounder species of approbation—the superior merit which private judgment has already assigned to it.[1]

I have the honour to be, Dear Sir,
Your very obliged obedient servant,
PERCY B. SHELLEY.

CCCVI
TO JOHN MURRAY
London

5 *Abbey Churchyard, Bath*,[1]
Oct. 30, 1816.

DEAR SIR,

I observe with surprise that you have announced the appearance of "Childe Harold" and "Prisoner of Chillon" for so early a date as the 23rd of November. I should not do my duty to Lord Byron, who entrusted me with the MSS. of his Poems, if I did not remind you that it was his particular desire that I should revise the proofs before publication. When I had the pleasure of seeing you in London, I think I stated his Lordship's wishes on this subject to you, remarking at the same time that his wishes did not arise from a persuasion that I should pay more attention to its accuracy than any other person whom you might select; but because he com-

---

[1] Although Shelley had brought the MS. of *Childe Harold*, Canto III, with him from Switzerland, Byron had sent another copy to John Murray, but he desired that in some particulars the MS. entrusted to Shelley should be preferred.

[1] Shelley wrote the following letters from 5 Abbey Churchyard, Bath, on October 10, 1816, to Brookes and Dixon, Bankers, Chancery Lane, London. "Gentlemen, Be so good as to send Thirty Pounds by return of Post addressed as above. I have the honor to be, Gentlemen, Your obed. H. Sert. Percy Bysshe Shelley"; also on November 5, 1816, to R. Hayward, Tooke's Court, requesting him to procure a loan on *post-obit*.

municated it to me immediately after composition, and did me the honour to entrust to my discretion, as to whether certain particular expressions should be retained or changed. All that was required was that I should see proofs before they were finally committed to the press. I wrote to you some weeks since, to this purpose. I have not received any answer.

Some mistake must have arisen, in what manner I cannot well conceive. You must have forgotten or misunderstood my explanations; by some accident you cannot have received my letter. Do me the favour of writing by return of Post, and informing me what intelligence I am to give Lord Byron respecting the commission with which I was entrusted.

I have the honour to be, Sir,
Your obedient servant,
PERCY BYSSHE SHELLEY.

P.S.—I remark that it is advertised as "The Prisoner*s* of Chillon." Lord Byron wrote it "Prisone*r*."

CCCVII

TO J. J. PASCHOUD
Geneva

12 *New Bond St.*,[1] *Bath,*
Nov. 9, 1816.

[FRAGMENT]

[*Directing the forwarding of some books.*]
    . . . The translation which I have engaged to make of "Political Justice" shall not be delayed, if I understand from you that you continue to wish that it should be done. . .

PERCY B. SHELLEY.

[Addressed]
MONSIEUR PASCHOUD,
Librarie,
Geneve, en Suisse

[1] This is the address where Clare Clairmont was lodging.

LETTERS

5, *Abbey Church Yard, Bath*,
November 20, 1816.

My dear Lord Byron,

It gives us pleasure to learn that you have arrived in safety at Milan, and that you have not relinquished your intention of revisiting England in the spring. The newspapers say that you have embarked for Albania. But I will hope that your own information is the most correct. Poor Clare's time approaches, and though she continues as well as women in that situation usually are, I think her spirits begin to fail. She has lost much of the animation and lightness which perhaps you do not ever remember in her. I shewed her your letter, which I should have withheld had I been aware of the wretched state into which it would have thrown her. I need not say that I do not doubt that you were as little aware of such an effect. But the smallest omission, or the most unpremeditated word often affects a person in a delicate state of health, or spirits. Any assurances which I could make to her of your correct intentions would be super-fluous; she expresses the most unbounded confidence in you; and, as is natural, considers every imagined defect of kindness in me, as a breach of faith to you. I need not entreat you to believe that neither Mary nor myself will be deficient in every requisite attention and kindness. If you do not like to write to Clare, send me some kind message to her, which I will, to give suspicion his due, throw into the fire as a sacrifice.

Of course you have received intimations of the tumultuous state of England. The whole fabric of society presents a most threaten-ing aspect. What is most ominous of an approaching change is the strength which the popular party have suddenly acquired, and the importance which the violence of demagogues has assumed. But the people appear calm, and steady even under situations of great excitement; and reform may come without revolution. Parlia-ment will meet on the 28th of January; until which—for the populace have committed no violence—they only meet, resolve and petition—all classes will probably remain in a sullen and moody expectation of what the session will produce. The taxes, it is said, cannot be collected—if so, the national debt cannot be paid—and are not the landed proprietors virtually pledged to the payment? I earnestly hope that, without such an utter overthrow as should leave us the prey of anarchy, and give us illiterate demagogues for masters, a most radical reform of the institutions of England may result from the approaching contest.

Murray, and another bookseller are skirmishing in the advertisement columns of the *Morning Chronicle*. The latter, a most impudent dog! affirming publickly that you sold him the copyright of some Poems for 500 guineas. By-the-bye, Murray refused to send me the sheets of your poems to superintend, under the plea of your having written to him committing them exclusively to Gifford's care. I saw them advertised for publication before I was aware of this; and in answer to my application to Murray, I received the above excuse. My situation with respect to Murray, claiming a duty to which I was not entitled, had some degree of awkwardness in it. Of course I cannot do, what otherwise I should most scrupulously have done, pay the attention to its correctness, which I doubt not to all practical purposes Mr. G. will do. I am not quite certain that Murray does not bear me some illwill, as the cause of the unexpected difference in his disbursements of £800. "Christabel" has been reviewed, and a most unfavourable judgment pronounced on it, by the *Edinburgh Review*. It suggests also that you were much to blame for praising it. In my opinion the *Edinburgh Review* is as well qualified to judge of the merits of a poet, as Homer would have been to write a commentary on the Newtonian System.

Accept our thanks for the curious account you give us of the Improvisators and the curiosities of Milan. We have no new things to tell.

> Believe me, my dear Lord Byron,
> Your very sincere friend,
> P. B. SHELLEY.

LETTERS

Bath,
Nov. 24, 1816.

SIR,

I lament exceedingly that you supposed it possible, or even esteem it right, that I should submit to such a proposal as Dawe's. I lament that you could even permit me to accede to such an imposture. You will therefore be disappointed at my refusal—you will think me insensible, unjust, insincere. I regret that I must inspire you with such feelings, but I am persuaded that it is my duty not to submit to terms of so exorbitant a nature.

The conclusion of your letter adds to the reluctance of my refusal, but it does not render it the less firm.

I enclose a letter to Hume written principally for the purpose of being shown to Dawe. Possibly he will change his tone when he finds his tricks ineffectual. For nothing is more evident than that all he says are the excuses and subterfuges of a money-broker.

You will observe from the rough calculation in my letter to H. that he asks very nearly 25 per cent., and that I should throw away not £1,000, but £2,800.

The principles which pronounce on the injustice of my hereditary rights, are such, as rightly limited and understood, are far dearer to me than life.

But these principles teach me to set a high value on the power with which their violation may one day intrust me. They instruct me to be more, not less, cautious in alienating it.

Indeed, it would be no inconsiderable evil if such a remorseless, mean-spirited wretch as Dawe were to be presented with £2,800!

My refusal is therefore firm.—But depend on it that what could be done in 1814 could be done, and that on even better terms, now. Do not despair. Even Dawe may retract and relent, or someone be found less exorbitant. I applied about a fortnight since to a quarter from which I had formerly obtained a supply, but have not received an answer.

LETTERS

The letters have arrived so late to-day, that I am obliged to write in haste if I would reply by return of post.

[Addressed]
W. GODWIN, Esq.,
41 *Skinner Street,*
Snow Hill,
London

CCCX
TO LEIGH HUNT
Hampstead

Marlow,[1]
Dec. 8, 1816

I have received both your letters yesterday and to-day, and I accuse myself that my precipitancy should have given you the vexation you express. Your letters, however, give me unmingled pleasure, and that of a very exalted kind. I have not in all my intercourse with mankind experienced sympathy and kindness with which I have been so affected or which my whole being has so sprung forward to meet and to return. My communications with you shall be such as to attempt to deserve this fortunate distinction. Meanwhile, let me lay aside preliminaries and their reserve; let me talk with you as with an old friend.

First I will answer your questions. By some fatality I have seen every *Examiner*,[2] but that of last week. Since I received your letter

[1] On December 1 Shelley received at Bath a letter from Leigh Hunt, to which this letter is obviously a reply. In Mary's journal on December 6, she says: "Letter from Shelley; he has gone to visit Leigh Hunt," but he went to Peacock's house at Marlow first, from which this letter was written. Shelley was staying here while seeking for a house, and Mary, writing from Bath to Marlow on December 6, gives him some advice on the subject. "But in the choice of a residence, dear Shelley," she says, "pray be not too quick or attach yourself too much to one spot. Ah! were you indeed a winged Elf, and could soar over mountains and seas, and could pounce on the little spot! A house with a lawn, near a river or lake, noble trees or divine mountains—that should be our little mouse-hole to retire to. But never mind this; give me a garden, and *absentia Claire*, and I will thank my love for many favours."
[2] The *Examiner* for December 1, 1816, contains the article entitled "Young Poets," in which Leigh Hunt refers to the work of Shelley, John Hamilton Reynolds (miscalled "John Henry Reynolds"), and John Keats. Of Shelley he says: "The object of the present article is merely to notice three young writers, who appear to us to promise a

207

yesterday, I have made every exertion to get a sight of it, unsuccessfully. All the people who take it in here have forwarded it to their friends at a distance. I hear there is one at a village five miles off; as it is very uncertain whether I shall be able to procure it, I will accept your kind offer of sending it to me. I take in the *Examiner* generally, and therefore will not trouble you to send your own copy.

Next, will I own the "Hymn to Intellectual Beauty?"[3] I do not care—as you like. And yet the poem was composed under the influence of feelings which agitated me even to tears, so that I think it deserves a better fate than the being linked with so stigmatised and unpopular a name (so far as it is known) as mine. You will say that it is not thus, that I am morbidly sensitive to what I esteem the injustice of neglect—but I do not say that I am unjustly neglected, the oblivion which overtook my little attempt of "Alastor" I am ready to acknowledge was sufficiently merited in *itself;* but then it was not accorded in the correct proportion considering the success of the most contemptible drivellings. I am undeceived in the belief that I have powers deeply to interest, or substantially to improve, mankind. How far my conduct and my opinions have rendered the zeal and ardour with which I have engaged in the attempt ineffectual, I know not. Self love prompts me to assign much weight to a cause which perhaps has none. But thus much I do not seek to conceal from myself, that I am an outcast from human society; my name is execrated by all who understand its entire import—by those very beings whose happiness I ardently desire. I am an object of compassion to a few more

considerable addition of strength to the new school. Of the first who came before us, we have, it is true, yet seen only one or two specimens, and these were no sooner sent us than we unfortunately mislaid them; but we shall procure what he has published, and if the rest answer to what we have seen, we shall have no hesitation in announcing him a very striking and original thinker. His name is Percy Bysshe Shelley, and he is the author of a poetical work entitled *Alastor, or the Spirit of Solitude.*" These lines probably comprise the first public recognition of Shelley as a poet. To the other two poets more space is devoted, and a specimen of their work is given. Keats had not then published a volume, but Leigh Hunt had the good fortune of printing in this article for the first time the sonnet "On first looking into Chapman's Homer."
[3] Shelley had sent Hunt his "Hymn to Intellectual Beauty" for insertion in the *Examiner,* where it appeared in the issue for January 19, 1817, with the signature "Percy B. Shelley." The poem was originally signed *Elfin Knight,* Mary's familiar name for Shelley, and was acknowledged by Hunt in the *Examiner* for October 6, 1816, p. 631, col. 1—"The ELFIN-KNIGHT, the first opportunity."

benevolent than the rest, all else abhor and avoid me. With you, and perhaps some others (though in a less degree I fear) my gentleness and sincerity find favour, because they are themselves gentle and sincere: they believe in self devotion and generosity, because they are themselves generous and self devoted. Perhaps I should have shrunk from persisting in the task which I had undertaken in early life, of opposing myself in these evil times and among these evil tongues, to what I esteem misery and vice. If I must have lived in the solitude of the heart, fortunately my domestic circle incloses that within it which compensates for the loss. But these are subjects for conversation, and I find that in using the privilege which you have permitted me of friendship, I have indulged in that garrulity of self-love which only friendship can excuse or endure.

When will you send me your poems? I never knew that you had published any other than "Rimini," with which I was exceedingly delighted. The *story* of the poem has an interest of a very uncommon and irresistible character,—though it appeared to me that you have subjected yourself to some rules in the composition which fetter your genius, and diminish the effect of the conceptions. Though in one sense I am no poet, I am not so insensible to poetry as to read "Rimini" unmoved.—When will you send me your other poems?[4]

Peacock is the author of "Headlong Hall,"—he expresses himself much pleased by your approbation—indeed, it is approbation which many would be happy to acquire! He is now writing "Melincourt" in the same style, but, as I judge, far superior to "Headlong Hall." He is an amiable man of great learning, considerable taste, an enemy to every shape of tyranny and superstitious imposture. I am now on the point of taking the lease of a house among these woody hills, these sweet green fields, and this delightful river—where, if I should ever have the happiness of seeing you, I will introduce you to Peacock. I have nothing to do in London, but I am most strongly tempted to come, only to spend one evening with you; and if I can I will, though I am anxious as soon as my employments here are finished to return to Bath.

---

[4] Besides the boyish collection of *Juvenilia*, 1801, the following volumes of Leigh Hunt's poetry had been published, *The Feast of the Poets*, 1814 and 1815, *The Descent of Liberty, a Mask*, 1815, and *The Story of Rimini*, 1816.

LETTERS

Last of all—you are in distress for a few hundred Pounds;[5]—I saw Lord Byron at Geneva, who expressed to me the high esteem which he felt for your character and worth. I cannot doubt that he would hesitate in contributing at least £100 towards extricating one whom he regards so highly from a state of embarrassment. I have heard from him lately, dated from Milan; and as he has entrusted me with one or two commissions, I do not doubt but my letter would reach him by the direction he gave me. If you feel any delicacy on the subject, may I write to him about it? My letter shall express that zeal for your interests which I truly feel, and which would not confine itself to those barren protestations if I had the smallest superfluity.

My friend accepts your *interest* and is contented to be a Hebrew for your sake. But a request is made in return which in courtesy cannot be refused. There is some little literary luxury, some enjoyment of taste or fancy you have refused yourself, because you have not felt, through the difficulty of your situation, that you were entitled to indulge yourself in it. You are entreated,—and a refusal would give more pain than you are willing to inflict—to employ the enclosed in making yourself a present of this luxury, that may remind you of this not unfriendly contest, which has conferred a value on £5 which I believe it never had before.

Adieu,

Most affectionately yours,

P. B. SHELLEY.

I will send you an "Alastor."

[Addressed]
LEIGH HUNT, Esq.,
Vale of Health,
Hampstead,
Near London

---

[5] In Mary's letter of December 6, quoted above, she there alludes to a sum of money that Shelley had already sent to Hunt. "Leigh Hunt has not written. I would advise a letter addressed to him at the *Examiner* office, if there be no answer to-morrow. He may not be at the Vale of Health, for it is odd that he does not acknowledge the receipt of so large a sum." Professor Dowden suggests that this money may have been conveyed to Hunt either for his private wants, or as a contribution to the relief of the distressed poor in Spitalfields, on whose behalf Hunt had pleaded in the *Examiner*."—*Life of Shelley*, Vol. II, p. 61.

LETTERS

TO MARY WOLLSTONECRAFT GODWIN

Bath

London,
December 16, 1816.[1]

I have spent a day, my beloved, of somewhat agonising sensations; such as the contemplation of vice and folly and hard heartedness exceeding all conception must produce. Leigh Hunt has been with me all day and his delicate and tender attentions to me, his kind speeches of you, have sustained me against the weight of the horror of this event. The children I have not got. I have seen Longdill, who recommends proceeding with the utmost caution and resoluteness. He seems interested. I told him I was under contract of marriage to you; and he said that in such an event all pretences to detain the

[1] Shelley returned to Bath on December 14, from his visit to Leigh Hunt at Hampstead, and was much pleased with his new friend. On the day following he received the tidings of Harriet Shelley's suicide. After her separation from Shelley, Harriet had lived for some time at her father's house in Chapel Street. Mary writes in her diary in April, 1815, "We hear that Harriet has left her father's house," and shortly afterwards there is a record of two visits paid to her by Shelley. But in June, 1816, she addressed a letter to Mr. Newton from 23 Chapel Street, from which it would seem that she was still on good terms with her family. It has been stated that her father's door was shut against her by order of her sister. In November Shelley had applied to Thomas Hookham for news of Harriet, but in vain. Her last lodgings were at a house in Queen Street, Brompton, from which place she disappeared on November 9, and about a month later, on December 15, Hookham wrote to Shelley to say that her body had been taken out of the Serpentine on December 10; that little information respecting her was laid before the jury at the coroner's inquest, and that her name had been given as that of Harriet Smith. (See *Shelley in England* for some recent information on Harriet's death.)

On the same day that Shelley received the news of Harriet's death he went to London to claim his two children; he could not, however, have arrived until the evening. This highly important letter has now been corrected, and the suppressed passage restored, by kind permission, from the original in the collection of Mr. T. J. Wise, who has given a facsimile of it in his *Shelley Library*. The date of the letter was formerly printed as December 15, but the figures are not very distinct, and I think Shelley may have written 15 and altered it to 16. The letter undoubtedly reached Mary, whose reply, dated December 17, 1816, was printed by Dowden from the original which is now in the Bodleian Library.

The postmarks on this letter are so puzzling that I have sought the help of officials at the General Post Office, London. After examining at my request Mr. Wise's facsimile of the letter they courteously confirmed my opinion that the indorsement *Not to be found* relates to when this letter, for some unexplained reason, passed through the post again in the year 1859; that is to say, eight years after Mary Shelley's death. The letter, which bears evidences of having been twice sealed, may have been one of those that Mary lost when she left Marlow. There is only a manuscript copy in the Bodleian Library.

children would cease. Hunt said very delicately that this would be soothing intelligence to you.—Yes, my only hope my darling love, this will be among the innumerable benefits which you will have bestowed upon me, and which will still be inferior in value to the greatest of benefits—yourself—it is thro' you that I can entertain without despair the recollection of the horrors of unutterable villainy that led to this dark, dreadful death.—I am to hear tomorrow from Desse[2] whether or no, I am to engage in a contest for the children.—At least it is consoling to know that if the contest should arise it would have its termination in your nominal union with me—that after having blessed me with a life, a world of real happiness, a mere form[3] appertaining to you will not be barren of good.

It seems that this poor woman—the most innocent of her abhorred and unnatural family—was driven from her father's house, and descended the steps of prostitution until she lived with a groom of the name of Smith, who deserting her, she killed herself.— There can be no question that the beastly viper her sister, unable to gain profit from her connexion with me—has secured to herself the fortune of the old man—who is now dying—by the murder of this poor creature. Every thing tends to prove, however, that beyond the mere shock of so hideous a catastrophe having fallen on a human being once so nearly connected with me, there would, in any case have been little to regret. Hookham, Longdill—every one, does *me* full justice;—bears testimony to the upright spirit and liberality of my conduct to her:—there is but one voice in condemnation of the detestable Westbrooks. If they should dare to bring it before Chancery, a scene of such fearful horror would be unfolded as would cover them with scorn and shame.

How is Clare? I do not tell her, but I may tell you how deeply I am interested in her safety. I [need] not recommend her to your care. Give her any kind message from me, and calm her spirits as well as you can.

I do not ask you to calm your own.—I am well in health tho' somewhat faint and agitated—but the affectionate attentions shown

[2] Mr. Westbrook's Attorney.
[3] Shelley had written "a form" and cancelled it for "a mere form."

me by Hunt have been sustainers and restoratives more than I can tell. Do you, dearest and best, seek happiness—where it ought to reside in your own pure and perfect bosom: in the thoughts of how dear and how good you are to me—how wise and how extensively beneficial you are perhaps destined to become. Remember my poor babes, Ianthe and Charles. How dear and tender a mother they will find in you—Darling William, too!—My eyes overflow with tears. To-morrow write a long letter, and give me some answer to Hunt's message.

P. B. SHELLEY.

[Addressed]
Mrs. SHELLEY,
12 *New Bond Street,*
Bath
[In another hand,] Not to be found.
[Postmarks]
Dec.   LONDON
16   *Mr.* 29
1816   59   C
BATH   BATH
Mr. 30   *Ap.* 1
59

CCCXII
TO CLARA MARY JANE CLAIRMONT
Bath

London,
December 30, 1816.

DEAREST CLARE,
Your letter to-day relieved me from a weight of painful anxiety. Thank you, too, my kind girl for not expressing much of what you must feel, the loneliness and the low spirits which arise from being entirely left. Nothing could be more provoking than to find all this unnecessary. However, they will now be satisfied and quiet.

213

LETTERS

We cannot come to-morrow, there being no inside place in any of the coaches, or in either of the mails. I have secured a place for Wednesday [January 1, 1817]—the day following that on which you will receive this letter—so that you will infalliably see us on that evening. I may say that it was by a most fortunate chance that I secured the places that I did.

The ceremony,[1] so magical in its effects, was undergone this morning at St. Mildred's Church in the City. Mrs. G[odwin] and G[odwin] were both present, and appeared to feel no little satisfaction. Indeed Godwin throughout has shown the most polished and courteous attentions to me and Mary. He seems to think no kindness too great in compensation for what has passed. I confess I am not entirely deceived by this, though I cannot make my vanity wholly insensible to certain attentions paid in a manner studiously flattering. Mrs. G. presents herself to me in her real attributes of affectation, prejudice and heartless pride. Towards her, I confess I never feel an emotion of anything but antipathy. Her sweet daughter is very dear to me.

We left the Hunts yesterday morning, and spent the evening at Skinner Street, not unpleasantly. We had a bed in the neighbourhood and breakfasted with them before the marriage. Very few inquiries have been made of you, and those not of a nature to show that their suspicions have been alarmed. Indeed, all is safe there.

I write to Clairmont by to-day's post, inclosing him £20. So that you see our expected advantage from added income this quarter comes to very little. Do not answer our letter, as we shall be on our way to you before it can reach London. The G.'s give the most singular account of Mrs. Boinville, etc.

I will not tell you how dreadfully melancholy Skinner Street appears with all its associations. The most horrid thought is how people can be merry there! But I am resolved to overcome such sensations. If I do not destroy them I may be myself destroyed.

The Baxters, we hear, have suddenly lost all their fortune, and are reduced to the lowest poverty.

Adieu, my dear. Keep up your spirits and manage your health

[1] Shelley's marriage to Mary Wollstonecraft Godwin, on the morning of December 30, 1816, the date of this letter.

214

LETTERS

till we come back. It will be Wednesday evening at nine o'clock.
Adieu, my dear—kiss Willy and yourself for me.

Ever affectionately yours,

P. B. SHELLEY.

Mary can't write, being all day with Mrs. G.

[Addressed]
MRS. CLAIRMONT,
12 *New Bond Street, Bath*

CCCXIII
TO MARY WOLLSTONECRAFT SHELLEY
Bath

London,
Jan. 11, 1816 [*error for* 1817.]

MY DEAR LOVE,

I will relate to you all that I have learned and all that has
happened first.

I saw Longdill early this morning and have spent the whole
day at his Chambers. From him I learned that after receiving
notice from Desse of Chancery proceedings he had made himself
acquainted with the *law of the point.* The only manner in which
I could get at the children in the *common course of law,* is by
Habeas Corpus, and that supposes a delay of some weeks. You
will see that the whole thing must be decided in Chancery
before that time, and that if I could succeed at common law my
situation would be still the same with respect to Chancery, and
that possession would in no manner ameliorate but rather the
contrary my situation. Their process is the most insidiously
malignant that can be conceived. They have filed a bill to say
that I published Queen Mab, that I avow myself to be an
atheist and a republican, with some other imputations of an
infamous nature. This, by Chancery Law I must *deny* or *admit*
upon oath and then it seems that it rests in the *mere* discretion of

215

the Chancellor to decide whether those are fit grounds for refusing me my children. They cannot have them at any rate; *my* father or *my* nearest relations are the persons whom the Chancellor will intrust with them if they must be denied me. It is therefore sheer revenge. If I admit myself or if Chancery decides that I ought not to have the children because I am an infidel; then the W[estbrook]s will make that decision a basis for a *criminal information* or common libel attack.

But there is hopes by watchful resistance that the whole of this detestable conspiracy will be overthrown—For if the Chancellor should decide not to hear their cause; and if our answer on oath is so convincing as to effect this, they are defeated. They do not tell Harriet's story: I mean the circumstances of her death, in these allegations against me.—They evidently [would][1] but that it make against themselves. They attack you and Godwin, by stating that I became acquainted with you whilst living with Harriet, and that Godwin is the author of *Political Justice* and other impious and seditious writings.

I learnt just now from Godwin that he has evidence that Harriet was unfaithful to me *four months* before I left England with you.[2] If we can succeed in establishing this, *our* connection will receive an additional sanction, and plea be overborne. On the 19th the Chancellor begins to sit and it must be decided instantly —from the nature of the case. I know not when, or whether at all, before that day I can return to Bath. How painful in these difficult and in one sense tremendous circumstances it is to me to be deprived of the counsel of your judgment and the consolation of your dear presence I must remain in London—I must attend to every, the minutest stage of the answer which is to be drawn up on my side. My story is what I have to tell. My evidence and my witnesses must be collected in the short space of five days. Besides I must be present. How much depends on this! Almost all besides that inviolable happiness which whilst you and your

[1] "The word 'would' seems to have been omitted."
[2] Godwin reiterated his charge in a letter to Baxter, May 12, 1817: "The late Mrs. Shelley has turned out to have been a woman of great levity—I know from unquestionable authority—wholly unconnected with Shelley—(though I cannot with propriety be quoted for this) that she had proved herself unfaithful to her husband before their separation."

LETTERS

affection remains to mc can never pass away is suspended perhaps
on the issue of this trial—[3]

CCCXIV
TO MARY WOLLSTONECRAFT SHELLEY
Bath

[? *London, January,* 1817.]

Cheer up, my beloved Mary. I have firm friends here. I am
not, as might have happened once, to be oppressed and crushed
in secrecy and solitude. Depend too, on the utmost foresight and
caution to be used on my part. I am to attend a consultation of
counsel early on Monday morning.

How is sweetest babe? How do his fair blue eyes look to-day?
Kiss him tenderly for me.

How is poor Clare? Give my love to her, and read her or tell
her the substance of my letter. I hope her spirits are not much

[3] The original letter, in the Bodleian, consists of 4 quarto pages and it ends at the foot
of the fourth page. Probably there was more that is missing. There is neither signature
nor address. Shelley was at Bath on January 3, 1817, as he addressed a note to his bankers
on that date from 5 Abbey Churchyard, but early in the month he again left Mary and
Clare Clairmont and proceeded to London, his object being to consult with his lawyers
regarding the case that was to come on shortly for hearing in the Court of Chancery
respecting the custody of his children by Harriet, Ianthe Eliza and Charles Bysshe.
The plaintiffs in the case were the children, who, at the time of their mother's death,
were in the care of a clergyman at Warwick. The defendants comprised John Westbrook and his daughter Eliza, Mr. Higham, Mr. Farthing Beauchamp (whom Eliza
Westbrook afterwards married), Shelley and Sir Timothy Shelley. The case was heard
before Lord Chancellor Eldon on Friday, January 24, 1817, his judgment being given
on March 27. He considered Shelley's "principles as highly immoral," and that he
would not be justified in delivering the children over to their father exclusively for
their education. It was not formally decided to whom the education of the children
should be entrusted until Shelley was in Italy. But he was allowed to propose the
names of persons for that office, and after the rejection of his solicitor, Longdill, Dr.
and Mrs. Hume of Hanwell were accepted. The boy was to be placed at a private
school until the age of seven, when he was to pass to a public school and one of the
universities: the girl was to be educated at home by Mrs. Hume. The allowance for
the children's maintenance was fixed at £200, £80 of which were to be paid by Mr.
Westbrook, and £120 by Shelley. Professor Dowden has given an exhaustive account
of these Chancery proceedings in his *Life of Shelley*, from which the brief particulars in
this note are derived.

During his absence, Clare Clairmont gave birth (on January 12) to a girl, the
daughter of Lord Byron, whom they called Alba, until later the names of Clara
Allegra were chosen.

[? ou[t]raged] in her present situation. She will see that in a matter so serious as that in which I am engaged I cannot return.— Now my darling Pecksie,[1] don't fancy I'm disquieted so as to be unwell. Dont think I have any of those misgivings and perturbations which vitally affect the heart. I am, it is true, earnest and active, but as far as relates to all highest hopes and you, my own only treasure, quite happy. So adieu—You shall hear tomorrow night if possible.

Your own affectionate

SHELLEY.

I've lost the list—send it again, and I'll send by the coach— Don't be disappointed if I send not by the mail. May be I can't.

CCCXV
TO LORD BYRON

London,
January 17, 1817.

I write to you, my dear Lord Byron, after a series of the most unexpected and overwhelming sorrows, and from the midst of a situation of peril and persecution. But I have good news to tell you. Clare is safely delivered of a most beautiful girl. Both the mother and the child are well, and Mary describes the latter to be a creature of the most exquisite symmetry, and as betraying, even at its birth, a vigour and a sensibility very unusual. But you will doubtless learn all, and more than can relate to this subject, from Clare's letters.

My late wife is dead. The circumstances which attended this event are of a nature of such awful and appalling horror, that I dare hardly avert to them in thought. The sister of whom you have heard me speak may be truly said (though not in law, yet in fact) to have murdered her for the sake of her father's money.

[1] Shelley's pet name for Mary. It has been suggested that he borrowed it from Mrs. Trimmer's tale of *The Robins.*

218

Thus did an event which I believed quite indifferent to me, following in the train of a far severer anguish, communicate a shock to me which I know not how I have survived. The sister has now instituted a Chancery process against me, the intended effect of which is to deprive me of my unfortunate children, now more than ever dear to me; of my inheritance, and to throw me into prison, and expose me in the pillory, on the ground of my being a REVOLUTIONIST, and an *Atheist*. It seems whilst she lived in my house she possessed herself of such papers as go to establish these allegations. The opinion of Counsel is, that she will certainly succeed to a considerable extent, but that I may probably escape entire ruin, in the worldly sense of it. So I am here, dragged before the tribunals of tyranny and superstition, to answer with my children, my property, my liberty, and my fame, for having exposed their frauds, and scorned the insolence of their power. Yet I will not fail; though I have been given to understand that I could purchase victory by recantation. Indeed, I have too much pride in the selection of their victim.

So here is an imperfect account of my misfortunes (yet one thing happened in the autumn that affected me far more deeply).[1] I should have written to you before, if I had been beaten down by any common griefs.

I had last month, an unexpected letter from your friend, Leigh Hunt, whom I have since visited. He is indeed a most friendly, and excellent man. I have found few such as he appears to be in the world. He was so kind as to listen to the story of persecution which I am now enduring from a libidinous and vindictive woman, and to stand by me as yet by his counsel, and by his personal attentions to me.

I have no other news to tell you, my dear Lord Byron, unless

---

[1] Early in October, Fanny Imlay had suddenly left Godwin's house, and had travelled through Bath and Bristol to Swansea. She did not visit Mary at Bath, but wrote from Bristol in such an alarming tone that Shelley immediately started for that town, but was unable to obtain any tidings of her. On Fanny's arrival at the Mackworth Arms Inn, Swansea, on the night of October 9, she retired to rest, and she was found the next morning lying dead, with a bottle of laudanum beside her. Shelley went again on the 10th to Bristol, but it was not until two days later that he brought Mary the news of her unhappy sister's death. " Hapless Woman! What a fate is thine!" Mary Woolstonecraft had exclaimed to her baby Fanny, in her *Letters Written During a Short Residence in Sweden and Denmark*, 1796, p. 66. Her words proved singularly prophetic.

you think this is news: that I often talk, and oftener think, of you; and that, though I have not seen you for six months, I still feel the burden of my own insignificance and impotence; as they must ever forbid my interest in your welfare from being put to the proof. Adieu.

Faithfully yours,

P. B. SHELLEY.

Hunt requests me to send you his remembrances.

CCCXVI
TO CLARA MARY JANE CLAIRMONT
Bath

[*London,*
Postmark] *Jan*[*uary*] 30, 1817.

Mary has written to you, dearest Clare, in better spirits, and as a reward of her good spirits, with better news than I. In fact, that about Hunt was overruled. It only serves to exhibit the malice of these monsters.

I have little doubt in my own mind but that they will finally succeed in the criminal part of the business. I mean that some such punishment as imprisonment and fine will be awarded me, by a jury. But do not disquiet yourself. Do not allow this to be a matter of present agitation to you. It is not a thing that can be decided within six months, an interval pregnant with many hopes and fears, and if well cultivated fruitful in joys which might make a bower of roses of the worst dungeon that tyranny could invent. Don't tease yourself, Clara. The greatest good you can do me is to keep well and quiet yourself, and of that you are well aware.

Mary tells me that she never engaged the lodgings for a month, or that if she did so, one fortnight of the time is already past.

[Addressed]
MISS JANE CLAIRMONT,
P. B. SHELLEY, Esq.,
12 *New Bond Street*,
Bath

LETTERS

CCCXVII
TO CHARLES OLLIER

February 22, 1817.

[FRAGMENT]

The bearer will wait for my revise.[1] Had you not better advertise the day (an exciting one) of publication? Advertise in *all* the morning papers of note. I think no more than 500 need be printed. You know best whether the sale of such a number would or would not pay the expenses—though this is a secondary matter.

CCCXVIII
TO WILLIAM GODWIN

[*Great Marlow*], Mar. 9, 1817.

MY DEAR GODWIN

I wish you knew me better than to be vexed or disappointed at anything I do. Either circumstances of petty difficulty and embarrassment find some peculiar attraction in me, or I have a fainter power of repulsion with regard to them. Certain it is, that nothing gives me serener and more pure pleasure than your society, and that if in breaking an engagement with you I have forced an exercise of your philosophy upon you, I have in my own person incurred a penalty which mine has not yet taught me to alleviate.

It gives me pain too that I cannot send the whole amount you want. I enclose a check to within a few pounds of my possessions. This in fact is the most unlucky time for me.—I shall never be so low again. I do much rely on loans, or indeed on any one besides Dawe.

We are immersed in all kinds of confusion here. Mary said you meant to come hither soon enough to see the leaves come out. Which leaves did you mean, for the wild-briar buds are already unfolded?—and what of "Mandeville" and how will he bear to be transplanted.[1]

[1] Of "A Proposal for Putting Reform to the Vote, &c." See Letter No. CCCXIX.

[1] A quarter of the last page here, and the signature have been cut away from the letter.

LETTERS

All my people, little Willy not excepted, desire their kindest love to you. I beg to unite in kind remembrances to Mrs. Godwin —whose health is I hope improved, and remain my dear friend.

[Addressed]
[MR. WILLIA]M GODWIN,   Postmark
    Skinner [Street],   MARL[OW]
    Snow H[ill],
    Lon[don]

CCCXIX
TO CHARLES OLLIER

[Before March 14, 1817.]

DEAR SIR

I inclose you the Revise[1] which may be put to press when corrected, and the sooner the better. I inclose you also a list[2] of persons to whom I wish copies to be sent *from the Author*, as soon as

[1] Shelley's pamphlet "A Proposal/for putting/Reform to the Vote/*Throughout the Kingdom.*/By the Hermit of Marlow."/For a full account of this pamphlet and of the public events that led Shelley to propose a plebiscite see Professor Dowden's *Life of Shelley*, Vol. II, p. 108, and Mr. H. Buxton Forman's preface to the Shelley Society facsimile of the manuscript of this tract, issued in 1887, in which this letter was first printed. Leigh Hunt was undoubtedly interested in the pamphlet, as it was printed and published by his friends Reynell and the Olliers.
[2 The list mentioned in the above letter.]

Sir Francis Burdett, M.P.*
Mr. Peters, of Cornwall.
Mr. Brougham, M.P.*
Lord Grosvenor.*
Lord Holland.*
Lord Grey.*
Mr. Cobbett.*
Mr. Waithman.*
Mr. Curran.
Hon. Douglas Kinnaird.*
Hon. Thos. Brand, M.P.*
Lord Cochrane, M.P.
Sir R. Heron, M.P.
The Lord Mayor.*
Mr. Montague Burgoyne.
Major Cartwright.*
Messrs. Taylor, Sen. and Jun., of Norwich.
Mr. Place, Charing Cross.*
Mr. Walker, of Westminster.
Lord Essex.*

Capt. Burnet, M.P.*
The Birmingham Hampden Club (five copies).
Mr. I. Thomas, St. Albans, Mon.
Mr. Philipps, Whitston, Mon.
Mr. Andrew Duncan, Provost of Arbroath.
Mr. Alderman Godbehere.*
Mr. Jones Burdett.*
Mr. Hallet, of Berkshire (five copies).
The London Hampden Club (ten copies).
The Editors of the *Statesman*,* the *Morning Chronicle*,* and the *Independent Whig*.*
Mr. Montgomery (the Poet), of Sheffield.
Mr. R. Owen, of Lanark.
Mr. Madocks, M.P.
Mr. George Ensor.
Mr. Bruce.
Mr. Sturch, of Westminster.*
Mr. Creevy, M.P.
Genl. Sir R. Ferguson, M.P.*

Mr. H. Buxton Forman stated that "against the names marked with the asterisks the

222

possible. I trust you will be good enough to take the trouble off my hands.—

Do not advertise sparingly: and get as many booksellers as you can to take copies on their own account. Sherwood Neely & Co., Hone of Newgate Street, Ridgeway, and Stockdale are people likely to do so.—Send 20 or 30 copies to Messrs. Hookham & Co., Bond Street without explanation. I have arranged with them.

Send twenty copies to me addressed to Mr. Hunt, who will know what to do with them if I am out of town.—

Your very obedient Ser^{t.}

P. B. SHELLEY.

[Addressed]
MR. OLLIER

CCCXX
TO CHARLES OLLIER

[Great Marlow],
March 14, 1817.

DEAR SIR,

Be so kind as to let the Books I ordered (so far as you have completed them) to be sent together with my prints immediately —by the Marlow Coach.

Mr. Hunt has, I believe, commissioned you to get me a *proof* impression of a print done from a drawing by Harlowe of Lord Byron: I said that it should be framed in oak, but I have changed my mind and wish it to be finished in black.

How does the pamphlet sell?

Dear sir, yours very truly,

P. B. SHELLEY.

Send in addition Mawe's *Gardening Calendar*.

word *sent* was written in the original list, and not by Shelley. This appears to have been done in Messrs. Olliers' office, and shows that the copies were really sent to the persons thus indicated." This list is interesting as giving the names of a number of men in whose opinions Shelley was more or less interested.

LETTERS

Marlow,
March 22, 1817.

MY DEAR GODWIN,

Marshall's proposal is one in which, however reluctantly, I must refuse to engage.[1] It is that I should grant bills to the amount of his debts, which are to expire in *thirty months*. This is a situation in which it might become me to place myself for the sake of some very dear friend, or some person who might have an irresistible public claim, but which, if it were only in the possible arrival of such emergencies, I feel that with respect to Marshall, I am bound to avoid. Do not infer that I deny him to have just claims on my assistance—which, if I were in possession of my paternal estate, I should hasten to fulfil.

It was spring when I wrote to you, and winter when your answer arrived. But the frost is very transitory, every bud is ready to burst into leaf. It is a nice distinction you make between the development and the complete expansion of the leaves—the oak and the chestnut, the latest and the earliest parents of foliage would afford you a still subtler subdivision which would enable you to defer the visit from which we expect so much delight, for six weeks. I hope we shall really see you before that time, and that you will allow the chestnut or any other impartial tree, as he stands in the foreground to be considered as a virtual representation of the rest.

Will is quite well and very beautiful. Mary unites with me in presenting her kind remembrances to Mrs. Godwin, and begs her most affectionate love to you.[2]

Have you read "Melincourt?"[3] It would entertain you—Will you

---

[1] Godwin had drawn up in 1816 an appeal for assistance on behalf of his friend, James Marshall.
[2] The signature has been cut away from the original letter.
[3] Peacock's novel, *Melincourt*, was published by Hookham in 1817. In 1856, when it was re-issued, it appeared with the title of *Melincourt, or Sir Oran Haut-Ton*.

224

be kind enough to pay Newberry the newsman, for me? I inclose cheque.

[Addressed]
W. GODWIN, Esq.,
41 *Skinner Street*,
Snow Hill,
London

[Postmarks]
MARLOW
[and]
24 MR
18 . . .

CCCXXII
TO WILLIAM HONE
London

Mr. Shelley's Compts to Mr. Hone—and his Messenger will wait for an answer on the subject of the Pamphlet.

[In pencil by another hand

PERCY BYSSHE SHELLEY

Marlow, April 20, 1817.][1]

[Addressed]
[MR. WILLIA]M HONE, Bookseller,
[*O*]*ld Bailey*

CCCXXIII
TO C. & J. OLLIER

Marlow,
April 23, 1817.

Mr. Shelley requests Messrs. Ollier will have the goodness to send the books and the little pictures as soon as they can.

In great haste,

---

[1] Shelley addressed the following note to "Brool es & Co., 27 Chancery Lane, London. Albion House, Great Marlow, Bucks, April 21, 1817. Gentlemen, Be so good as to send me by return of post. Thirty pounds. Your obedient Sert. Percy Bysshe Shelley."

LETTERS

Albion House,
Marlow,
Bucks.
April 23rd, 1817.

MY DEAR LORD BYRON,

This letter goes out on an adventure to meet you, though nothing is more improbable than that it should succeed. Rumour says that you are at Venice, and determines that you should make an expedition into Greece and Asia. I wrote to you last under the impression of some horrible circumstances which had occurred to me; and in the midst of a legal persecution, the most material blow of which I need not inform you has taken effect, though another, viz. that of criminal information against "Queen Mab," yet remains suspended. But all human evils either extinguish or are extinguished by the sufferer, and I am now living with my accustomed tranquillity and happiness in a house which I have taken near this town.

But I was incited to write to you, not that I might relate anything concerning myself, but that I might say something of Clare, and of a little being whom we—in the absence of all right to bestow a *Christian* designation—call Alba, or the Dawn. She is very beautiful, and though her frame is of somewhat a delicate texture, enjoys excellent health. Her eyes are the most intelligent I ever saw in so young an infant. Her hair is black, her eyes deeply blue, and her mouth exquisitely shaped. She passes here for the child of a friend in London, sent into the country for her health, while Clare has reassumed her maiden character. Indeed all these precautions have now become more necessary than before, on account of our renewed intimacy with Godwin, which has taken place in consequence of my marriage with Mary, a change (if it be a change) which had principally her feelings in respect to Godwin for its object. I need not inform you that this is simply with us a measure of convenience, and that our opinions as to the importance of this pretended sanction, and all the prejudices connected with it, remain the same.

And now, what are your plans with respect to the little girl? I need not assure you of the pleasure which both Mary and myself would feel in contributing all our care to it during your absence, or indeed during any period convenient to you. But we find it indispensable that Clare should reside with us; and a perpetual danger of discovery that it is hers impends. Nothing would be easier than to own that it was hers, and that it is the offspring of a private marriage in France. But the wise heads suppose that such a tale would make people consider it as mine, and that the inhabitants of this most Christian country would not suffer me to dwell among them under such an imputation. The answer to these difficulties, which would be most satisfactory to us, would be your own speedy return. We hear that the plague rages in Albania, and hope that you will thus be delayed from proceeding into a country from which it is always questionable whether an European will ever return.

As to this country, you will have heard that the ministers have gained a victory, which has not been disturbed by a single murmur; if I except those of famine, which they have troops of hireling soldiers to repress. Other news of course I cannot know. We spend our time here in that tranquil uniformity which presents much to enjoy and leaves nothing to record. I have my books, and a garden with a lawn, enclosed by high hedges, and over-shadowed with firs and cypresses intermixed with apple trees now in blossom. We have a boat on the river, in which, when the days are sunny and serene, such as we have had of late, we sail. May we hope that you will ever visit us? Clare would be the most rejoiced of all of us at the sight of a letter written by you. I do not tell her that I write to you now. Mary desires to be affectionately remembered to you; and I remain,

Always yours very faithfully,

P. B. Shelley.

LETTERS

[? *Marlow*] *April* 1817.

[FRAGMENT]

I wish you could contrive to make your visit here early. Hunt is with me at present, and will remain at least three weeks. May Peacock expect you during that period? My τετραπους has been metamorphosed since you were here into a featherless biped; he lives, and inhabits his father's house, but he has ceased to crawl. He walks with great alacrity.

Very sincerely yours,

P. B. SHELLEY.

CCCXXVI
TO LEIGH AND MARIANNE HUNT
London

Great Marlow,
June 29, 1817.

MY DEAR FRIENDS,

I performed my promise, and arrived here the night after I set off. Everybody up to this minute has been and continues well. I ought to have written yesterday, for to-day, I know not how, I have so constant a pain in my side, and such a depression of strength and spirits, as to make my holding the pen whilst I write to you an almost intolerable exertion. This, you know, with me is transitory. Do not mention that I am unwell to your nephew[1]; for the advocate of a new system of diet is held bound to be invulnerable by disease, in the same manner as the sectaries of a new system of religion are held to be more moral than other people, or as a reformed parliament must at least be assumed as

[1] The son of Leigh Hunt's brother John, also mentioned in this letter, Henry L. Hunt was afterwards a London publisher. His name appears with his father's on the title page of Shelley's *Posthumous Poems*, 1824.

228

the remedy of all political evils. No one will change the diet, adopt the religion, or reform parliament else.

Well, I am very anxious to hear how you get on, and I intreat Marianne to excite Hunt not to delay a minute in writing the necessary letters, and in informing me of the result. Kings are only to be approached through their ministers; who indeed, as Marianne should know to her cost, if she don't take care, are responsible not only for all their commissions, but, a more dreadful responsibility, for all their *omissions*. And I know not who has a right to the title of King, if not according to the Stoics, he to whom the King of Kings had delegated the prerogative of lord of the creation.

Let me know how Harry gets on, and make my best respects to your brother and Mrs. Hunt. Adieu.

Always most affectionately yours,

P. B. S.

[*By Mary Wollstonecraft Shelley*]

You may see by this letter that Shelley is very unwell—he always writes in this manner when ill. He was well yesterday until the evening, but to-day he is worse than I have known him for some time. Perhaps the decrease of heat in the weather has to do with it.

The babes are all well. John has been a very good boy, and Mary better within the last day or two. Swynburne [*sic*] is quite well.

What about the Alpha Cottage? It is dear and I should think too far from the theatres, is there another choice?

Please Mary Anne send flannel for petticoats and flannels, and a pattern of the latter, and lawn not too expensive with a pattern shirt and cap.

The statues are not of a snowy but of a milky whiteness, but I think begin to look more creamy to-day.

Miss Kent is very attentive to the children. She bids me tell you that they are well, and that she does not write to-day.

LETTERS

How do you like Canova—one of you write and tell me a little news of yourselves.

You know the news we have had concerning the little faithless Clare is of course unhappy and consequently cross or so. I do not wonder that she should be unhappy. I suppose she is over head and ears in love with some Venetian. Give our love to Thornton.[2]

Adieu, little babes.—Take care not to loose one another in the streets for fear one of you should be kidnapped, but take hold of one another's hands and walk pretty.

Affectionately yours,

M. W. S.

[Postmark] 10 *o'clock*, Jy. 1, 1817.
[Addressed]
    LEIGH HUNT, Esq.,
    J. HUNT, Esq.,
    Maida Vale, Paddington,
    London

CCCXXVII
TO THOMAS JEFFERSON HOGG

Marlow,
July 6, 1817.

MY DEAR HOGG,

Peacock and I shall be very glad to see you in this part of the Country; and I regret that you had not contrived to visit it earlier when Hunt would have contributed his musical powers to your amusement.—

At present we have little else than clouds and rain. We have a water chariot drawn by the coursers of Notus, but except some fine warm days, and soft moonlight evening[s] which lost heir way in this abominable climate as they were crossing from Italy to Greece, it has been of little use to us. I hope your coming will be like that of Alcuone in storms, to this wintry season.

[2] John, Mary and Swinburne, were children of Leigh Hunt who had evidently been staying with the Shelleys. Marianne (usually so spelt) was Leigh Hunt's wife, Miss (Bessy) Kent, her sister, and Thornton was the Hunts' eldest son.

I have [been] reading little else but Homer. I am now in the 23rd book; you can imagine, the wonders of poetry which I have enjoyed in the five preceding books. Indeed this part of the Iliad, the Patrocleiad, seems to me to surpass all other portions of the Iliad, as that production considered as a whole surpasses any other single production of the human mind. Familiarity with Homer increases our admiration and astonishment—I can never believe that the Odyssy is a work of the same author.

I am well acquainted with Lucretius, and am happy to find that you have cultivated an intimacy with him. The 4th book is perhaps the finest. The whole of that passage about love is full of irresistible energy of language as well as the profoundest truth.

I am weak enough to employ myself in writing, tho' half conscious that my time might be better employed. I have therefore read very little. I have been reading Arrian. His history of Alexander is very inferior to Q. Curtius but his Historia Indica is attractive from the singularity of the subject. It is a kind of abstract of the Pæriplus of Nearchus, (I know not if such a book yet exist) who commanded the expedition sent by Alexander from the mouth of the Ganges to that of the Euphrates.

We are all, my blue eyed boy included, very well.

Yours ever sincerely,

P. B. SHELLEY.

[Addressed]
JEFFERSON HOGG, Esq.,
7 *Garden Court,*
Temple,
London

LETTERS

Marlow,
July 9th, 1817.

My dear Lord Byron,

I called on Rogers[1] the other day, on some affairs relating to Hunt, and heard some news of you, viz. that you had been to Rome, and that you had returned to Venice. I had already acquired the preceding piece of information from the Coliseum scene in "Manfred." How is it that I have not heard from you? At first I drew from your silence a favourable augury of your early return. This is in a degree confirmed by the circumstance of Newstead being advertised for sale. I shall be among the first to greet you on your return.

At present I write only to enquire what are you plans with regard to little Alba. She continues to reside with us under a feigned name. But we are somewhat embarrassed about her. We are exposed to what remarks her existence is calculated to excite. At least a period approaches when it will be impossible to temporize with our servants or our visitors. There are two very respectable young ladies in this town, who would undertake the charge of her, if you consent to this arrangement. Clare would then be able to superintend her; and I cannot but recommend this measure to you as a provisional one, if any other is at present inconvenient to you. If you return to England in the autumn, or even in the winter, we should experience no inconvenience from deferring the question until that period.

I ought to tell you that your little girl is in excellent health and spirits. She improves very much, and although small for her age, has an extraordinary degree of animation and intelligence Our Genevese nurse walks about with her and William all the day in the garden; and she is bathed, like him, in cold water.

---

[1] "Before meeting Shelley in Italy, I had seen him only once. It was at my own house at St. James's Place, where he called upon me—introducing himself—to request the loan of some money which he wished to present to Leigh Hunt; and he offered me a bond for it. Having numerous claims upon me at that time, I was obliged to refuse the loan. Both in appearance and in manners Shelley was the perfect gentleman."— *Recollections of the Table-Talk of Samuel Rogers* [by Alexander Dyce]. Third Edition, 1856, p. 240.

I suppose you know that the tyranny, civil and religious, under which this country groans, has visited me somewhat severely. I neither like it the worse nor the better for this. It was always the object of my unbounded abhorrence. But it may become necessary that I should quit the country. It is possible that the interference exercised by Chancery in the instance of my two other children might be attempted to be extended to William. Should this be the case, I shall depart. And in this case, what shall I do with Alba?

I have read "Manfred" with the greatest admiration. The same freedom from common rules that marked the 3rd Canto and "Chillon" is visible here; and it was that which all your earlier productions, except "Lara," wanted. But it made me dreadfully melancholy, and I fear other friends in England, too. Why do you indulge this despondency? "Manfred," as far as I learn, is immensely popular; it is characterized as a very daring production.

Hunt has been with me here, and we have often spoken of you. Hunt is an excellent man, and has a great regard for you.

How is your health—and—the resolutions on which it depends? I am anxious to know whether you are free from the disorder by which you were threatened. I have lately had a kind of relapse of my constitutional disease, and if the Chancellor should threaten to invade my domestic circle, I shall seek Italy; as a refuge at once from the stupid tyranny of these laws and my disorder.

I suppose Clare will write to you herself. Mary desires her kind remembrances to you, and I am,

Ever sincerely yours,

P. B. SHELLEY.

Alba has blue eyes, and had dark hair, which has fallen off, and there is now a dispute about the colour. Clare says that it is auburn; William and she are very good friends.

LETTERS

Marlow,
July 13, 1817.

DEAR SIR,

Be so obliging as to send me *immediately* "Sibylline Leaves,"[1] by S. T. Coleridge." I should secure it the same night if on receipt of this you will have the goodness to send wherever it is published, and direct the messenger to take it to the Marlow courier before he returns.

Dear Sir,
Your very obedt. Sevt.
PERCY B. SHELLEY.

[Addressed]
MESSRS. OLLIER,
Welbeck Street,
London

Marlow,
August 3, 1818 [*for* 1817].

DEAR SIR,

I send you with this letter a manuscript[1] which has been consigned to my care by a friend in whom I feel considerable interest. I do not know how far it consists with your plan of business to purchase the copyrights, or a certain interest in the copyrights of any works which should appear to promise success. I

[1] *Sibylline Leaves* was published in 1817.

[1] Of Mary Shelley's novel, which John Murray and Ollier declined to publish. It was afterwards issued by another firm of publishers with the following title: "Frankenstein; /or,/The Modern Prometheus,/in three volumes./[quotation from *Paradise Lost*] Vol. I, etc./Printed for/Lackington, Hughes, Harding, Mavor & Jones,/Finsbury Square,/ 1818."

should certainly prefer that some such arrangement as this should be made if on consideration you could make any offer which I should feel justified to my friend in accepting. How far that can be you will be the better able to judge after a perusal of the MS. Perhaps you will do me the favour of communicating your decision to me as early as you conveniently can.

I remain, dear sir,
Your faithful, obedient servant,

PERCY B. SHELLEY.

Do you know is Taylor's "Pausanias"[2] to be procured, and at what price?

Be so kind as to tell me also, is Martyn's "Georgics"[3] of Virgil, printed in a very large octavo edition, to match with the "Eclogues?" I wish an octavo edition of Moore's new poem[4] to be half-bound for me. I enclose a note to Mr. Hunt which you will have the kindness to put in the post for me.

[Endorsed]
MR. OLLIER.

CCCXXXI
TO LEIGH HUNT

Marlow,
August 3, 1817.

MY DEAR FRIEND,

You tell me nothing of what it most interests me to hear. I want to know if you have made any, and what progress in such a negotiation as I endeavoured to effectuate in Town for you? I cannot tell whether you deserve forgiveness for your trip over the brook until I know how this is. To be sure it would be a very

[2] "The Description of Greece by Pausanias, with notes, 1794, translated by Thomas Taylor the Platonist (1758-1835)."
[3] See note, Letter No. CLXIV.
[4] Thomas Moore's poem, *Lalla Rookh*, published in 1817.

235

horrid thing if you have done nothing towards such a complete settlement, and yet have put £60 out of your possession, and that with I don't know how many bills coming due, and that odious November frowning the last object in this vista. In fact I should imagine among your intimate friends nothing could be more easy than to arrange a loan on the terms and in the manner that I suggested. Your Brother[1] I do not doubt will or can do nothing. But there is Keats, who certainly *can*, and Alsager, from whom I should expect much. The persons to whom I applied, as you well know, were merely men of business. I have no private friends. My applications, of course, were unsuccessful, and my resources for applications soon exhausted. If you have done nothing; all that remains is Horace Smith; and if we are reduced to make applications to him, by the pressure of the difficulties that approach you with November, you and I must consider what we must say to him. He is not in Town now, but I suppose will soon arrive.— Meanwhile, my dear Hunt, pray answer me on this subject; as all other bills and affairs are comparatively of small importance. If I were not persuaded that my own quarters of application are entirely exhausted, at least until H. Smith arrives, I should have come to Town before this time.—Meanwhile let me trust you to yourself.—

Nothing gives me greater pleasure than to learn your comfortable mode of life. I shall feel the greatest satisfaction in paying you an early visit. I scarcely needed to hear that you are economical. But I am glad to discover that you are actively employed, and that on some original work. My best wishes also for the success of all criminals, even though invisible. It is the most comical thing in the world: You write accounts of your good behaviour to me as if I were some antient and wrinkled, but rather good-natured grand-uncle. Now this is a new feeling for me. I have been accustomed to consider myself as the most imprudent and [un]accountable of mankind.

Many kind thanks for the expected parcel. The contents will be highly prized by the individuals to whom they are addressed. Clare forgot to thank you, which she does very sincerely, for the

[1] John Hunt, joint-proprietor with Leigh Hunt, of the *Examiner*.

236

music. Mayen continues pretty well and sends her kind love and thanks for all favours. Bye-the-bye I have sent an MS.[2] to Ollier concerning the true author of which I entreat you to be silent, if you should be asked any questions. Mary's love to Marianne. She is very anxious about a nurse, and hopes Marianne will be kind enough to send an answer to her letter as soon as she can.

I have arrived at the 380th stanza of my Poem.[3]

Ever my dear Hunt,
Most faithfully and affectionately yours.
P. B. S

[Addressed]
LEIGH HUNT, Esq.,
13 *Lisson Grove,*
Paddington

CCCXXXII
TO CHARLES OLLIER
London

Marlow,
August 8, 1817.

DEAR SIR,
I wish you to send me together with "Lalla Rookh," if it will be ready in a few days, a copy of Dr. Percy's "Northern Antiquities." If the former is not at present ready I wish the latter to come immediately.

May I trouble you with a commission, and is it in your range of transactions to undertake it? I published some time since a poem

---

[2] Mary Shelley's *Frankenstein.*
[3] "Laon and Cythna;/or/The Revolution/of/The Golden City:/a vision of the Nineteenth Century./In the Stanza of Spenser./By/Percy B. Shelley. / ΔΟΣ ΠΟΥ ΣΤΩ ΚΑΙ ΚΟΣΜΟΝ ΚΙΝΗΣω/Archimedes./London./Printed for Sherwood, Neely & Jones, Paternoster-/Row; and C. and J. Ollier, Welbeck Street:/By B. McMillan, Bow-Street, Covent-Garden./1818." Mrs. Shelley says, in her note to this poem, that it "was written in his boat, as it floated under the beech groves at Bisham, or during his wanderings in the neighbouring country, which is distinguished for its peculiar beauty." According to Peacock, Shelley wrote *Laon and Cythna* in the summer of 1817, "chiefly on a seat on a high prominence in Bisham wood, where he passed whole mornings with a blank book and a pencil." Shelley tells us in his preface that little more than six months were occupied in its composition. "That period has been devoted to the task with unremitting ardour and enthusiasm." It was completed by September 23, 1817.

called "Alastor," at Baldwin's: the sale, I believe, was scarcely
anything, but as the printer has sent me in his account I wish to
know also how my account stands with the publisher. He had no
interest in the Work, nor do I know that anyone else had. It is
scarcely worth while to [do]¹ anything else with it, other than to
try to procure a business-like reply on the subject of the state of
what is to pay or receive. In case this commission is unusual or
disagreeable to you for any reason of which I may be ignorant, I
beg you will not scruple to decline it.

I hope "Frankenstein" did not give you too bad dreams, and
remain, Dear Sir,

Your very obedient servant,

P. B. SHELLEY.

Can you lend me the sixth volume of Gibbon's "Rome"?

[Addressed]
MR. OLLIER,
  Bookseller,
  3 *Welbeck Street, London*

CCCXXXIII
TO MARIANNE HUNT

[*Written by Mary Wollstonecraft Shelley*]

Marlow,
August 16, 1817.

MY DEAR MARIANNE,

In writing your congratulations to Shelley on his birthday did not your naughty
heart smite you with remorse? Did you not promise to look at some brooches, and
send me the descriptions and prices?—But the 4th of August arrived and I had no
present!

I am exceedingly obliged to you for the loan of the caps. But a nurse. I have a
great aversion to the having a Marlow woman,—but I must be provided by the 20th.
What am I to do? I dare say Mrs. Lucas is out at present, but she may be disengaged
by that time.

I am sorry to observe by your letter that you are in low spirits. Cheer up, my dear
little girl, and resolve to be happy. Let me know how it is with you, and how your
health is as your time advances. If it were of any use I would say a word or two against
your continuing to wear stays. Such confinement cannot be either good for you or the
child; and as to shape, I am sure they are very far from becoming.

We are all well here. Our dog, who is a malicious beast whom we intend to send

¹ Word torn off.

away, has again bitten poor little William without any provocation, for I was with him, and he went up to him to stroke his face when the dog snapped at his fingers. Miss Alba is perfectly well and thriving. She crows like a little cock, although (as Shelley bids me say) she is a hen.

Our sensations of indignation have been a little excited this morning by the decision of the Master of Chancery. He says the children are to go to this old clergyman in Warwickshire, who is to stand instead of a parent. An old fellow whom no one knows, and [who] never saw the children. This is somewhat beyond credibility did we not see it in black and white. Longdill is very angry that his proposition is rejected, and means to appeal from the Master to the Lord Chancellor.

I cannot find the sheet of Mrs. T. W. I send you two or three things of yours—the stone cup and the soap dish must wait until someone goes up to town.

I am afraid Hunt takes no exercise or he would not be so ill. I see, however, that you go to the play tolerably often. How are you amused?

The gown must not be dear. But you are as good a judge as I of what to give Milly as a kind of payment from Miss Clifford's mamma for the trouble she has had.

Longdill thought £100 per annum sufficient for both Shelley's children, to provide them with clothes and everything. Why then should we pay £70 for A[llegra]?

The country is very pleasant just now, but I see nothing of it beyond the garden. I am *ennuied*, as you may easily imagine, from want of exercise which I cannot take. The cold bath is of great benefit to me. By-the-bye, what are we to do with it? Have you a place for its reception? It is of such use for H[unt]'s health that you ought not to be without it; we can easily get another. If you should chance to hear of any very amusing book send it in the parcel if you can borrow it from Ollier.

Adieu. Take care of yourself, and do not be dispirited. All will be well one day I do not doubt.

I send you £3.

Shelley sends his love to you all, and thanks for your good wishes and promised present. Pray when is this intended parcel to come?

Affectionately yours,
M. W. S.

[*Written by Shelley*]

I will write to Hunt to-morrow or the day after. Meanwhile kindest remembrances to all, and thanks for your dreams in my favour. Your incantations have not been *quite* powerful enough to expel evil from all revolutions of time. Poor Mary's book came back with a refusal, which has put me rather in ill spirits. Does any kind friend of yours, Marianne, know any bookseller, or has any influence with one? Any of those good tempered Robinsons? All these things are affairs of interest and preconception.

You have seen Clarke about this loan. Well, is there any proposal—Anything in bodily shape? My signature makes any security infallible in fact though not in law,—even if they would not take Hunt's—I shall have more to say on this.

The while—   Your faithful friend,
P. B. S.

239

LETTERS

Great Marlow, Bucks,
August 22, 1817.

GENTLEMEN,

I ought to have mentioned that the novel[1] which I sent you is not my own production, but that of a friend who not being at present in England cannot make the correction you suggest. As to any mere inaccuracies of language I should feel myself authorized to amend them when revising proofs. With respect to the terms of publication, my first wish certainly was to receive on my friend's behalf an adequate price for the copyright of the MS. As it is, however, I beg to submit the following proposal, which I hope you will think fair, particularly as I understand it is an arrangement frequently made by Booksellers with Authors who are new to the world.—It is that you should take the risk of printing, advertising, etc., entirely on yourselves and, after full deduction being made from the profits of the work to cover these expenses that the clear produce, both of the first edition and of every succeeding edition should be divided between you and the author. I cannot in the author's part disclaim all interest in the first edition, because it is possible that there may be no demand for another, and then the profits, however small, will be all that will accrue.

I hope on consideration that you will not think such an arrangement as this unreasonable, or one to which you will refuse your assent.

Gentlemen, I am,
Your very obt. sert.,
PERCY B. SHELLEY.

[Addressed]
MESSRS. LACKINGTON, ALLEN & CO.,
Finsbury Square,
London

---

[1] Mrs. Shelley's *Frankenstein.*

240

LETTERS

Marlow,
September 20, 1817.

My Lord,

I trust you will think the natural affection of a parent for his Children a sufficient excuse for my troubling your Lordship with this letter. At the time your Lordship was sitting in Lincoln's Inn Hall, my Solicitor, Mr. Longdill, in an interview with Mr. Morphett, Mr. Westbrook's Solicitor, informed him that it was my intention, in case your Lordship should not during the Sittings deliver your Judgment on the Petition before you respecting my Children, to apply to your Lordship with a request that during the vacation the Children might be permitted to go on a visit to the family of Mr. Longdill for a fortnight, that I might have an opportunity of seeing them, Mr. Morphett on that occasion stated that there was no necessity of troubling your Lordship on the subject, as he saw no objection to the proposed arrangement. On the 9th instant Mr. Longdill wrote a note to Mr. Morphett requesting that the Children might be permitted to come to him, and having sent several times to Mr. Morphett for an answer without being able to obtain one, Mr. Longdill sent one of his Clerks to Mr. Westbrook's house to request that an answer might be sent, when he was informed that the family and the Children had left town, and on inquiring to what place they were gone, the servant said she had particular directions not to answer that question. Mr. Morphett afterwards informed Mr. Longdill that they were gone to Hastings, and that he had immediately forwarded Mr. Longdill's first and his subsequent letters; but to this moment the only answer which Mr. Longdill has been able to obtain from Mr. Morphett is that Miss Westbrook has not answered his letters. Not having seen one of my children for more than two years, and never having seen the other, I cannot conceive that your Lordship will deem my anxiety for a short and unrestrained intercourse with them either unnatural or improper. From several circumstances,

[1] It does not appear to be certain whether this letter, which was draughted by Longdill, was sent to the Chancellor.—See Dowden's *Life of Shelley*, Vol. II, p. 92 footnote.

with the detail of which I will not trouble your Lordship, I have no hopes of obtaining this gratification without your Lordship's interference, and I therefore hope that your Lordship will do me the favour to cause it to be communicated to Mr. Westbrook's Solicitor that it is your Lordship's desire that the Children may be permitted to make the proposed visit immediately.

I have the honour to remain
Very truly
Your Lordship's most obedient servant,

P. B. S.

To the RIGHT HONOURABLE
THE LORD HIGH CHANCELLOR.

CCCXXXVI
TO LACKINGTON & CO.

Mr. Leigh Hunt's,
13 Lisson Grove North,
Wednesday, Sep. 22, 181[7].

Mr. Shelley presents his Compts—to Messrs. Lackington & Co. and begs to inform them that he expects to remain in Town for a week or fortnight and that during that [time?] the proofs may be addressed as[1] a[bove].

[1] The letter is mutilated; the word "below" has been cancelled here. The proofs referred to must have been for *Frankenstein.*

XIII

SEPTEMBER 24, 1817, TO MARCH 12, 1818

MARLOW—THE REVOLT OF ISLAM

CCCXXXVII
TO LORD BYRON

*13, Lisson Grove North (Leigh Hunt's),
Paddington,
September 24, 1817.*

MY DEAR LORD BYRON,

Since I received your letter, my own destination has been so uncertain, that I have taken no steps about the little girl. I shall, if possible, spend this winter at Pisa, and in that case I shall be myself the lion to the little Una. If I am compelled to remain in England, I shall commit her to the charge of some person on whom I can entirely depend. My health is in a miserable state, so that some care will be required to prevent it speedily terminating in death. Such an event it is my interest and duty to prevent; nor am I indifferent to the pleasures of this scene of things. They recommend Italy as a certain remedy for my disease.[1]

I told you what I thought of "Manfred." The impression of the public seems, as far as I can judge, to be the same. "The Lament of Tasso" I do not think so perfect and sustained a composition. There are passages, indeed, most wonderfully impressive; and those lines in which you describe the youthful feelings of Tasso; that indistinct consciousness of its own greatness, which a heart of genius cherishes in solitude, amid neglect and contempt, have a profound and thrilling pathos which I will confess to you, whenever I turn to them, make my head wild with tears. The *Edinburgh*

---

[1] Shelley went to London on September 23 (with the manuscript of his poem *Laon and Cythna*) accompanied by Clare, to consult Mr. William Lawrence, a pupil of Abernethy, with regard to his health. He stayed with Hunt at his new residence, 13 Lisson Grove, apparently until October 13. The physician recommended change of air and scene, and Shelley was inclined towards spending the winter in Italy, on his own account, and in order to place Alba (the name by which Allegra was known at this time) under her father's care.

LETTERS

Review praises "Manfred" excessively, yet far less than it deserves; because their praise, though unbounded, is studied and cold. You know I live out of the world, and hear nothing. Hunt, who has a very great esteem and interest for you, thinks with me that the 3rd Canto[2] is the finest specimen of your powers yet exhibited. His taste considerably differs from mine in some other respects. He does not like "Manfred," not because it is defective in power and imagination, but because, as he alleges, it administers to a diseased view of things. I should say that some of your earlier writings had that tendency, but that "Manfred" was free from it. We are all most anxious for the 4th Canto, and hope to hear some news of the fair Venetian.

Since I wrote to you last, Mary has presented me with a little girl.[3] We call it Clara. Little Alba and William, who are fast friends, and amuse themselves with talking a most unintelligible language together, are dreadfully puzzled by the stranger, whom they consider very stupid for not coming to play with them on the floor.

I have been engaged this summer, heart and soul, in one pursuit. I have completed a poem which, when it is finished, though I do not tax your patience to read it, I will send you. It is in the style and for the same object as "Queen Mab," but interwoven with a story of human passion, and composed with more attention to the refinement and accuracy of language, and the connexion of its parts. Some friends speak favourably of it, and particularly Hunt, whose opinion is very flattering. It *is* to be *published*—for I am not of your opinion as to religion, &c., and for this simple reason, that I am careless of the consequences as they regard myself. I only feel persecution bitterly, because I bitterly lament the depravity and mistake of those who persecute. As to me, I can but die; I can but be torn to pieces, or devoted to infamy most undeserved; and whether this is inflicted by the necessity of nature, and circumstances, or through a principle, pregnant, as I believe, with important benefit to mankind, is an alternative to which I cannot be indifferent.

[2] *Childe Harold*, canto iii.
[3] Shelley's daughter, Clara Everina, born on September 2, 1817, and named after Clare Clairmont, and (apparently) Mary Shelley's aunt, Everina Wollstonecraft.

246

I see Newstead has been advertised for sale, and not found a purchaser. So the papers say. Can nothing save Newstead? I wish it had so happened that I had the redemption of it.

Clare is well, but anxious. I have said nothing to her which you do not authorize. Mary is recovering from her accouchement; she is one of those many persons who, together with myself, remember you with interest and regard.

Most sincerely yours,

P. B. SHELLEY.

CCCXXXVIII
TO MARY WOLLSTONECRAFT SHELLEY
Marlow

[13 *Lisson Grove North, London*],
October 6, 1817.

MY OWN DEAREST LOVE—

You will not see me tomorrow—I will try if possible to come by the Wednesday's coach, if I do not hear any thing in the mean time from you to detain me.

My own Mary would it not be better for you to come to London at once? I think we could quite as easily do some thing with the house if you were in London: that is to say all of you; as in the Country. In that case I would advise the packing up of all the books which we determine to take with us in a large box, and sending them here in the first instance. I would then lock up the library and leave the cook in the house until something was done; first seeing Madocks, and putting the safety of the whole in his charge. I mean you should do that, if you like this proposal. If not write instantly, directing to Longdills, or else I shall not get your letter in time. Write at all events and if you negative my proposal I will come down the same evening, if possible: or at least will write by the coach and come down the next.

We must go to Italy, on every ground. This weather does me

247

great mischief. I nurse myself, and these kind people nurse me with great care. I think of you, my own beloved, and study the minutest things relative to my health. I suffer to day with violent bowl complaint attended with pain in the side which I dare say will relieve me but which prevents me to day from going out at all. I have thus put off engagements with Longdill and Godwin, which must be done to-morrow.

I have borrowed £250 from H[orace] S[mith],[1] which is now at my banker's.

Dearest and best of living beings how much do your letters console me when I am away from you.—Your letter today gave me the greatest delight. So soothing so powerful and quiet are your expressions, that it is almost like folding you to my heart. To-morrow therefore beloved I shall n[ot co]me, but the day after, certainly, if you decide on that.

I should take rather spacious lodgings if you come up.

I shall forget none of your commissions.

Kiss all the little ones, poor little William—is he so cold?—and Alba and Clara.

My most affect. love to Clare, and tell her that I have offered her book to Lackingtons and to Taylor and Hessey, and that they have both declined.

I can scarcely write to day, but shall be better to-morrow. Adieu only dearest love take twenty kisses to your sweet lips.

P. B. S.

[Addressed]
MRS. SHELLEY,
Albion House,
Marlow, Bucks
[Postmarks]
OC. 6. 1817
[and]
CRAWFOR[D] STREET

[1] On October 2, 1817, Shelley paid Smith a cheque for £60, and on July 25, 1818, he wrote his bankers, Brookes & Co., from Bagni di Lucca: "Gentlemen, three bills drawn by me upon Mr. Horatio Smith, I request you will be so good as to pay when presented. They are each for fifty Pounds. I have the honour to be, Gentlemen, your most obed. Sert., Percy Bysshe Shelley."

LETTERS

[13 *Lisson Grove North, London,*
October 8, 1817.]

MY SWEETEST AND ONLY LOVE,

The anxiety which I have suffered for the last two days has been very great. I did not get your letter till this morning, or rather this evening when I went to Longdill's. I sent and went in vain to Hookham's. I am now relieved, and perhaps she whom I love far more than myself, and whose anxieties are far more painful to me than my own, is at this moment wondering if I shall come this evening, and will be so disappointed if I do not—I shall not come. I waited and waited for your letter, and was too late for the Coach.

Now, dearest, let me talk to you. I think we ought to go to Italy. I think my health might receive a renovation there, for want of which perhaps I shall never entirely overcome that state of diseased action which is so painful to my beloved. I think Alba ought to be with her father—This is a thing of incredible importance to the happiness perhaps, of many human beings. It might be managed without our going there. Yes, but not without an expense which would in fact suffice to settle us comfortably in a spot where I might be regaining that health which you consider so valuable. It is valuable to you my own dearest I see too plainly that you will never be quite happy till I am well. Of myself I do not speak, for I feel only for you.

First, then, Money.—I am sure that if I ask Horace Smith he will lend me 200 or even 250 more. I did not like to do it from delicacy, and a wish to take only just enough. But I am quite certain he would lend me the money.

Next—the House. We have decided at all events to quit it.[1] Let us look the truth boldly in the face. We gave we will say 1200 for the house—Well—we can get if we like £60 a year for the bare walls, and sell the furniture so as to realize £75 for every 100.

---

[1] In a letter from Marlow to Mr. W. T. Baxter, December 3, 1817, Mary Shelley says: "This house is very damp; all the books in the library are mildewed. We must quit it. Italy is yet uncertain."

This is losing scarcely any thing especially if we consider it in fact only so much money borrowed on Post-Obit—which in fact is cheaper than ever before.

But all this is nothing. Godwin!—Well, I am trying what I can do now, and I am not quite hopeless. I forgot about the house to mention the other side of the alternative which is, to let it furnished. This is not so well. My advice is that you should come to Town, and prepare for departure.

I shall be with you my beloved tomorrow evening; but I *may* not, as I have an appointment with Longdill, which it is *barely possible* should not be . . .[2]

CCCXL
TO A PUBLISHER[1]

13 *Lisson Grove North,*
October 13, 1817.

SIR,

I send you the four first sheets of my poem entitled "Laon and Cythna, or the Revolution of the Golden City."

I believe this commencement affords a sufficient specimen of the work. I am conscious, indeed, that some of the concluding cantos, when "the plot thickens" and human passions are brought into more critical situations of development, are written with more energy and clearness; and that to see a work of which unity is one of the qualifications aimed at by the author in a disjointed state is, in a certain degree, unfavourable to the general impression. If, however, you submit it to Mr. Moore's judgment, he will make due allowance for these circumstances. The whole poem, with the exception of the first canto and part of the last, is a mere human

[2] The letter, which is in the Bodleian Library, consists of four quarto pages and is evidently incomplete, as it breaks off in the middle of a sentence at the end of the fourth page. There is neither date, address, nor signature.

[1] It is not known to whom this letter was addressed, but Professor Dowden suggests a member of the firm of Longman & Co., who had lately published Moore's *Lalla Rookh.*

story without the smallest intermixture of supernatural interference. The first canto is indeed in some measure a distinct poem,
though very necessary to the wholeness of the work. I say this
because if it were all written in the manner of the first canto, I
could not expect that it would be interesting to any great number
of people. I have attempted in the progress of my work to speak to
the common elementary emotions of the human heart, so that
though it is the story of violence and revolution, it is relieved by
milder pictures of friendship and love and natural affections. The
scene is supposed to be laid in Constantinople and modern Greece,
but without much attempt at minute delineation of Mahometan
manners. It is in fact a tale illustrative of such a Revolution as
might be supposed to take place in an European nation, acted
upon by the opinions of what has been called (erroneously, as I
think) the modern philosophy, and contending with antient notions and the supposed advantage derived from them to those who
support them. It is a revolution of this kind that is the *beau ideal*,
as it were, of the French Revolution, but produced by the influence
of individual genius and not out of general knowledge. The
authors of it are supposed to be my hero and heroine, whose names
appear in the title. My private friends have expressed to me a very
high, and therefore I do not doubt, a very erroneous judgment of
my work. However, of this I can determine neither way. I have
resolved to give it a fair chance, and my wish, therefore, is, first, to
know whether you would purchase my interest in the copyright—
an arrangement which, if there be any truth in the opinions of my
friends Lord Byron and Mr. Leigh Hunt of my powers, cannot be
disadvantageous to you; and, in the second place, how far you are
willing to be the publisher of it on my own account if such an
arrangement, which I should infinitely prefer, cannot be made.

I rely, however, on your having the goodness at least to send the
sheets to Mr. Moore, and ask his opinion of their merits.

I have the honour to be, Sir,
Your very obedient servant,
PERCY B. SHELLEY.

251

LETTERS

Albion House, [Marlow],
October 28, 1817.

GENTLEMEN,

I thought it necessary just to say that I shall not find it necessary in future to trouble the printer with any considerable alteration such as he will find in the present sheet, and that which immediately preceded it. But the alterations will be found of the last importance to the interest of the tale.[1]

Gentlemen,
Your obedt. Servt.,
P. B. SHELLEY.

[Addressed]
MESSRS. LACKINGTON & CO.

19 Mabledon Place, [Euston Road, London],
November 12, 1817.

DEAR SIR,

I inclose what I have written of a pamphlet[1] on the subject of our conversation the other evening. I wish it to be sent to press without an hour's delay—I don't think the whole will make a pamphlet larger [or] so large as my last, but the printer can go on with this and send me a proof and the rest of the MSS. shall be sent

[1] Mary Shelley's *Frankenstein.*

[1] Apparently his pamphlet entitled "An address to the People on the Death of the Princess Charlotte. By the Hermit of Marlow." It has been stated that the pamphlet was not published and that not more than twenty copies were printed. If printed, no copy of the original address is known to have survived, but what is described as a "reprint," by Thomas Rodd (not later than 1843) with the motto "We pity the Plumage, but forget the Dying Bird," is not uncommon.

before evening. If you should have any objections to publish it you can state them as soon as the whole is printed before the title goes to press, though I don't think that you will, as the subject though treated boldly is treated delicately.

Your obedient servant,

P. B. SHELLEY.

CCCXLIII
TO CHARLES OLLIER
London

Marlow,
Nov. 25, 1817.

DEAR SIR,
I have not yet seen the announce[ment] of "Laon and Cythna" in the public papers.—Be so good as not to let it be delayed a day longer, as the books are now ready.

I wish a parcel of *twelve* to be sent to me as soon as you can get them put in boards. If you will send me the account of the expense of the advertisements I will transmit you the money the moment they appear. Dear Sir,

Your most obet.,

PERCY B. SHELLEY.

Send one of Hunt's *Examiner*[1] the first thing.—Dante? and the "Spectator"?

[Addressed]
MR. OLLIER,
Bookseller,
3 *Welbeck Street,*
London
[Postmark] 26 Nov., 1817

[1] The *Examiner* for November 30 contained a long extract from *Laon and Cythna*: ". . . . a poem just published by Percy Shelley," beginning "I had a little sister whose fair eyes" down to "the enchanted waves that child of glory sung." Shelley may have contributed this quotation, or perhaps he was aware that Hunt intended to print it, and wished to have a copy of the paper as soon as it appeared. Dante and the *Spectator* may have been books that Shelley had ordered.

LETTERS

Marlow,
Nov. 28, 1817.

MY DEAR HOGG,

Mary desires me to say that she has received your letter, and that she unites with me in saying that she shall be happy to see you as soon as you can get free from the numberless briefs which no doubt are pouring into your vestibule.

The weather is delightful and so unseasonably fine that yellow and blue flowers are blooming in the hedges, and the primroses are blowing in the garden as if it was spring: a few days may cover them all with snow.

Peacock has finished his poem,[1] which is a story of classical mystery and magic—the transfused essence of Lucian, Petronius, and Apuleius. I have not heard it all, but in a few days he will send it to the Press.

I am at this moment not very classically employed, nor have I summoned courage to accept Scapula as my mentor and guide thro' the bowers of Greek delight.

Might I not, by a confidence in Scapula, lose the end while busied about the means; and exchange the embraces of a living and tangible Calypso for the image of a Penelope, who, though wise, can never again be young.

Adieu.   Yours very sincerely,

P. B. SHELLEY

[Addressed]
  T. JEFFERSON HOGG,
    1 *Garden Court,*
      Temple.   London

---

[1] *Rhododaphne,* published in 1818.

LETTERS

Marlow,
Dec. 1, 1817.

MY DEAR GODWIN,

Mandeville has arrived this evening. Mary is now reading it—and I am like a man on the brink of a precipice, or a ship whose sails are all to wind for the storm.

What do you mean by saying that you shall be in a state of unusual disquiet for the next two weeks? Is it money or literary affairs? I am extremely sorry to hear that Iveson has put you off. I am to the last degree serious and earnest in the affair, and I can place no trust but in Evans. I have written to Longdill as enclosed.

My health has suffered somewhat of a relapse since I saw you, attended with pulmonary symptoms. I do not found much hope on physicians—their judgments are all dissimilar, and their prescriptions alike ineffectual. I shall, at all events quit this damp situation, as soon as an opportunity offers; and I am strongly impelled to doubt whether Italy might not decide in my frame the contest between disease and youth in favour of life. The precariousness arising out of these considerations makes me earnest that something should be done, and speedily, with Evans. I shall then be free, whatever I ought to do. Until then I consider myself bound to you.

Adieu. Most affectionately yours,

P. B. S.

My best respects to Mrs. Godwin—does she think of paying us a visit?

Clare bids me say that the enclosed thing is a measure, and that she sends her love to her mother.

[Addressed]
W. GODWIN, Esq.

255

LETTERS

CCCXLVI
TO LACKINGTON & CO.
London

Marlow,
Dec. 3, 1817.

GENTLEMEN,

Inclosed is a dedication which has been transmitted to me by the author of "Frankenstein,"[1] and which should be printed as is customary immediately subsequent to the Title. How soon do you propose to publish it?

Your very obed. Servant,

PERCY B. SHELLEY.

[Addressed]
MESSRS. LACKINGTON & CO.,
Finsbury Square,
London

CCCXLVII
TO CHARLES OLLIER
London

Marlow,
Dec. 3, 1817.

DEAR SIR,

That M°Millan[1] is an obstinate old dog and as troublesome as he is impudent; 'tis a mercy, as the old women say, that I got him thro' the poem at all.

Let him print the errata, and say at the top if he likes, that it was all the Author's fault, and that he is as immaculate as the Lamb of God. Only let him do it directly, or if he won't, let someone else.

I forgot to say that Alastor might be advertised at the end of the

---

[1] The dedication appeared in the book in the following words: "To William Godwin, author of *Political Justice, Caleb Williams*, etc. These volumes are respectfully inscribed by the author."

[1] The printer of *Laon and Cythna*, who produced an edition of 750 copies at Shelley's expense. McMillan had probably drawn attention to some of these passages in the poem to which Ollier afterwards took objection.

256

advertisement of this poem. If there should be a demand for a second edition of Alastor, I should reprint it with many others in my possession now.

I should be glad to hear any news that is authentic and that would mark the feeling of people public or private respecting the Poem.

I am totally indifferent as to whether it be good or bad.

On the opposite page you will find a thing to print with the errata.

Will you be so obliging as to charge yourself with sending the enclosed advertisement to the Morning Chronicle and the Times, to be inserted twice in each. I enclose this letter in a parcel to London. Dear Sir,

Your obliged servant,

PERCY B. SHELLEY.

CCCXLVIII
TO CHARLES OLLIER
London

Marlow,
Dec. 7, 1817.

DEAR SIR,
Pray be so good as to send me if possible by return of coach, the "Purgatorio" and "Paradiso"[1] of Dante, in English and Italian, by Carey [*sic*] and what other books may be ready, also the "Dionysiaca" of Nonnus. It is likeliest to be found at Priestley's, the classical bookseller.

I am, Sir, your obliged

PERCY B. SHELLEY.

[1] The translation of Dante, by the Rev. Henry Francis Cary (1772–1844). The *Inferno* was published in 1805, and was followed by the *Purgatorio* and *Paradiso* in 1814.

257

LETTERS

Marlow,
Dec. 7, 1817.

MY DEAR GODWIN

To begin with the subject of most immediate interest.—Close with Richardson. And when I say this what relief should I not feel from a thousand distressing emotions if I could believe that he was in earnest in his offer! I have not heard from Longdill, though I wrote urgently for information.

My health has been materially worse. My feelings at intervals are of a deadly and torpid kind, or awakened to a state of such unnatural and keen excitement that only to instance the organ of sight, I find the very blades of grass and the boughs of distant trees present themselves to me with microscopical distinctness. Towards evening I sink into a state of lethargy and inanimation, and often remain for hours on the sofa between sleep and waking a prey to the most painful irritability of thought. Such with little intermission is my condition. The hours devoted to study are selected with vigilant caution from among these periods of endurance. It is not for this that I think of travelling to Italy, even if I knew that Italy would relieve me. But I have experienced a decisive pulmonary attack, and, although at present it has past away without any very considerable vestige of its existence, yet this symptom sufficiently shows the true nature of my disease to be consumptive. It is to my advantage that this malady is in its nature slow, and, if one is sufficiently alive to its advances is susceptible of cure from a warm climate. In the event of its assuming any decided shape, it *would be my duty* to go to Italy without delay; and it is only when that measure becomes an indispensable duty that, contrary both to Mary's feelings and to mine as they regard you, I shall go to Italy. I need not remind you, besides the mere pain endured by the survivors, of the train of evil consequences which my death would cause to ensue. I am thus circumstantial and explicit because you seem to have misunderstood me. It is not health, but life, that I should seek in Italy, and that, not for my own sake—I feel that I am capable of trampling on all such weakness—but for the sake of those to whom my life may be a source of happiness, utility, security, and honour, and to some of whom my death might be all that is the reverse.

I ought to say I cannot persevere in the meat diet.

What you say of Malthus fills me, as far as my intellect is concerned, with life and strength. I believe that I have a most anxious desire that the time should quickly come that, even so far as you are personally concerned, you should be tranquil and independent. But when I consider the intellectual lustre with which you clothe this world, and how much the last generation of mankind may be benefited by that light flowing forth without the intervention of one shadow, I am elevated above all thoughts which tend to you or to myself as an individual, and become, by sympathy, part of those distant and innumerable minds to whom your writings must be present.

I meant to have written to you about Mandeville[1] solely. But I was so irritable and weak that I could not write, although I thought I had much to say. I have read Mandeville, but I must read it again soon. For the interest is of that irresistible and overwhelming kind, that the mind in its influence is like a cloud borne on by an impetuous wind, like one breathlessly carried forward, who has no time to pause or observe the causes of his career. I think the *power* of Mandeville is inferior to nothing you have done, and, were it not for the character of Falkland,[2] no instance in which you have exerted that power of *creation* which you possess beyond all contemporary writers might compare with it. Falkland is still alone; power is in Falkland not as in Mandeville. Tumult hurried onward by the tempest, but Tranquillity standing unshaken amid its fiercest rage. But "Caleb Williams" never shakes the deepest soul like Mandeville. It must be said of the latter, you rule with a rod of iron. The picture is never bright, and we wonder whence you drew the darkness with which its shades are

---

[1] Shelley's critique of Godwin's *Mandeville*, which had been recently published, appeared in the form of a letter in the last number of the *Examiner* for 1817, with the initials E. K., that is, Elfin Knight, Mary's familiar name for Shelley. See Letter No. CCCLII, p. 265.
[2] In Godwin's novel, *Caleb Williams*.

259

deepened, until the epithet of tenfold might almost cease to be a metaphor. The *noun smorfia*[3] touches some cord within us with such a cold and jarring power, that I started, and for some time could scarce believe but that I was Mandeville, and that this hideous grin was stamped upon my own face. In style and strength of expression, Mandeville is wonderfully great, and the energy and the sweetness of the sentiments scarcely to be equalled. Cliffords character as mere beauty is a divine and soothing contrast; and I do not think, if perhaps, I except (and I know not if I ought to do so) the speech of Agathon in the Symposium of Plato—that there ever was produced a moral discourse more characteristic of all that is admirable and lovely in human Nature—more lovely and admirable in itself—than that of Henrietta to Mandeville as he is recovering from madness. Shall I say that, when I discovered that she was pleading all this time secretly for her lover, and when at last she abandoned—weakly abandoned poor Mandeville, I felt an involuntary and, perhaps, an unreasonable pang? Adieu

Always most affectionately yours,

P. S.

We will speak another time, of what is deeply interesting both to Mary and to myself, of your William.

[*Written by Mary*]

Will you ask Mamma to be so kind as to get next door to 41 a yard and a nail of gold band for little Willy's hat and send it by ye next coach. All our loves.

[Addressed]
WILLIAM GODWIN, Esq.,
41 *Skinner St., Holborn,*
London
[Postmark]
MARLOW
[and]
8 DE 8
1817

[3] Italian for "grimace."

LETTERS

TO WILLIAM THOMAS BAXTER

Marlow,
Dec. 10, 1817.

MY DEAR SIR,
We have neither heard from you announcing any intelligence of your own family, or, what is of far less consequence, the receipt of my cheque for 7£.[1] We heard at once of Mr. Booth's illness and recovery,[2] and I hope he is so far recovered and so much at leisure as to make it no compliment to say that we wish you would visit us here once more. Mary desires me to give you her kindest remembrances, and to ask if you have heard from Isabel and the others in the North and how they are.

Most truly yours,

P. B. SHELLEY.

[Addressed]
W. T. BAXTER, Esq.,
117 *Dorset Street,*
Salisbury Square, Fleet Street

[1] This amount was in payment for some blankets (such as were supplied to the British officers while serving in the Peninsula) that Shelley had asked Baxter to obtain for him from Scotland, for distribution to the poor at Marlow. Mrs. Shelley says that while visiting the poor in the winter of 1817-18 he sustained a severe attack of ophthalmia.
[2] David Booth, a brewer of Newburg, Fifeshire, was a man of advanced political and religious opinions, and a friend of William Godwin, to whom he introduced his friend William Thomas Baxter, a Dundee merchant, when he visited London in 1809. Baxter, who had five daughters of his own, invited Mary Godwin to Scotland, where she arrived in June, 1812, and she stayed there some months. Isabel Baxter, the youngest of the family, became a close friend of Mary, with whom she corresponded on her return to London until July, 1814, when, after another visit to Scotland, Mary eloped with Shelley. In the meantime David Booth married Isabel Baxter, who was twenty-nine years his junior, and insisted that the correspondence between his wife and Mary should cease. In 1817, after Shelley's marriage with Mary, the correspondence was renewed, and in the autumn of that year Mr. Booth and Mr. Baxter came to London. During September Baxter visited Marlow and was most favourably impressed by Shelley. Mr. Booth, however, declined to meet the poet, and when he heard that his wife had been invited to accompany the Shelleys on their proposed visit to the Continent, he insisted that her correspondence with Mary (which had been resumed without his knowledge) should be discontinued. On December 3 Mrs. Shelley had addressed a chatty letter (mentioning the cheque) to Mr. Baxter, asking why Mrs. Booth had not written to her. As Baxter did not reply, Shelley wrote him the above letter. An account of Shelley's association with the Baxter family, from which the particulars in this note are derived, was contributed by Miss Isobel Stuart to the *Star* in February and March, 1894. Shelley's two letters are here reprinted from these articles by kind permission of the editor of that newspaper.

LETTERS

TO CHARLES OLLIER
London

Marlow,
December 11, 1817.

DEAR SIR,

It is to be regretted that you did not consult your own safety and advantage (if you consider it connected with the non-publication of my book)[1] before your declining the publication, after having accepted it, would have operated to so extensive and serious an injury to my views as now. The instances of abuse and menace which you cite were such as you expected, and were, as I conceived, prepared for. If not, it would have been just to me to have given them their due weight and consideration before. You foresaw, you foreknew, all that these people would say. You do your best to condemn my book before it is given forth, because you publish it, and then withdraw; so that no other bookseller will publish it, because one has already rejected it. You must be aware of the great injury which you prepare for me. If I had never consulted your advantage, my book would have had a fair hearing. But now it is first published, and then the publisher, as if the

---

[1] *Laon and Cythna*. Peacock says: "In this poem he [Shelley] had carried the expression of his opinions, moral, political and theological, beyond the bounds of discretion. The terror which, in those days of persecution of the Press, the perusal of the book inspired in Mr. Ollier, the publisher, induced him to solicit the alterations of many passages which he had marked. Shelley was for some time inflexible; but Mr. Ollier's refusal to publish the poem as it was, backed by the advice of all his friends, induced him to submit to the required changes. Many leaves were cancelled, and it was finally published" as "The Revolt of Islam;/a Poem,/In twelve cantos./By Percy Bysshe Shelley./ London:/Printed for C. and J. Ollier, 3 Welbeck-Street;/By B. M'Millan, Bow-Street, Covent Garden."/ Of *Laon and Cythna* "only three copies had gone forth. One of these had found its way to the *Quarterly Review*, and the opportunity was readily seized of pouring out on it one of the most malignant effusions of the *odium theologicum* that ever appeared even in those days, and in that periodical." Peacock adds that when Ollier positively refused to publish the poem as it was, "Shelley had no hope of another publisher. He for a long time refused to alter a line: but his friends finally prevailed on him to submit. Still he could not, or would not, sit down by himself to alter it, and the whole of the alterations were actually made in successive sittings of what I may call a literary committee. He contested the proposed alterations step by step: in the end, sometimes adopting, more frequently modifying, never originating, and always insisting that his poem was spoiled." (*Fraser's Magazine*, January, 1860, March, 1862.) It would appear that the alterations were practically made on December 15 when Ollier was at Marlow (see Letter No. CCCLIII). Shelley, however, may have discussed the subject previously with Peacock, who was probably at Shelley's house when the alterations were actually made.

author had deceived him as to the contents of the work—and as if the inevitable consequence of its publication would be ignominy and punishment—and as if none should dare to touch it or look at it—retracts, at a period when nothing but the most extraordinary and unforeseen circumstances can justify the retraction.

I beseech you to reconsider the matter, for your sake no less than for my own. Assume the high and secure ground of courage. The people who visit your shop, and the wretched bigot who gave his worthless custom to some other bookseller, are not the public. The public respect talent; and a large portion of them are already undeceived with regard to the prejudices which my book attacks. You would lose some customers, but you would gain others. Your trade would be diverted into a channel more consistent with your own principles. Not to say that a publisher is in no wise pledged to all the opinions of his publications, or to any; and that he may enter his protest with each copy sold, either against the truth or the discretion of the principles of the books he sells. But there is a much more important consideration in the case. You are, and have been to a certain extent, the publisher. I don't believe that, if the book was quietly and regularly published, the Government would touch anything of a character so refined, and so remote from the conceptions of the vulgar. They would hesitate before they invaded a member of the higher circles of the republic of letters. But, if they see us tremble, they will make no distinctions; they will feel their strength. You might bring the arm of the law down upon us by flinching now. Directly these scoundrels see that people are afraid of them, they seize upon them and hold them up to mankind as criminals already convicted by their own fears. You lay yourself prostrate, and they trample on you. How glad they would be to seize on any connection of Hunt's by his most powerful of all their arms—the terrors and self-condemnation of their victim. Read all the *ex officio* cases, and see what reward booksellers and printers have received for their submission.

If, contrary to common sense and justice, you resolve to give me up, you shall receive no detriment from a connection with me in small matters, though you determine to inflict so serious a one on me in great. You shall not be at a farthing's expense. I shall still, so far as my powers extend, do my best to promote your interest. On the contrary supposition, even admitting you derive no benefit from the book itself—and it should be my care that you shall do so—I hold myself ready to make ample indemnity for any loss you may sustain.

There is one compromise you might make, though that would be still injurious to me. Sherwood and Neely wished to be the principal publishers. Call on them, and say that it was through a mistake that you undertook the principal direction of the book, as it was *my wish* that it should be theirs, and that I have written to you to that effect. This, if it would be advantageous to you, would be detrimental to, but not utterly destructive of, my views. To withdraw your name entirely, would be to inflict on me a bitter and undeserved injury.

Let me hear from you by return of post. I hope that you will be influenced to fulfil your engagement with me, and proceed with the publication, as justice to me, and, indeed, a well-understood estimate of your own interest and character, demand. I do hope that you will have too much regard to the well-chosen motto of your seal[2] to permit the murmurs of a few bigots to outweigh the serious and permanent considerations presented in this letter. To their remonstrances you have only to reply, "I did not write the book; I am not responsible; here is the author's address— state your objections to him. I do no more than sell it to those who inquire for it; and, if they are not pleased with their bargain, the author empowers me to receive the book and to return the money." As to the interference of Government, nothing is more improbable [than] that in any case it would be attempted; but, if it should, it would be owing entirely to your perseverance in the groundless apprehensions which dictated your communication received this day, and conscious terror would be perverted into an argument of guilt.

I have just received a most kind and encouraging letter from Mr. Moore on the subject of my poem. I have the fairest chance of the public approaching my work with unbiassed and unper-

2 "In omnibus libertas."

verted feeling: the fruit of reputation (and you know for *what purposes* I value it) is within my reach. It is for you, now you have been once named as publisher, and have me in your power, to blast all this, and to hold up my literary character in the eye of mankind as that of a proscribed and rejected outcast. And for no evil that I have ever done you, but in return for a preference which, although you falsely now esteem injurious to you, was solicited by Hunt, and conferred by me, as a source and a proof of nothing but kind intentions.

Dear Sir,
I remain your sincere well-wisher,

PERCY B. SHELLEY.

CCCLII
TO WILLIAM GODWIN
London

Marlow,
Dec. 11, 1817.

MY DEAR GODWIN
I have received the two parts of your long and interesting letter and will speak of it, the moment I have dispatched a word about business. I have had a letter from Longdill, saying no more than that he has had one communication with Gordon's attorney, in which the price of the farm was fixed by him at £4000 and that they are now pausing to consider this proposal. The rental of the farm scarcely exceeds £200 a year,—therefore if Longdill's proposal succeeds it is obvious how great will be our advantage in point of terms.—I am very anxious to hear of Richardson and Iveson.

If I had believed it possible you should send any part of my letter to the *Chronicle*, I should have expressed more fully my sentiments of Mandeville, and of the author. As it is, I cannot but be gratified that you should think any opinion of mine relating to your book worthy of being presented to the public. The effect of your favourable considerations of my powers, as they relate to the judgement of the degree and kind of approbation due to the intellectual exertions of others has emboldened me to write—not a volume, but a more copious statement of my feelings as they were excited by Mandeville. This I have sent to the Examiner. If Hunt does not insert it, I will send it to you for your own reading, though it was so written as to be more interesting to the public than to yourself.

I have read and considered all that you say about my general powers, and the particular instance of the Poem in which I have attempted to develop them. Nothing can be more satisfactory to me than the interest which your admonitions express. But I think you are mistaken in some points with regard to the peculiar nature of my powers, whatever be their amount. I listened with deference and self suspicion to your censures of "Laon and Cythna;" but the productions of mine which you commend hold a very low place in my own esteem, and this reassured me, in some degree at least. The poem was produced by a series of thoughts which filled my mind with unbounded and sustained enthusiasm. I felt the precariousness of my life, and I engaged in this task resolved to leave some records of myself. Much of what the volume contains was written with the same feeling, as real, though not so prophetic, as the communications of a dying man. I never presumed indeed to consider it any thing approaching to faultless, but when I considered contemporary productions of the same apparent pretensions, I will own that I was filled with confidence. I felt that it was in many respects a genuine picture of my own mind. I felt that the sentiments were true, not assumed. And in this have I long believed that my power consists in sympathy and that part of imagination which relates to sentiment and contemplation. I am formed, if for anything not in common with the herd of mankind, to apprehend minute and remote distinctions of feeling, whether relative to external nature, or the living beings which surround us, and to communicate the conceptions which result from considering either the moral or the material universe as a whole. Of course I believe these faculties, which perhaps comprehend all that is sublime in man, to exist very imperfectly in my own mind. But when you advert to my Chancery paper, a cold, forced, unimpassioned, insignificant piece of cramped and cautious argument; and to the little scrap about Mandeville, which expressed my feelings indeed, but cost scarcely two minutes thought to express, as specimens of my powers, more favourable than that which grew as it were from "the agony and bloody sweat" of intellectual travail—surely I must feel that in some manner, either I am mistaken in believing that I have any talent at all, or you in the selection of the specimens of it. Yet, after all, I cannot but be conscious, in much of what I write, of an absence of that tranquillity which is the attribute and accompaniment of power. This feeling alone would make your most kind and wise admonitions on the subject of the economy of intellectual force, valuable to me. And, if I live, or if I see any trust in coming years, doubt not but that I shall do something whatever it might be, which a serious and earnest estimate of my powers will suggest to me, and which will be in every respect accommodated to their utmost limits.

This dry and frosty weather fills me with health and spirits; I wish I could believe that it would last: Shall we not see you soon? Why could you not at least for a day or two leave Town? Mrs. Godwin too, how is she and does she not mean to take embargo off her own person? Mary unites with me in best love to all.

> My dear Godwin,
> Most affectionately yours,
> P. B. S.

[Addressed]
WILLIAM GODWIN, ESQ.,
41 Skinner Street,
Snow Hill,
London

[Postmark]
MARLOW
[and]
12 DE 12
1817

LETTERS

CCCLIII
TO CHARLES OLLIER
London

Marlow,
December 13, 1817.

DEAR SIR,

The contents of your letter this morning certainly alters the question.[1] No one is to be blamed, however heavy and unexpected is my disappointment. It is of the greatest importance that we should meet immediately, and, if the state of my health would have permitted I should have come to Town immediately on the receipt of your letter. As it is, I send my servant (that no delay or mistake may take place) with this note.

I need not say that I should be happy to see you if you could contrive to spend a few days with us. But my present letter is written under the persuasion that you could spare no day [letter torn ? so or as] conveniently as Sunday, and in a strong feeling of the *necessity of instant communication with you.*

The mails which pass within a short distance of my house leave Piccadilly at eight o'clock, and you will find a friendly welcome and a warm fire at the end of your journey.

I ought to say that I have received no parcel from you.

Your very obliged sert.,

PERCY B. SHELLEY.

---

[1] In regard to altering certain passages in *Laon and Cythna,* Mary states in her journal that Ollier came down to Marlow on Sunday, December 14; on December 15 the alterations were made in the poem, and finished on the following day, when Ollier returned to London.

LETTERS

CCCLIV
TO THOMAS MOORE
Devizes

Albion House, Marlow,
Dec. 16, 1817.

DEAR SIR,

The present edition of "Laon and Cythna" is to be suppressed, and it will be republished in about a fortnight under the title of "The Revolt of Islam," with some alterations which consist in little else than the substitution of the words *friend* or[1] *lover* for that of *brother* and *sister*. The truth is, that the seclusion of my habits has confined me so much within the circle of my own thoughts, that I have formed to myself a very different measure of approbation or disapprobation for actions than that which is in use among mankind; and the result of that peculiarity, contrary to my intention, revolts and shocks many who might be inclined to sympathise with me in my general views.—As soon as I discovered that this effect was produced by the circumstance alluded to, I hastened to cancel it—not from any personal feeling of terror, or repentance, but from the sincere desire of doing all the good and conferring all the pleasure which might flow from so obscure a person as myself. I don't know why I trouble you with these words, but your kind approbation of the opening of the Poem has emboldened me to believe that this account of my motives might interest you.

The little volume[2] which you have been quicksighted enough to attribute to its real authors is composed of two letters written by[3] me signed *S.*, and some other letters and the Journal signed M., written by Mrs. Shelley. I ought to say that the Journal was written some years ago—the style of it is almost infantine, and it was published in the idea that the Author would never be recognized.—The letters from Geneva were written in the summer of 1816, and the voyage round the lake, described in one of them was made in the society of Lord Byron, and its memory derives from that circumstance the light of an enchantment which can never be

[1] Originally written "&."
[2] *History of a Six Weeks' Tour,* etc., London, 1817.
[3] The original holograph reads "to."

dissolved. I mention this because *you* were often the theme of our conversations, from which I learned that you were intimate with him. I ought to say that Mrs. Shelley, tho' sorry that her secret is discovered, is exceedingly delighted to hear that you have derived any amusement from our book.—Let me say in her defence that the Journal of the Six Weeks' Tour was written before she was seventeen, and that she has another literary secret which I will in a short time ask you to *keep* in return for having *discovered* this.

What right have I to have written all this to you?

Dear Sir. Y[ours][4] very obliged
and sin[cerely],

PER[CY B. SHELLEY].

[Addressed]
[THOMA]s MOORE, ESQ.,
*Sloperton Cottage,
Devizes, Wilts*
[Endorsed by another hand] "MR. SHELLEY."

CCCLV
TO LORD BYRON

*Marlow,
December* 17, 1817.

MY DEAR LORD BYRON,
Since I last wrote to you, I have remained in weekly expectation of leaving England, in which case I should have brought you your little girl in person. But my affairs have been so uncertain that after this constant and gradual delay, it is decided that I must abide in England. So soon as this became evident, I looked about for some respectable person to whom I could confide the little Alba. But here is a difficulty which I cannot overcome. You may conceive how scrupulous I should be in the selection; and you know my secluded mode of life. These circumstances have

---

[4] The letter is torn: I have supplied the words in brackets.

prevented me from finding any person fit for this purpose. I write therefore to ask,—can you suggest any plan? Have you any friend, or person of trust, who is leaving England for Italy? You have a number of powerful friends all devoted to your interests, and anyone of these would be able to procure her conveyance in security to you, if you desired it. I have only to solicit one caution—that under this arrangement Clare's name ought not to be mentioned.

Little Alba, or Clara, as she is now to be called, is grown exquisitely beautiful, and her temper has lost much of its *vivacité*, and has become affectionate, and mild. She is William's playmate, who is so fond of her, that he will be among the many sincere mourners at her departure. They sit on the floor together and amuse themselves for hours in the most sociable way; little William putting more than half the raisins, &c., that are given to him into her mouth. Clare thinks of christening her after herself, but she delays this *important ceremony* until I hear whether you have a predilection for any other name.

From such a recluse and valetudinarian as me you cannot expect news. I intend, however, in a short time to send you a parcel of books (in about a week), which will speak for themselves; and if I find that they will escape the embargo, I will inclose some newspapers. My long Poem under the title of "The Revolt of Islam" is almost printed. You will receive in addition to this Godwin's "Mandeville," a Satanic likeness of Childe Harold the first, and two of three other new books.

We should (I need not say) be extremely happy to hear how you are getting on, and what you are doing—whether you are yet in love, or have been out, and in again. But sincerely, if you knew the interest felt by some of your English friends, I doubt whether you would adhere so severely to the maxim of old—*periturae parcere chartae*, whilst you are so little disposed to spare those which your genius may make eternal. . . .

We *hear* of the 4th and *last* Canto,[1] but have not yet seen it.

Adieu, my dear Lord Byron.

Most sincerely yours,

P. B. SHELLEY.

[1] *Childe Harold.*

LETTERS

CCCLVI
TO CHARLES OLLIER
London

Marlow,
Monday Night. [Probably December 22, 1817.]

DEAR SIR,

I cannot but say that I am extremely desirous that all the copies that have been given forth should, if possible, be returned. If it is *not* possible, I cannot help it.

Do just as you like about Mr. Barton.[1]

I wish, on publication, copies to be sent to all the principal Reviews.

Your obliged sert.,

PERCY B. S.

MR. OLLIER.

CCCLVII
TO LACKINGTON & CO.

I wish to add to the books below, Carey's Dante, the Paradiso and the Purgatorio. I have the Inferno.

Great Marlow,
Albion House—Dec. 23 1817.

GENTLEMEN

Be so good at to let me have copies of Frankestein as soon as they can be put in boards—I think I said, that in addition to the six stipulated for, I wished nine to be sent to make in all fifteen, and the extra copies to be placed to mine or the author's account.— On what day do you propose to publish it?

Be so good as to send me, "Discours sur les Sciences et les Arts

---

[1] This may have been Bernard Barton, the Quaker poet, Charles Lamb's friend and one of the earliest admirers of Shelley's poems. Barton's volume of *Poems*, 1820, contains some verses "To Percy Bysshe Shelley, on His Poems," and in 1822 he published as a pamphlet his *Verses on the Death of Percy Bysshe Shelley.*

par Rousseau, avec les Responses" and the "Dionysiaca" of Nonnus, A Greek Poem of the 5th Century, printed I think at Paris—I owe you 8*s.* I will send the —— [1] when there is enough to make it worth while to write a check.

Your obedient Servant,

P. B. SHELLEY.

[Addressed]
MESSRS. LACKINGTON & CO.,
Finsbury Square

CCCLVIII
TO CHARLES OLLIER
London

Marlow,
December 27, 1817.

DEAR SIR,
I am surprised that I have not received the remainder of the proofs of the Poem.[1] I wish them to be sent immediately; and as soon after as possible, perfect copies of the Book. I have succeeded in procuring the return of two of the copies from Ebers's.[2] Have you been equally fortunate in the application I requested you to make to the other purchaser?

It ought to be *now* advertised as to be published January 10th.

Dear Sir,

Your obliged servant,

P. B. SHELLEY.[3]

[Addressed]
MR. CHAS. OLLIER,
73 *Welbeck St.,*
London

[1] Word indecipherable.
[1] Presumably the cancelled sheets for *The Revolt of Islam.*
[2] Ebers's British and Foreign Circulating Library, 27 Old Bond Street.
[3] From the original holograph in the Wrenn Library, University of Texas, Austin, Texas, U.S.A.

LETTERS

CCCLIX
TO WILLIAM THOMAS BAXTER

Marlow,
December 30, 1817.

MY DEAR SIR,

Your candid explanation is very welcome to me,[1] as it relieves me from a weight of uncertainty, and is consistent with my own mode of treating those who honour me with their friendship—which is, either to maintain with them a free and unsuspicious intercourse, or explicitly to state to them my motives for interrupting or circumscribing it, as soon as they arise within my own mind.

I understand by your letter that you decline, in the name of your family, an intercourse which I believe had its sole foundation in

---

[1] Mr. Booth had influenced his father-in-law (who was his junior by ten years) to break off all relations with Shelley, and Baxter had hoped to do so by leaving his letters unanswered. But on December 25 Shelley wrote again; his letter has not been preserved, but he appears to have complained that Baxter had changed in his manner and not only declined to visit him, but did not think his invitations worth the formality of a refusal. Baxter in his reply of December 29 repudiated the charge of having changed in his manner, and though oppressed with a sense of Shelley's kindness and attention, he excused himself for not visiting Marlow on account of business. He added: "The station your rank and fortune gives you in society, the sphere which it entitled you to move in, are such as I cannot in good conscience introduce my family into, as it could only tend to give them notions and habits of life wholly unsuited to my circumstances, and the humility of their expectations. This independence of fortune, too, has given you a freedom of thought and action entirely inconsistent with the customs, manners, and prejudices of European society with which I have been at pains to imbue their minds, and which I wish not to see eradicated. On all these accounts, although I had not been withheld by business, I should have found myself called on to refrain from visiting you, and to allow that such intimacy to gradually die away, which had nothing in common between us to support it." On receiving the above letter of December 30, Baxter showed it to Mr. Booth, who wrote to Shelley in January 2, 1819: "You have amused yourself in sketching the characters of Mr. Baxter and me. They are composite pictures, and, as a pair of portraits, form together a ludicrous mystical divinity, combining the abstract principles of good and evil, of divinity and demon. With Mr. Baxter you are perhaps entitled to use such freedom, but I apprehend that you have had too little intimacy with me to authorise you to become my calumniator. I have never been yours. I have never accused you of an opinion or of an action which I have not seen avowed and vindicated by your name. I know you only as a stranger. I have never sought your friendship or your correspondence, I have therefore violated no presumptive compact in declining either." After referring to Mary's elopement with Shelley, and her estrangement from her father and Mrs. Booth, and to the renewal of her correspondence with his wife at Godwin's request, he concludes by saying that Baxter's last letter was sent off without him seeing it, and that he "certainly should not have suggested any expression which could have called forth remarks about rank or station. In these I never would acknowledge inferiority." On March 2, before Shelley left England, he took leave of Mr. Baxter; but Mrs. Booth, although in town, neither called nor communicated with Mary Shelley.

the intimacy of Isabel and Mary. This intercourse entirely originated in an unsolicited advance on their part; a change in their opinions and feelings produced it then, and now concludes it. Mary renewed with pleasure the friendship of her early years. I considered her friends as mine, and found much satisfaction, distinct from that duty, in discovering in you, the first of the new circle to whom I was introduced, a man of virtue and talent with whose feelings and opinions I perpetually found occasions of sympathy. To me, a secluded valetudinarian, all this was quite an event. Mary for three whole years had been lamenting the loss of her friend, and was made miserable and indignant that her friendship had been sacrificed to opinions which she supposed had already received their condemnation in the mind of every enlightened reasoner on moral science. Young and ardent spirits confound theory and practice. I saw that all this was in the natural order of things, and it is neither my habit to feel indignation or disappointment at the inconsistencies of mankind. People who had one atom of pride or resentment for injury or neglect would have refused the renewal of an intimacy which had already been once dissolved on a plea, in their conception, to the last degree unworthy and erroneous.

I thus see your determination to deprive Mary of the intercourse of her friend, and most highly respect the motives, as I know they must exist in your mind, for this proceeding. May I ask *precisely what* those motives are? You do not distinctly say, but only allude to certain free opinions which I hold, inconsistent with yours. We had a good deal of discussion about all sorts of opinions, and I thought we agreed on all—except matters of taste; and I don't think any serious consequences ought to flow from a controversy whether Wordsworth or Campbell be the greater poet. Yet I would not be misapprehended. Though I have not a spark of pride or resentment in this matter, I disdain to say a word that should tend to *persuade* you to change your decision. On any such change you know where to find a man constant and sincere in his predilections. But all I now want is to know the plain truth.

Mr. Booth is no doubt a man of great intellectual acuteness and consummate skill in the exercise of logic. I never met a man by

275

whom, in the short time we exchanged ideas, I felt myself excited to so much severe and sustained mental competition, or from whom I derived so much amusement and instruction. It would have given me much pleasure to have cultivated his acquaintance. But I know that this desire could not be reciprocal. Nor is it difficult to apprehend the cause of this distinction. Am I not right in my conjecture in attributing to Mr. Booth the change in your sentiment announced in your letter? His keen and subtle mind, deficient in those elementary feelings which are the *principles* of all moral reasoning, is better fitted for the detection of error than the establishment of truth, and his pleadings, urged or withdrawn with sceptical caution and indifference, may be employed with almost equal force as an instrument of fair argument or sophistry. In matters of abstract speculation we can readily recur to the first principles on which our opinions rest, and thus confute a sophism or derive instructioh from an argument. But in the complicated relations of private life, it is a practice difficult, dangerous, and rare to appeal to an elementary principle; the motives of the sophist are many and secret; the resources of his ingenuity as numerous as the relations respecting which it is exercised. Mr. Booth's reasonings *may* be right; they *may* be sincere; he *may* be conscientiously impressed with views widely differing from mine. But be frank with me, my dear sir, is it not Mr. Booth who has persuaded you to see things in this way since your last visit, when no such considerations as you allege in your letter were present to your thoughts? The only motive that suggests this question is an unwillingness to submit to the having my intimacies made the sport of secret and unacknowledged manœuvres.

I need not say that your expressions of kindness and service are flattering to me, and that I can say with great truth that I should consider myself honoured if at any time it were possible that you should make the limited power which I possess a source of utility to you.

My dear Sir,
Yours most sincerely,
P. B. SHELLEY.

LETTERS

[*Written by Mary Shelley*]

MY DEAR SIR,

You see I prophesied well three months ago, when you were here. I then said that I was sure that Mr. Booth was averse to our intercourse, and would find some means to break it off. I wish I had you by the fire here in my little study, and it might be "double, double, toil and trouble," but I could quickly convince you that your girls are not below me in station, and that in fact I am the fittest companion for them in the world; but I postpone the argument until I see you, for I know (pardon me) that *viva voce* is all in all with you.

CCCLX
TO CHARLES OLLIER

Marlow,
Jan. 2, 1818.

DEAR SIR,

The advertisements of the "Revolt of Islam" ought to contain a notice of "Alastor."

Pray send me copies as quickly as you can—And send me Hunt's new Poems and Lord Byron's New Canto the moment they come out.—Please also to send Altham.

I send a copy of Frankenstein to be bound for me in some neat and appropriate binding. I am curious to know whether your binder will let me have Montaigne, Rousseau, and the Spectator, Theocritus, etc.

I should like to hear your opinion of Frankenstein.

Your very obliged serv.,

PERCY B. SHELLEY

Pray send the accompanying notes to the 2nd Post.[1]

[Endorsed in another hand]
MRS. LAMBERT,
40 *Wigmore St.*

[1] From the original holograph in the Carl H. Pforzheimer collection.

LETTERS

CCCLXI
TO LACKINGTON, ALLEN & CO.

[*January* 2, 1818¹].

GENTLEMEN,

I send a check for £3 on account. I remain your debtor yet a few shillings.

I wish ten additional copies of Frankenstein to be sent which may be placed to mine or to the author's account, as you please. I am not at liberty to send any of these or of those already sent except to the personal friends of the Author. None of these are officially connected with any of the Reviews, and if any of them should express their opinions of the work to the public, it would be solely through the newspapers. I have no influence in any other quarter.

Gentlemen, your obedient sert.

PERCY B. SHELLEY.

CCCLXII
TO ROBERT WAITHMAN¹

Marlow,
4 *January*, 1818.

Mr. Percy Shelley's compliments to Mr. Waithman and send the enclosed check for Mr. Hone's subscription.

¹ Among the collection of Shelley's cheques, formerly in the possession of Mr. W. T. Spencer, there was one in favour of Messrs. Lackington & Co. for £3, dated January 2, 1818, which is possibly the cheque referred to in this letter.

¹ Robert Waithman, Alderman of London 1818, Lord Mayor 1822, M.P. of London 1818–20, 1826–33. His name figures on the list of persons to whom Shelley desired Ollier to send copies of his pamphlet, "A Proposal for putting Reform to the Vote" (see p. 222). *The Champion* for January 11, 1818, contains the notice of a "Subscription for Mr. Hone" and of a meeting of the Friends of the Liberty of the Press and Trial by Jury, held at the City of London Tavern, on Monday, December 29, 1817, Mr. Waithman in the Chair: at which it was resolved unanimously—That the extensive knowledge; the varied talents; the manly intrepidity; the energy of mind; and the unshaken perseverance which enabled Mr. William Hone so dauntlessly to resist the reiterated assaults of Ministerial persecution, entitle him to the gratitude and support of every friend to constitutional freedom.—That a Subscription be now opened, and that the money which may be subscribed, be placed in the hands of a Committee, to promote the permanent welfare of Mr. Hone and his family." Among the subscribers are "Percy B. Shelley, Marlow, £5. 5. 0."; "Leigh and John Hunt, Examiner Office, not what they would, but what they could £5." Shelley's cheque for £5, to the order of Robert Waithman, dated January 5, 1818, was formerly in Mr. W. T. Spencer's possession.

278

LETTERS

Marlow,
Jan. 11, 1818.

DEAR SIR,

I ought to have received copies of the "Revolt of Islam"—
send six—be sure. Pray send them instantly, as I ought to have
exchanged the other for them long ago. Keep it well *advertised*, and
write for money directly the other is gone—"Alastor" may be
adv[ertised] *with it.*

I enclose this note by the Coach.

Your obedient servant,

PERCY B. SHELLEY.

[Addressed]
MR. CHARLES OLLIER,
    Bookseller,
        3 *Welbeck St.,*
            Cavendish Square

Marlow,
Jan. 15, 1818.

DEAR SIR,

Pray send me the copies of my Poem which I requested
immediately or write and assign some reason for their detention.
On second thoughts I wish ten, not six to be sent. I should have
written before, but that I have expected their arrival every night
by the coach.

Inclosed is ten pounds—which be so good as to say that you
have received safe—that no delay may take place in vigorously

advertising. I think I said that I wish under the new circumstances that a copy should be sent to each of the Reviews.

Your obedient servant,

Percy B. Shelley.

Do you hear anything said of "Frankenstein"?

[Addressed]
Mr. Charles Ollier,
  Bookseller,
    3 *Welbeck Street*,
      Cavendish Sq.,
        London

CCCLXV
TO CHARLES OLLIER
London

Marlow,
Jan. 16, 1818.

Dear Sir,

Enclosed is a check for (within a few shillings) the amount of your bill. Can't you *make* the Booksellers subscribe more of the Poem?

Your most obedient servt.,

Percy Bysshe Shelley.

LETTERS

Marlow,
January 22d 1818.

DEAR SIR,

I write now simply to request you to send me *Chapman's Hymns* as they have been published by Triphook—together with any of the numbers of the Collection of Poetry which he is printing—Pray send them immediately without waiting for the other books—I mean *if possible* by tomorrow's Coach—

Munday, An Oxford Bookseller happened to call on me and I requested him to send for some copies of the *Poem,* and advertise it in the Oxford Paper. He will probably use my name with yours for that purpose.

Don't relax in the advertising—I suppose at present that it scarcely sells at all—If you see any reviews or notices of it in any periodical paper pray send it me, it is part of my reward—the amusement of hearing the abuse of the bigots.

Dear Sir Yours very obliged Sert

PERCY B. SHELLEY.

[Addressed]
MR. CHAS. OLLIER,
Bookseller,
3 *Welbeck St.,*
London

Corrections from the original letter in the Miriam Stark collection, University of Texas.

LETTERS

CCCLXVII
TO CHARLES OLLIER
London

Marlow,
Jan. 22, 1818.

DEAR SIR,

I take the opportunity of a parcel to town to say that I have no objections—or rather that it is my wish that a copy of the "Revolt of Islam" should be sent to Valpy.[1]

Pray send me Hunt's new poems[2] as soon as they appear, as well as "Altham."[3]

Dear Sir, your faithful servant,

P. B. SHELLEY.

Will the books ever be bound?

[Addressed]
MR. CHAS. OLLIER,
3 *Welbeck St.,*
Cavendish Square

CCCLXVIII
TO CHARLES OLLIER[1]
London

Marlow,[2]
Jan, 25, 1818.

DEAR SIR,

Be so good as to send copies of the Poem with my compliments to Mr. Co[u]lson and Sir James Mackintosh. Do you think you could get for me for copies some original drawings in Indian

---

[1] Probably John Abraham Valpy (1787–1854), the editor and printer.
[2] Leigh Hunt's volume, *Foliage; or Poems, Original and Translated,* was published early in 1818, by C. & J. Ollier.—See Shelley's letter to Hunt, March 22, 1818.
[3] *Altham and his Wife : a Domestic Tale,* by Charles Ollier, was issued this year, also by C. and J. Ollier.
[1] This letter is in the writing of Mrs. Shelley.
[2] Miss Clairmont notes in her journal that the house at Marlow was sold on this day.
Dr. F. J. Furnivall contributed to the *Academy,* in October 1889, Shelley's lodging

ink, etc.? There are such things to be had, I know, but I do not know exactly where.

You ought to continue to advertsise the poem vigorously.

Shall be glad to receive the bound books.

Your obedient sert.,

P. B. SHELLEY.

Last No. of the *Quarterly*.

[Addressed]
  MR. CHARLES OLLIER,
    3 *Welbeck St.,*
      Cavendish Square,
      London

bill in London, apparently 119 Great Russell Street, February 1818, from which it appears that he must have taken the rooms before Mary arrived in town. Dr. Furnivall adds, on the authority of Mr. Kegan Paul, that T. H. Godwin was no relation of William Godwin.

Percy Shelly, Esq.
  Dr. To T. H. Godwin
  Took Apartments from February 9, 1818 and came into Ditto 10th of Do., at £3. 0. 0 per week, and to find their own Linen and plate.
  To Cash Paid first day for Mr. Shelley

		£	s.	d.
Feb. 10.	2 half Quarterns of Bread . . .	0	1	2
„ „	2 half lb. of Butter .	0	1	7½
„ 11.	Paid carriage [*sic*] of Trunks & Porter	0	8	0
„ „	Cash Lent Mr. Shelly . . .	0	3	0
„ 12.	Paid for Parcel Miss C[lairmont] . .	0	2	0
„ „	Cash to P. Shelly, Esq.	0	2	6
„ „	Amelia Broke a Dish	£0	18	3½
„ 13.	Cash to Do Do Do			

[sum cut off]

"Up the side of the figures," said Dr. Furnivall, "is 'Clairmont's Letter 7*d.*' and 'Glass.' On the back of Shelley's bill is another one in the same hand, of extra articles bought, I suppose, for Shelley's rooms."

		£	s.	d.
Feb. 10.	Bought of Mr. Little 2 pair of Blankets and one Counter- pane Rug . . .	[no sum]		
„	Bought of Mr. Dover 1 Looking Glass .	0	12	0
„	Bason and Ewer, Blue figures . .	0	4	6
„	2 Blankets . . .	1	0	0
„	1 Pillow . . .	0	4	6
	This due to Mr Dover .	2	1	0

283

LETTERS

London, Jan. 31, 1818.

SIR,

You having lent me on security a sum of Money and Insured my Life, the Policy of which Insurance will be void if I leave England without giving you notice so that you may increase your insurance if you think fit, I hereby promise you not to leave England without giving you sufficient previous Notice for that purpose.

I am, Sir,

Your Obedt. Servt.,

PERCY BYSSHE SHELLEY.

Witness: Wm. Richardson, Clement's Inn.
George Adams, Fore Street.
Thos. Dignam, Clerk to Wm. Richardson,
Clement's Inn.

CCCLXX
TO BROOKES & CO.
London

Dover,
March 12, 1818.

GENTLEMEN,

In my absence I wish no other bill to be honoured but the following:

Mr. Peacock	..	£30—15 days.
Mr. Godwin	..	150—one month.
Mr. Ollier	..	30— Do.
Mr. Madocks		
(for accounts at Marlow)	117—four months.	

[1] The signature and date only of this letter are in Shelley's handwriting.

LETTERS

Should any other be presented for payment, I request that payment be refused, as they depend upon Conditional engagements
with friends in England who ought to be prepared to meet them.

Gentlemen, I have the honour to be,

Your most obed. Sert.,

PERCY BYSSHE SHELLEY.

[Addressed]
MESSRS. BROOKES & CO.,
 Bankers,
  Chancery Lane, London
[Postmark]
 Dover
  72
13 *Mar.* 13
 1818

From the extracts in Mary Shelley's journal printed by Professor Dowden (*Life of Shelley*, Vol. II, pp. 183–4) it appears that Shelley left Marlow for London on February 7; Clare followed with Willy and Allegra on the 9th; Mary departed on the following day. Shelley's last days in England were spent in the pleasant society of Hunt, Hogg, Peacock and Horace Smith. He took lodgings at 119 Great Russell Street, Bloomsbury. Mary Lamb was a visitor. He also saw Keats, Novello, Baxter, and Godwin; and he went to the theatre and opera. Peacock says: "I saw him for the last time on Tuesday, the 10th of March. The evening was a remarkable one, as being that of the first per-formance of an opera of Rossini in England, and of the first appearance here of Mali-bran's father, Garcia. He performed *Count Almaviva* in the 'Barbiere di Siviglia'; Fodor was *Rosina*; Naldi, *Figaro*; Ambrogetti, *Bartolo*; and Angrisani, *Basilio*. I supped with Shelley and his travelling companions after the opera. They departed early the next morning."

Two days before leaving England, on March 9, Mary writes in her journal, "Chris-tening the children." The register at St. Giles in the Fields records the baptism of William, and Clara Everina, children of Percy Bysshe Shelley, Esq., and Mary Woll-stonecraft, his wife, of Great Marlow, co. Bucks (late of Great Russell Street); the first born January 24, 1816, the second September 2, 1817; also Clara Allegra, reputed daughter of Rt. Hon. George Gordon, Lord Byron, Peer, of no fixed residence, travel-ling on the Continent, by Clara Mary Jane Clairmont, born January 17, 1817. The officiating clergyman was Charles Macarthy.

XIV

MARCH 13 TO NOVEMBER 10, 1818

EARLY ITALIAN IMPRESSIONS

"ROSALIND AND HELEN"

TO LEIGH HUNT
London

Calais,[1]
March 13, 1818.
[*Friday*.]

MY DEAR FRIEND,

After a stormy but very short voyage we have arrived at Calais, and are at this moment on the point of proceeding. We are all very well, and in excellent spirits. Motion has always this effect upon the blood, even when the mind knows that there are causes for dejection.

With respect to Tailor and Hessy [*sic*][2] I am ready to certify,

[1] Mary Shelley's journal tells us that they arrived at Calais on March 12, and departed on the following day, and travelled through Douay, La Fere, Rheims, Dizier, Langres, Dijon, Macon, and reached Lyons on Saturday, the 21st, at half-past eleven. The following day Shelley wrote to Byron, "who had refused to correspond with Clare, informing him that Allegra had come thus far on the way." (Dowden's *Shelley*, Vol. II, p. 108.) On the 25th they left Lyons.

[2] Leigh Hunt was still in financial difficulties, and being unable to repay Taylor & Hessey a sum advanced by them in expectation of a new book, which Hunt had not produced, he had endeavoured to transfer the profits of *Rimini* to them. This proposal did not appeal to Taylor, who was visited by Shelley, on Hunt's behalf in March. In a letter from Taylor & Hessey, written from 91 New Bond Street on March 23, 1818, Taylor refers to a second visit from Shelley, who offered Taylor one of his own poems, but that on that occasion "not a word was said of *Rimini*." An unpublished letter from Hunt to Taylor, written while Hunt was staying with the Shelleys at Great Marlow, in January 1817, refers to this question of the assignment of the copyright.

Albion House, Marlow, Bucks,
9 June, 1817.

DEAR SIR,

I have to apologize to you very sincerely for not sooner settling this little matter between us; but I have been waiting from day to day, and am still so, in expectation of a settlement in my own affairs, which will relieve me finally from all my difficulties, and enable me to shew my sense of your kindness. At any rate, it will not be more than a if necessary in a Court of Justice, that one of them said he would give up his copyright for the £20; and that in lieu of that he would accept the profits of "Rimini" until it was paid.

Yours ever affectionately,

P. B. SHELLEY.

Pray write to Milan.

[*Written by Mary Shelley*]

Shelley is full of business, and desires me to finish this hasty notice of our safety. The children are in high spirits and very well. Our passage was stormy but very short. Both Alba and William were sick, but they were very good and slept all the time. We now depart for Italy, with very fine weather and good hopes. Farewell, my dear Friend, may you be happy.

Your affectionate friend,

MARY W. S.

[Addressed]
MR. LEIGH HUNT,
13 *Lisson Grove North,*
Paddington, London
Angleterre

few weeks longer before I do so;—and till then I must beg your further indulgence. In the mean while, I have sent to Mr. Triphook, the chief publisher of the new edition of *Rimini,* which is now coming out, to put yours and Mr. Hessey's name in the title-page, according to your acceptance of my offer on that subject; I trust, that your connexion with me in this and perhaps other matters will at least make you amends for the delay of which I have been guilty in the present one.

I am, dear Sir, yours very truly,
LEIGH HUNT.

LETTERS

Lyons,
March 22, 1818.

My dear Friend,

Why did you not wake me that night before we left England, you and Marianne?[1] I take this as rather an unkind piece of kindness in you; but which, in consideration of the six hundred miles between us, I forgive. We have journeyed towards the spring, that has been hastening to meet us from the south; and though our weather was at first abominable, we have now warm sunny days, and soft winds, and a sky of deep azure, the most serene I ever saw. The heat in this city to-day is like that of London in the midst of summer. My spirits and health sympathize in the change. Indeed, before I left London, my spirits were as feeble as my health, and I had demands upon them which I found difficult to supply.

I have read "Foliage—"[2] with most of the poems I was already familiar. What a delightful poem "The Nymphs" is! especially the second part. It is truly *poetical*, in the intense and emphatic sense of the word. If six hundred miles were not between us, I should say what a pity that *glib*[3] was not omitted, and that the poem is not as faultless as it is beautiful. But, for fear I should *spoil* your next poem I will not let slip a word upon the subject.

Give my love to Marianne and her sister, and tell Marianne she defrauded me of a kiss by not waking me when she went away, and that as I have no better mode of conveying it, I must take the best, and ask you to pay the debt. When shall I see you all again? Oh, that it might be in Italy! I confess that the thought of how

---

[1] Shelley's last day in London, Tuesday, March 10, 1818, was spent at his lodgings at No. 119 Great Russell Street, in the company of Leigh Hunt and his wife. Mary adds in her journal: "Mary Lamb calls, Papa in the evening; our adieus." During the evening Shelley fell into a sleep from which he was not awakened, and his friends departed without taking leave of him.
[2] *Foliage; or, Poems Original and Translated.* By Leigh Hunt. Published by Ollier in 1818. The volume contains a poem "To Percy Shelley."
[3] In the phrase, "the glib sea-flowers," towards the end of Part I of *The Nymphs.*

291

LETTERS

long we may be divided makes me very melancholy. Adieu, my dear friends. Write soon.

Ever most affectionately yours,

P. B. S.

To LEIGH HUNT, Esq.

CCCLXXIII
JOURNAL: PASSAGE OF THE ECHELLES

Thursday, March 26, [1818].

We travel towards the mountains, and begin to enter the valleys of the Alps. The country becomes covered again with verdure and cultivation, and white chateaux and scattered cottages among woods of old oak and walnut trees. The vines are here peculiarly picturesque; they are trellissed upon immense stakes, and the trunks of them are moss-covered and hoary with age. Unlike the French vines, which creep lowly on the ground, they form rows of interlaced bowers, which, when the leaves are green and the red grapes are hanging among those hoary branches, will afford a delightful shadow to those who sit upon the moss underneath. The vines are sometimes planted in the open fields, and sometimes among lofty orchards of apple and pear trees, the twigs of which were just becoming purple with the bursting blossoms.

We dined at Les Echelles, a village at the foot of the mountain of the same name, the boundaries of France and Savoy. Before this we had been stopped at Port Bonvoisin, where the legal limits of the French and Sardinian territories are placed. We here heard that a Milanese had been sent back all the way to Lyons, because his passport was unauthorised by the Sardinian Consul, a few days before, and that we should be subjected to the same treatment. We, in respect to the character of our nation I suppose, were suffered to pass. Our books, however, were, after a long discussion, sent to Chambery, to be submitted to the censor; a priest, who admits nothing of Rousseau, Voltaire, etc., into the dominions of the King of Sardinia.[1] All such books are burned.

After dinner we ascended Les Echelles, winding along a road cut through perpendicular rocks, of immense elevation, by Charles Emanuel, Duke of Savoy, in 1582. The rocks, which cannot be less than a thousand feet in perpendicular height, sometimes overhang the road on each side, and almost shut out the sky. The scene is like that described in the Prometheus of Æschylus. Vast rifts and caverns in the granite precipices, wintry mountains with ice and snow above; the loud sounds of unseen waters within the caverns, and walls of toppling rocks, only to be scaled as he described, by the winged chariot of the ocean nymphs.

Under the domination of this tyranny, the inhabitants of the fertile valleys, bounded by these mountains, are in a state of most frightful poverty and disease. At the foot of this ascent, were cut into the rocks at several places, stories of the misery of the inhabitants, to move the compassion of the traveller. One old man, lame and blind, crawled out of a hole in the rock, wet with the perpetual melting of the snows of above, and dripping like a shower-bath.

The country, as we descended to Chambery, continued as beautiful; though marked with somewhat of a softer character than before: we arrived a little after night-fall.

CCCLXXIV
TO THOMAS LOVE PEACOCK

Milan,
April 1818.

My dear Peacock,

Behold us arrived at length at the end of our journey—that is, within a few miles of it—because we design to spend the summer on the shore of the Lake of Como. Our journey was somewhat painful from the cold and in no other manner interesting until we passed the Alps: of course I except the Alps themselves but no

[1] A canon who had met Sir Timothy Shelley at the Duke of Norfolk's happened to be present at the inspection, and so the books were allowed to pass.—Professor Dowden's *Life of Shelley*, Vol. II, p. 189.

sooner had we arrived at Italy than the loveliness of the earth and the serenity of the sky made the greatest difference in my sensations—I depend on these things for life; for in the smoke of cities and the tumult of human kind and the chilling fogs and rain of our own country I can hardly be said to live. With what delight did I hear the woman who conducted us to see the triumphal arch of Augustus at Susa, speak the clear and complete language of Italy, tho half unintelligible to me, after that nasal and abbreviated cacophony of the French! A ruined arch of magnificent proportions in the Greek taste, standing in a kind of road of green lawn, overgrown with violets and primsoses, and in the midst of stupendous mountains, and a *blonde* woman, of light and graceful manners, something in the style of Fuseli's Eve were the first things we met in Italy.

This city is very agreeable. We went to the opera last night— which is a most splendid exhibition. The opera itself was not a favourite, and the singers very inferior to our own. But the Ballet, or rather a kind of melodrame or pantomimic drama, was the most splendid spectacle I ever saw. We have no Miss Milanie [*sic*][1] here —in every other respect Milan is unquestionably superior. The manner in which language is translated into gesture, the complete and full effect of the whole as illustrating the history in question, the unaffected self possession of each of the actors, even to the children, made this choral drama more impressive than I sould have conceived possible. The story is *Othello*, and strange to say it left no disagreeable impression.

I write but I am not in the humour to write; and you must expect longer, if not more entertaining, letters soon—that is, in a week or so—when I am a little recovered from my journey. Pray tell us all the news with regard to our own offspring, whom we left at nurse in England; as well as those of our friends. Mention Cobbet and politics too—and Hunt—to whom Mary is now writing; and particularly your own plans and yourself—re *Mariame*. You shall hear more of me and my plans soon. My health is improved

---

[1] Peacock says that in the season of 1817 he persuaded Shelley to accompany him to the opera. "The performance was 'Don Giovanni' . . . followed by a ballet, in which Mlle. Melanie was the principal *danseuse*. He was enchanted with this lady; said he had never imagined such grace of motion; and the impression was permanent."

already—and my spirits something—and I have many literary
schemes and one in particular—which I thirst to be settled that I
may begin. I have ordered Ollier to send you some sheets, etc.,
for revision.

Adieu.—Always faithfully yours,
P. B. S.

Mary and Clare desire their best regards.

[Addressed]
  THOMAS PEACOCK, Esq.,
    Great Marlow,
     Bucks,
      Angleterre
Inghilterra
[Postmark]
  F.P.O
  AP. 23
   1818

CCCLXXV
TO LORD BYRON

(Hotel Reale) Milan,
April 13, 1818.

MY DEAR LORD BYRON,
    I write chiefly to inquire whether you have received a letter
from me dated Lyons;[1] and to inform you that your little girl has
arrived here in excellent health and spirits, with eyes as blue as the
sky over our heads.
    Mary and I have just returned from the Lake of Como, where
we have been seeking a house for the summer. If you have not
visited this sublime and lovely scene, I think it would repay your
toil. Will you spend a few weeks with us this summer? Our mode
of life is uniform, and such as you remember it at Geneva, and the
situation which I imagine we have chosen (the Villa Pliniana) is
solitary, and surrounded by scenery of astonishing grandeur, with

---

[1] This letter has not been traced.

295

the lake at our feet. If you would visit us—and I don't know where you could find a heartier welcome—little Allegra might return with you.

Mary unites with me in best regards, and Clare bids me ask if you have received a lock of Allegra's hair which she sent in the winter.

Most sincerely yours,

P. B. SHELLEY.

P.S. I have got some books for you, packed up at the bottom of a large box of my own. Shall I send them to Venice?

I cannot conceive how my letter from Lyons should have failed.

CCCLXXVI
TO THOMAS LOVE PEACOCK

Milan,
April 20, 1818.

MY DEAR PEACOCK,

I had no conception that the distance between us, measured by time in respect of letters, was so great. I have but just received yours dated the 2d—and when you will receive mine written from this city somewhat later than the same date, I cannot know. I am sorry to hear that you have been obliged to remain at Marlow; a certain degree of society being almost a necessary of life, particularly as we are not to see you this summer in Italy. But this, I suppose, must be as it is. I often revisit Marlow in thought. The curse of this life is, that whatever is once known, can never be unknown. You inhabit a spot, which before you inhabit it, is as indifferent to you as any other spot upon earth, and when, persuaded by some necessity, you think to leave it, you leave it not; it clings to you and with memories of things, which, in your experience of them, gave no such promise, revenges your desertion. Time flows on, places are changed; friends who were with us, are no longer with us; but what had been, seems yet to be, but barren and stript of life. See, I have sent you a study for Night Mare Abbey.

LETTERS

Since I last wrote to you we have been to Como, looking for a house. This lake exceeds anything I ever beheld in beauty, with the exception of the arbutus islands of Killarney. It is long and narrow, and has the appearance of a mighty river winding among the mountains and the forests. We sailed from the town of Como to a tract of country called the Tremezina, and saw the various aspects presented by that part of the lake. The mountains between Como and that village, or rather cluster of villages, are covered on high with chestnut forests (the eating chestnuts, on which the inhabitants of the country subsist in time of scarcity), which sometimes descend to the very verge oft he lake overhanging it with their hoary branches. But usually the immediate border of this shore is composed of laurel-trees, and bay, and myrtle, and wild fig-trees, and olives which grow in the crevices of the rocks, and overhang the caverns, and shadow the deep glens, which are filled with the flashing light of the waterfalls. Other flowering shrubs, which I cannot name, grow there also. On high, the towers of village churches are seen white among the dark forests. Beyond, on the opposite shore, which faces the south, the mountains descend less precipitously to the lake, and although they are much higher, and some covered with perpetual snow, there intervenes between them and the lake a range of lower hills, which have glens and rifts opening to the other, such as I should fancy the *abysses* of Ida or Parnassus. Here are plantations of olive, and orange, and lemon trees, which are now so loaded with fruit, that there is more fruit than leaves—and vineyards. This shore of the lake is one continued village, and the Milanese nobility have their villas here. The union of culture and the untameable profusion and loveliness of nature is here so close, that the line where they are divided can hardly be discovered. But the finest scenery is that of the Villa Pliniana so called from a fountain which ebbs and flows every three hours described by the younger Pliny which is in the courtyard. This house which was once a magnificent palace, and is now half in ruins, we are endeavouring to procure. It is built upon terraces *raised from* the bottom of the lake, together with its garden, at the foot of a semicircular precipice, overshadowed by profound forests of chestnut. The scene from the colonnade is the most extraordinary at once, and the most lovely that eye ever beheld. On one side is the mountain, and immediately over you are clusters of cypress trees, of an astonishing height which seem to pierce the sky. Above you, from among from the clouds, as it were, descends a waterfall of immense size, broken by the woody rocks into a thousand channels to the lake. On the other side is seen the blue extent of the lake and the mountains, speckled with sails and spires. The apartments of the Pliniana are immensely large, but ill furnished and antique. The terraces, which overlook the lake, and conduct under the shade of such immense laurel trees as deserve the epithet of Pythian, are most delightful. We stayd at Como two days, and have now returned to Milan, waiting the issue of our negotiation about a house. Como is only 6 leagues from Milan, and its mountains are seen from the cathedral. This cathedral is a most astonishing work of art. It is built of white marble, and cut into pinnacles of immense height, and the utmost delicacy of workmanship, and loaded with sculpture. The effect of it, piercing the solid blue with those groups of dazzling spires, relieved by the serene depth of this Italian Heaven, or by moonlight when the stars seem gathered among those clustered shapes, is beyond anything I had imagined architecture capable of producing. The interior, tho very sublime, is of a more earthly character, and with its stained glass and massy granite columns overloaded with antique figures, and the silver lamps, that burn for ever under the canopy of black cloth beside the brazen altar and the marble fretwork of the dome, give it the aspect of some gorgeous sepulchre. There is one solitary spot among these aisles, behind the altar, where the light of day is dim and yellow under the storied window, which I have chosen to visit, and read Dante there.

I have devoted this summer, and indeed the next year, to the composition of a tragedy on the subject of Tasso's madness, which I find upon inspection is, if properly treated, admirably dramatic and poetical.[2] But, you will say, I have no dramatic talent. Very true, in a certain sense; but I have taken the resolution to see what

[2] Mrs. Shelley tells us in her note on *Prometheus Unbound* that during the first year of Shelley's residence in Italy "the poetical spirit within him speedily revived with all the power, and with more than all the beauty of his first attempts. He meditated three subjects as the groundwork for lyrical dramas. One was the story of Tasso; of this a

kind of a tragedy a person without dramatic talent could write. It shall be better morality than Fazio,[3] and better poetry than Bertram,[4] at least. You tell me nothing of Rhododaphne,[5] a book from which, I confess, I expected extraordinary success.

Who lives in my house at Marlow now, or what is to be done with it? I am seriously persuaded that the situation was injurious to my health, or I should be tempted to feel a very absurd interest in who is to be its next possessor. The expense of our journey here has been very considerable—but we are now living at the Hotel here, in a kind of pension, which is very reasonable in respect of price, and when we get into a menage of our own, we have every reason to expect that we shall experience something of the boasted cheapness of Italy. The finest bread, made of a sifted flour, the whitest and the best I ever tasted, is only *one English penny* a pound. All the necessaries of life bear a proportional relation to this. But then the luxuries, tea, etc., are very dear,—and the English, as usual, are cheated in a way that is quite ridiculous, if they have not their wits about them. We do not know a single human being, and the opera, until last night, has been always the same. Little Alba is still with us, but I suppose will soon cease to be.—Lord Byron we hear has taken a house for three years, at Venice; whether we shall see him or not, I do not know, as it depends partly on whether we get such a house as we can invite him to. The number of English who pass through this town is very great. They ought to be in their own country in the present crisis. Their conduct is wholly inexcusable. The people here, though inoffensive enough, seem both in body and soul a miserable race. The men are hardly

slight fragment of a song of Tasso remains. The other was one founded on the book of Job, which he never abandoned in idea, but of which no trace remains among his papers. The third was the *Prometheus Unbound*.
[3] By Henry Hart Milman (1791–1868), Dean of St. Paul's. This tragedy was produced at Covent Garden in 1815. Peacock said that he remembered Shelley's absorbed attention to Miss O'Neill's performance of "Bianca" in *Fazio*, "and it is evident to me that she was always in his thoughts when he drew the character of 'Beatrice' in the *Cenci*. With the exception of *Fazio*, I do not remember his having been pleased at any performance at an English theatre."
[4] *Bertram*, a tragedy by the Rev. Charles Robert Maturin, was produced with success at Drury Lane in 1816, through the influence of Byron.
[5] *Rhododaphne, or The Thessalian Spell*, a poem by Peacock, which was published anonymously in 1818 by Hookham. Shelley's review of this book was probably the last piece of literary work done by him in England. Mary records in her journal for Friday, February 20, 1818, "copy Shelley's critique on *Rhododaphne*."

299

men; they look like a tribe of stupid and shrivelled slaves, and I do not think that I have seen a gleam of intelligence in the countenance of man since I passed the Alps. The women in enslaved countries are always better than the men; but they have tight-laced figures, and figures and mien which express (O how unlike the French!) a mixture of the coquette and prude, which reminds me of the worst characteristics of Englishwomen.[6] Everything but humanity is in much greater perfection here than in France. The cleanliness and comfort of the Inns is sometimes quite English; the country is beautifully cultivated; and altogether, if you can, as one ought always to do, find your happiness in yourself, it is a most delightful and commodious place to live in.

Adieu—

Mary and Clare send their kindest remembrances—

Your affectionate friend

P. B. S.

Clare requests you to write a history of Mademoiselle Millane.

[*Written by Mary*]

Mary requests you to send with your midsummer parcel, several papers of pins a few sticks of sealing wax a brush like Mrs. Hunt's and a tortoise-shell comb 3 inches across and teeth 2 inches.

[Addressed]
  T. L. PEACOCK, Esq.,
    Great Marlow,
      Bucks,
        Angleterre
[Postmark]
  F.P.O
  MY. 7
  1818

---

[6] These impressions of Shelley, with regard to the Italians, formed in ignorance, and with precipitation, became altogether altered after a longer stay in Italy. He quickly discovered the extraordinary intelligence and genius of this wonderful people, amidst the ignorance in which they are carefully kept by their rulers, and the vices, fostered by a religious system, which these same rulers have used as their most successful engine. —Note by Mrs. Shelley.

300

LETTERS

Milan,
April 22, 1818.

MY DEAR LORD BYRON,

Clare will write to you herself a detail of her motives and feelings relating to Allegra's being absent as you desire. Her interference as the mother of course supersedes *mine*, which was never undertaken but from the deep interest I have ever felt for all the parties concerned. Here my letter might well close, but that I would not the affair should finish so.

You write as if from the instant of its departure all future intercourse were to cease between Clare and her child. This I cannot think you ought to have expected, or even to have desired. Let us estimate our own sensations, and consider, if those of a father be acute, what must be those of a mother? What should we think of a woman who should resign her infant child with no prospect of ever seeing it again, even to a father in whose tenderness she entirely confided? If she forces herself to such a sacrifice for the sake of her child's welfare, there is something heroically great in thus trampling upon the strongest affections, and even the most unappeasable instincts of our nature. But the world will not judge so; she would be despised as an unnatural mother, even by those who might see little to condemn in her becoming a mother without the formalities of marriage. She would thus resign her only good, and take to herself, in its stead, contempt on every hand. Besides, she might say, " What assurance have I of the tenderness of the father for his child, if he treats the feelings of the mother with so little consideration?" Not to mention, that the child itself would, on this supposition, grow up either in ignorance, or in contempt of one of its parents; a state of things full of danger. I know the arguments present in your mind on this subject; but surely, rank and reputation, and prudence are as nothing in comparison to a mother's claims. If it should be recorded that you had sought to violate these, the opinion of the world might indeed be fixed on you, with such blame as your friends could not justify; and wholly unlike those ridiculous and unfounded tales which are told of every person of eminent powers, and which make your friends so many in England, at the expense of those who fabricated them. I assure you, my dear Lord Byron, I speak earnestly, and sincerely. It is not that I wish to make out a case for Clare; my *interest*, as you must be aware, is entirely on the opposite side. Nor have I in any manner influenced her. I have esteemed it a duty to leave her to the impulse of her own feelings in a case where, if she has no feeling, she has no claim. But in truth, if she is to be brought to part with her child, she requires reassurance and tenderness. A tie so near the heart should not be rudely snapt. It was in this persuasion that I hoped (I had a thousand other reasons for wishing to see you) that you would have accepted our invitation to the Pliniana. Clare's pain would then have been mitigated by the prospect of seeing her child with you, and she would have been reassured of the fears which your letter has just confirmed, by the idea of a repetition of the visit. Your conduct must at present wear the aspect of great cruelty, however you justify it to yourself. Surely, it is better if we err, to err on the side of kindness, than of rigour. You can stop when you please; and you are not so infirm of purpose that soothing words, and gentle conduct need betray you in essential matters further than you mean to go.

I am a third person in this painful controversy, who, in the invidious office of mediator, can have no interest, but in the interests of those concerned. I am now deprived of the power to act; but I would willingly persuade.

You know my motives, and therefore I do not fear to ask you again to come to see me at Como; and, for the sake of your child's welfare, to soothe Clare's wounded feelings by some reassurances in the meanwhile. As I understand her, with these assurances she would send the child. You are afraid, perhaps, that she might be inclined to tease you; but her first impression on seeing your letter (which, by-the-bye, I did not mean her to see) was that if your coming to see her depended upon her absence, she would willingly place herself *en pension* in the city, during that period. But in fact, so far as gossip is concerned, if you have any motive for caring about it, they cannot say more at Como than they do at Venice.

You have no idea of the absurd stories which the multitude believe of you; but which every person of sense, and indeed every enlightened circle of our own countrymen, laugh at. This is the common lot of all who have distinguished themselves among men. When Dante walked through the streets, the old women pointed at him, and said, "That is the man who went to Hell with Virgil; see how his beard is singed." Stories unlike this, but to the full as improbable and monstrous, are propagated of you at Venice; but I know not wherefore you should regard them. With us you would find a sincere, and frank welcome; and as we should be all unknown, or might be, I can see no loophole for calumny.

If your messenger arrives before Clare and you have come to an understanding on this subject, I shall detain him until further orders, unless your instructions are explicit that he shall not stay. Allegra has an English nurse, a very clean and good-tempered young woman, whom, in case of a termination of these melancholy differences, I can safely recommend to you.

The expenses of which you speak have been in our family so extremely trifling, that I know not how to name any sum that will not leave me, what I cannot accept, a pecuniary profit. Perhaps you will be kind enough not to place me in so degrading a situation, as to estimate a matter of this kind.

I feel confident that you will attribute to its right motive the earnestness with which I have written on this painful subject; and believe me, my dear Lord B., most sincerely attached to your interest and honour,

P. B. SHELLEY.

Allegra is daily improving in beauty, but she is suffering just now from cutting her teeth.

LETTERS

Milan,
April 30, 1818.

MY DEAR LORD BYRON,

It certainly gave me much pleasure to be able to bring your little girl to Italy, as indeed I was puzzled to find a person to trust her with; but the purpose of my journey was, I lament to say, in no manner connected with it. My health, which has always been declining, had assumed such symptoms that the physicians advised me to proceed without delay to a warmer climate. Allow me also to *repeat* my assertion that Clare's late conduct with respect to the child was wholly unconnected with, and uninfluenced by me. The correspondence from which these misinterpretations have arisen was undertaken on my part solely because you refused to correspond with Clare. My conduct in the affair has been simple, and intelligible. I am sorry that I misunderstood your letter; and I hope that on both sides there is here an end of misunderstandings.

You will find your little Allegra quite well. I think she is the most lovely and engaging child I ever beheld. Tell us what you think of her, and whether, or no, she equals your expectations. Her attendant is not the servant whom I alluded to in my last letter; but a Swiss, who has attended my own children, in whom Mrs. S[helley] entirely confides, and who even quits us somewhat unwillingly, and whom Mary parts with solely that Clare and yourself may be assured that Allegra will be attended almost with a mother's care.

Clare, as you may imagine, is dreadfully unhappy. As you have not written to her, it has been a kind of custom that she should see your letters; and I daresay you know that you have sometimes said things which I do not think you would have addressed to her. It could not in any way compromise you to be cautious in this respect, as, unless you write to her, I cannot well refuse to let her see your letters. I have not seen any of those which she has written to you; nor even have I often known when they were sent.

You will receive your packets of books. Hunt sends you one he

304

has lately published; and I am commissioned by an old friend of yours to convey "Frankenstein" to you, and to request that if you conjecture the name of the author, that you will regard it as a secret. In fact, it is Mrs. S[helley]'s. It has met with considerable success in England; but she bids me say, "That she would regard your approbation as a more flattering testimony of its merit."

Address your next letter "Poste Restante, Pisa," as we leave Milan for that city to-morrow. We have been disappointed in our house at Como; and indeed, I shall attempt to divert Clare's melancholy by availing myself of some introductions at Pisa. Clare is wretchedly disconsolate, and I know not how I shall calm her, until the return of post. I ought to say that we shall be at Pisa long before the return of post—when we expect (pray don't disappoint us) a letter from you to assure us of the safe arrival of our little favourite. Mary begs to unite with me in best regards; and to express her affection, and anxiety, about little Allegra, whom she has been accustomed to regard almost as one of her own children.

I ought to say that by an unfortunate mistake I left behind me the 2nd part of the "Voyage to Corea," and a poem called "Beppo," which Murray had sent to me for you. Peacock has a parcel for me, which I expect at midsummer, in which these will be included. Elsie's wages with us were 20 louis.

My dear Lord Byron, yours always sincerely,

P. B. SHELLEY.

CCCLXXIX
TO THOMAS JEFFERSON HOGG
London

Milan,
April 30, 1818.

MY DEAR FRIEND,

I received your note a few hours before I left England, and have designed to write to you from every town on the route, but the difficulty not so much of knowing what to say as how to say it prevented me till this moment. I was sorry that I did not see you again before my departure.[1] On my return, which will not perhaps take place so soon as I at first expected, we shall meet again; meanwhile my letters to Hunt and Peacock are, as it were, common property, of which, if you feel any curiosity about me which I neglect to satisfy myself, you are at liberty to avail yourself. To-morrow we leave this city for Pisa, where, or in its neighbourhood, we shall remain during the summer.

The Italians—at least those whom I have seen—are a very different people from the French. They have less character; and the women especially seem a very inferior race of beings. Their manners, so far as I can judge from their mien and physiognomy, are at once prudish and coquettish, their features bony; their figures thin, and those who have any claims to beauty, have a beauty superficial, and of a cold and unfeeling character. Their voices have none of that winning persuasiveness of those of France, but are hard, and without inflexion or variety of tone. But this holds good, as far as I know, only to Milan, as my experience extends no further. The Architecture of the Cathedral of this city exceeds anything I ever saw in the Gothic style, it is far superior to York Minster or Westminster Abbey. The Opera is very good and the house larger or at least as large as that of London. They have Mad. Camporese here as the *prima donna*—a cold and unfeeling singer and a bad actress. The best singer is a man called David. Their ballets, which are a kind of pantomimic dance illustrative of some story, are much superior to anything of the kind in England. Indeed, they are wholly unlike anything represented on our stage; being a combination of a great number of figures, grouped with the most picturesque and even poetical effect, and perpetually changing with motions the most harmoniously interwoven and contrasted with great effect. *Othello* is represented in one of these ballets, and the story is so well told in action as to leave upon the mind an impression as of a real tragedy.—

We have been to the Lake of Como, and indeed have since thought of taking our residence there for the summer. The scenery is very beautiful, abounding among other things with those green

[1] Hogg dined with Shelley in London (apparently in Great Russell Street) on Sunday, February 15, 1818. Perhaps their final meeting was on February 17 when, Mary records in her journal, Hogg spent the evening with them.

banks for the sake of which you represented me as wandering over the world. You are more interested in the human part of the experience of travelling; a thing of which I see little, and understand less, and which, if I saw and understood more, I fear I should be little able to describe. I am just reading a Novel of Wieland called "Aristippus," which I think you would like. It is very Greek, tho' perhaps not religious enough for a true Pagan. If you can get it, otherwise, do not read it in the French translation, as the impudent translator has omitted much of the original, to accommodate it, as he says, to the "fastidious taste and powerful understanding of his countrymen."

I have read some Greek but not much on my journey—two or three plays of Euripides and among them the "Ion," which you praised and which [I think][2] is exquisitely beautiful. But I have also made some Italian book my companion from my desire to learn the language so as to speak it. I have been studying the history of Tasso's life with some idea of making a drama of his adventures and misfortunes. How such a subject would suit English poetry, I cannot tell.—
Address Poste Restante, Pisa.

Most sincerely yours,

P. B. SHELLEY.

If you see Miss Lamb[3] present my compts., and tell her that I did not pass thro' Paris, but that I put her letter in the nearest post. remember me also to the Dr. . .

---

[2] Part of the letter is injured. Most of the address of this letter is carefully scored through, but some words can still be deciphered. It seems to have been—
[THOMAS J. HOGG], Esq.,
    [8 *Garden Court*],
        Temple, Lond n, Angleterre.
Endorsed, probably in Hogg's writing, "The first letter Shelley wrote from Italy."
[3] See footnote on p. 291.

LETTERS

TO THOMAS LOVE PEACOCK

Milan,
April 30, 1818.

MY DEAR PEACOCK,

I write simply to tell you to direct your next letters, Poste Restante, Pisa. We have engaged a vetturino for that city, and leave Milan tomorrow morning: our journey will occupy six or seven days. Pisa is not six miles from the Mediterranean with which it communicates by the river Arno. We shall pass by Piacenza, Parma, Bologna, the Apennines, and Florence, and I will endeavour to tell you something of these celebrated places in my next letter; but I cannot promise much for though my health is much improved my spirits are unequal, and seem to desert me when I attempt to write.

Pisa, they say, is uninhabitable in the midst of summer—we shall therefore do what other people do retire to Florence or to the mountains. But I will write to you our plans from Pisa, when I shall understand them better myself.

You may easily conjecture the motives which led us to forego the divine solitudes of Como. To me whose chief pleasure in life is the contemplation of nature, you may imagine how great is this loss.

Let us hear from you *once a fortnight.* Do not forget those who do not forget you.

Adieu.—Ever most sincerely yours,

P. B. SHELLEY.

[*Written by Mary*]

P.S. If you see Hunt give my love—to him and his Marianne —Tell him I am going to buy some airs for him from an opera we saw here.

Be so kind as to remember the things I mentioned in S's last for our midsummer parcel and add Beppo—(if possible) Le proces de Sualdest.

[Addressed]
T. L. PEACOCK, Esqr.,
Great Marlow,
Bucks,
Angleterre

[Postmark]
F.P.O
MY. 14
1818

LETTERS

Livorno,[1]
June 5, 1818.

MY DEAR PEACOCK,

We have not heard from you since the middle of April—that is, we have received only *one* letter from you since our departure from England. It necessarily follows that some accident has intercepted them. Address, in future, to the care of Mr. Gisborne, Livorno—and I shall receive them, though sometimes somewhat circuitously, yet always securely.

We left Milan on the 1st of May, and travelled across the Apennines to Pisa. This part of the Apennines is far less beautiful than the Alps; the mountains are wide and wild, and the whole scenery broad and undetermined—the imagination cannot find a home in it. The Plain of the Milanese, and that of Parma, is exquisitely beautiful; it is like one garden, or rather cultivated wilderness; because the corn and the meadow-grass grow under high and thick trees, fastened to one another by regular festoons of vines. On the seventh day we arrived at Pisa, where we remained three or four days. A large disagreeable city, almost without inhabitants. We then proceeded to this great trading town, where we have remained a month, and which, in a few days, we leave for I Bagni di Lucca, a kind of watering place situated in the depths of the Apennines; the scenery surrounding this village is very fine.

We have made some acquaintance with a very amiable and accomplished Lady, Mrs. Gisborne, who is the sole attraction in this most unattractive of cities. We had no idea of spending a month here, but she has made it even agreeable. Italian society seems sufficiently worthless. We shall see something of it at the Bagni di Lucca, where the most fashionable people resort.

[1] According to Shelley's statement in this letter, they would have reached Pisa on May 7. Professor Dowden says that Shelley, unaccompanied by Mary or Clare, "went to the Bagni di Lucca towards the end of May, probably in quest of a house. Mary's journal tells us that they arrived at Leghorn on May 9, and on that day they made the acquaintance of Mrs. Gisborne, who 'calls in the evening with her husband; she is reserved yet with easy manners.' Throughout the ensuing week they meet the Gisbornes every day."—Dowden's *Life of Shelley*, Vol. II, p. 209.

LETTERS

When you send my parcel—which, by-the-bye, I should request you to direct to Mr. Gisborne—I wish you could contrive to enclose the two last parts of Clarke's Travels,[2] relating to Greece, and belonging to Hookham. You know I subscribe there still. And I have determined to take the Examiner here. You would, therefore, oblige me, by sending it weekly, after having read it yourself, to the same direction, and so clipped, as to make as little weight as possible.—Also to send our linen which you will find at Mrs. Hunts and of which we have very great need. Send *all* except the cotton sheets. If the sheets are not at Mrs. Hunt's they are at the lodgings which we occupied in London last.

I write as if writing where perhaps my letter may never arrive. With every good wish from all of us,

Believe me most sincerely yours,

P. B. S.

[Addressed]
 T. PEACOCK, Esqr.,
  Great Marlow,
  Bucks,
   Inghilterra
[In another hand]
 MR. SHELLEY ALLA CURADI
 SIGNOR GISBORNE
  via Genesi fuori dalla
  porta Cappucino,
   Livorno.
[Postmark]
 F.P.O
 JU. 20
 1818

---

[2] Rev. Edward Daniel Clarke (1769–1822), whose *Travels* in six volumes were published in 1810–1823.

LETTERS

Bagni di Lucca,
June 28, 1818.

"In great haste"

DEAR SIR,
I write simply to request you to pay ten pounds on my account to a person who will call on you, and *on no account* to mention my name. If you have no money of mine still pay it at all events and cash the enclosed at the bank.

Ever most truly yours,

P. B. SHELLEY.

The person will bring a note without date signed A. B. It is of so great consequence that this note should be paid that I hope if there is any mistake with Brookes you will pay it for me, and if you have none of mine in your hands, that you will rely on my sending it you by return of Post.

CCCLXXXIII
TO JOHN AND MARIA GISBORNE
Leghorn

Bagni di Lucca,[1]
July 16, 1818.

You cannot know, as some friends in England do, to whom my silence is still more inexcusable, that this silence is no proof of forgetfulness or neglect.

I have, in truth, nothing to say, but that I shall be happy to see you again, and renew our delighted walks, until the desire or the duty of seeing new things hurries us away. We have spent a month here already in our accustomed solitude, (with the exception of one night at the Casino) and the choice society of all ages, which I took

[1] On June 11 the Shelleys moved to the Baths of Lucca. This date is clearly written in the original, but it cannot be correct as the postmark is July 13. Mrs. Shelley dates the letter July 10 in her edition.

311

care to pack up in a large trunk before we left England, have re-visited us here. I am employed just now, having little better to do, in translating into my fainting and inefficient periods the divine eloquence of Plato's Symposium; only as an exercise or perhaps to give Mary some idea of the manners and feelings of the Athenians —so different on many subjects from that of any other community that ever existed.

We have almost finished Ariosto—who is entertaining and grace-ful, and *sometimes* a Poet. Forgive me, worshippers of a more equal and tolerant divinity in poetry, if Ariosto pleases me less than you. Where is the gentle seriousness, the delicate sensibility, the calm and sustained energy without which true greatness cannot be? He is so cruel too, in his descriptions; his most prized virtues are vices almost without disguise. He constantly vindicates and embellishes revenge in its grossest form; the most deadly superstition that ever infested the world. How different from the tender and solemn enthusiasm of Petrarch—or even the delicate moral sensibility of Tasso, though somewhat obscured by an assumed and artificial style.

We read a good deal here and we read little in Livorno. We have ridden, Mary and I, once only, to a place called Prato Fiorito, on the top of the mountains: the road, winding through forests, and over torrents, and on the verge of green ravines, affords scenery magnificently fine. I cannot describe it to you, but bid you, though vainly, come and see. I take great delight in watching the changes of the atmosphere here, and the growth of the thunder showers with which the moon is often over shadowed, and which break and fade away towards evening into flocks of delicate clouds. Our fire flies are fading away fast; but there is the planet Jupiter, who rises majestically over the rift in the forest-covered mountains to the south, and the pale summer lightning which is spread out every night, at intervals, over the sky. No doubt Providence has con-trived these things, that, when the fire flies go out, the low-flying owl may see her way home.

Remember me kindly to the Machinista.[2]

---

[2] Henry Reveley, Mrs. Gisborne's son by a former marriage, so called on account of his occupation, that of an engineer.

With the sentiment of impatience until we see you again in the Autumn.

I am, yours most sincerely,

P. B. SHELLEY.

[Addressed]
 MR. & MRS. GISBORNE,
  1091 *Via Genesi,*
   Fuore della porta di Capucini,
   Livorno
[Endorsed by another hand]
 Recd. 14. July. 1818
  Mr. Shelley
[Postmarks]
 13 LUGLIO
   [&]
 LUCCA

CCCLXXXIV
TO THOMAS LOVE PEACOCK

Bagni di Lucca,
July 25, 1818.

MY DEAR PEACOCK,

I received on the same day your letters marked 5 and 6, the one directed to Pisa, and the other to Livorno, and I can assure you that they are most welcome visitors.

Our life here is as unvaried by any external events as if we were at Marlow, where a sail up the river or a journey to London makes an epoch. Since I last wrote to you, I have ridden over to Lucca, once with Clare, and once alone; and we have been over to the Casino, where I cannot say there is anything remarkable, the women being far removed from anything which the most liberal annotator could interpret into beauty or grace, and apparently possessing no intellectual excellences to compensate the deficiency. I assure you it is well that it is so, for these dances, especially the waltz, are so exquisitely beautiful that it would be a little dangerous to the newly unfrozen senses and imaginations of us migrators from the neighbourhood of the pole. As it is—except in the dark—there could be no peril. The atmosphere here, unlike that of the rest of

313

Italy, is diversified with clouds, which grow in the middle of the day, and sometimes bring thunder and lightning, and hail about the size of a pigeon's egg, and decrease towards the evening, leaving only those finely woven webs of vapour which we see in English skies, and flocks of fleecy and slowly-moving clouds, which all vanish before sunset; and the nights are for ever serene, and we see a star in the east at sunset—I think it is Jupiter—almost as fine as Venus was last summer; but it wants a certain silver and aerial radiance, and soft yet piercing splendour, which belongs, I suppose to the latter planet by virtue of its at once divine and female nature. I have forgotten to ask the ladies if Jupiter produces on them the same effect. I take great delight in watching the changes of the atmosphere. In the evening Mary and I often take a ride, for horses are cheap in this country. In the middle of the day, I bathe in a pool or fountain, formed in the middle of the forests by a torrent. It is surrounded on all sides by precipitous rocks, and the waterfall of the stream which forms it falls into it on one side with perpetual dashing. Close to it, on the top of the rocks, are alders, and above the great chestnut trees, whose long and pointed leaves pierce the deep blue sky in strong relief. The water of this pool, which, to venture an unrythmical paraphrase, is "sixteen feet long and ten feet wide,"[1] is as transparent as the air, so that the stones and sand at the bottom seem, as it were, trembling in the light of noonday. It is exceedingly cold also. My custom [is] to undress, and sit on the rocks, reading Herodotus, until the perspiration has subsided, and then to leap from the edge of the rock into this fountain—a practice in the hot weather excessively refreshing. This torrent is composed, as it were, of a succession of pools and waterfalls, up which I sometimes amuse myself by climbing when I bathe, and receiving the spray over all my body, whilst I clamber up the moist crags with difficulty.

I have lately found myself totally incapable of original composition. I employed my mornings, therefore, in translating the

---

[1] Mr. Buxton Forman pointed out that Shelley was thinking of an early version of Wordsworth's poem "The Thorn":

> You see a little muddy pond of water, never dry;
> I've measured it from side to side:
> 'Tis three feet long, and two feet wide.

"Symposium," which I accomplished in ten days. Mary is now transcribing it, and I am writing a prefatory essay. I have been reading scarcely anything but Greek, and a little Italian poetry with Mary. We have finished Ariosto together—a thing I could not have done again alone.

"Frankenstein" seems to have been well received; for although the unfriendly criticism of the *Quarterly* is an evil for it, yet it proves that it is read in some considerable degree, and it would be difficult for them with any appearance of fairness, to deny it merit altogether. Their notice of me, and their exposure of the true motives for not noticing my book, shews how well understood an hostility must subsist between me and them.

The news of the result of the elections, especially that of the metropolis, is highly inspiring. I received a letter, of two days' later date, with yours, which announced the unfortunate termination of that of Westmoreland. I wish you had sent me some of the overflowing villainy of those apostates. What a beastly and pitiful wretch that Wordsworth! That such a man should be such a poet! I can compare him with no one but Simonides, that flatterer of the Sicilian tyrants, and at the same time the most natural and tender of lyric poets.

What pleasure would it have given me if the wings of imagination could have divided the space which divides us, and I could have been of your party. I have seen nothing so beautiful as Virginia Water—in its kind. And my thoughts for ever cling to Windsor Forest, and the copses of Marlow, like the clouds which hang upon the woods of the mountains, low trailing, and though they pass away, leave their best dew when they themselves have faded. You tell me that you have finished "Nightmare Abbey." I hope that you have given the enemy no quarter. Remember, it is a sacred war. We have found an excellent quotation in Ben Jonson's "Every Man in his Humour." I will transcribe it, as I do not think you have these plays at Marlow.

"MATTHEW. O, it's only your fine humour, sir. Your true melancholy breeds your fine wit, sir. I am melancholy myself divers times, sir; and then do I no more but take pen and paper presently, and overflow you half a score or a dozen of sonnets at a sitting.

LETTERS

"ED. KNOWELL. Sure, he utters them by the gross.
"STEPHEN. Truly, sir; and I love such things out of measure.
"ED. KNOWELL. I' faith, better than in measure, I'll undertake.
"MATTHEW. Why, I pray you, sir, make use of my study; it's at your service.
"STEPHEN. I thank you, sir; I shall be bold, I warrant you. *Have you a stool there to be melancholy upon?*"—"Every Man in his Humour," Act 3, scene i.
The last expression would not make a bad motto.[2]

CCCLXXXV
TO WILLIAM GODWIN
London

Bagni di Lucca,
July 25, 1818.

MY DEAR GODWIN

We have, as yet, seen nothing of Italy which marks it to us as the habitation of departed greatness. The serene sky the magnificent scenery the delightful productions of the climate are known to us indeed as the same with those which the antients enjoyed. But Rome and Naples—even Florence are yet to see; and if we were to write you at present a history of our impressions it would give you no idea that we lived in Italy.

I am exceedingly delighted with the plan you propose of a book illustrating the character of our calumniated Republicans.[1] It is precisely the subject for Mary, and I imagine that but for the fear of being excited to refer to books not within her reach, she would attempt to begin it here, and order the works you notice. I am

---

[2] In the 1837 edition Peacock adopted this passage as a second motto (omitting E. Knowell's interlocutions) for his novel, *Nightmare Abbey*, which was first published in 1818.

[1] In Godwin's letter to Shelley from Skinner Street, June 18, 1818, he sketches the plan of a book "to be called The Lives of the Commonwealth's Men." Godwin says that he will never write it himself, but he thought that Mary might like to do so, and he adds a list of books to be consulted. Godwin, however, did write some years later a *History of the Commonwealth of England*, 1824–1828.

unfortunately little skilled in English history, and the interest which
it excites in me, is so feeble, that I find it a duty to attain merely to
that general knowledge of it which is indispensable.

Mary has just finished Ariosto with me, and, indeed has attained
a very competent knowledge of Italian. She is now reading Livy.
I have been constantly occupied in literature but have written
little—except some translations from Plato in which I exercised
myself in the despair of producing anything original. The Symposium of Plato, seems to me, one of the most valuable pieces of
all antiquity whether we consider the intrinsic merit of the composition or the light which it throws on the inmost state of manners and opinions among the antient Greeks. I have occupied myself in translating this, and it has excited me to attempt an Essay
upon the cause of some differences in sentiment between the
Antients and Moderns, with respect to the subject of the dialogue.

Two things give us pleasure in your late letters. The resumption
of Malthus, and the favourable turn of the general election.[2] If
Ministers do not find some means, totally inconceivable to me, of
plunging the nation in war, do you imagine that they can subsist?
Peace is all that a country in the present state of England seems to
require, to afford it tranquillity and leisure for attempting some
remedy—not to the universal evils of all constituted society, but to
the peculiar system of misrule under which those evils have been
exasperated now. I wish that I had health or spirits that would
enable me to enter into public affairs, or that I could find words to
express all that I feel and know.

[2] Godwin writes to Mary on July 7, 1818, that "I am now over head and ears in my
answer to Malthus." This book, *On Population*, was published by Longman on November 25, 1820, at the author's expense. In the same letter he says, "The Westminster
election closes on Saturday, and the result of the whole in this division is, that the
metropolis, which sends eight members—four for London, two for Westminster, and
two for Southwark—has not sent, in its whole number, one old supporter of the present
Administration. The members for Westminster are Romilly and Burdett; for Southwark, Calvert, a veteran Foxite, and Sir Robert Wilson; and for London Alderman
Wood, Alderman Morp, and Waithman (all staunch Oppositionists), and Mr. Wilson,
a new man, who will in all probability vote for Government, but who is at least not an
old supporter. Sir William Curtis for London—their right-hand man—is thrown out.
The consequence of all this is, that everybody is of opinion that, if time had been given,
and these examples had been sufficiently early, the general defeat of the Ministry
would have been memorable. As it is, it is computed that the Ministerial majority will
immediately be diminished by forty or fifty votes; and sanguine people say, nobody can
tell what that may end in."

LETTERS

The modern Italians seem a miserable people, without sensibility or imagination, or understanding. Their outside is polished, and an intercourse with them seems to proceed with much facility—tho it ends in nothing, and produces nothing. The women are particularly empty, and though possessed of the same kind of superficial grace, are devoid of every cultivation and refinement. They have a ball at the Casino here every Sunday, which we attend—but neither Mary nor Clare dances. I do not know whether they refrain from philosophy or protestantism.

I hear that poor Mary's book, "Frankenstein," is attacked most violently in the Quarterly review. We have heard some praise of it, and among others an article of Walter Scott's in Blackwood's Magazine.[3]

If you should have anything to send us—and, I assure you, anything relating to England is interesting to us—commit it to the care of Ollier the bookseller, or Peacock—they send me a parcel every quarter.

My health is, I think, better, and, I imagine, continues to improve, but I still [have] busy thoughts and dispiriting cares, which I would shake off—and it is now summer.——A thousand good wishes to yourself and your undertakings.

Ever most affectionately yours,

P. B. S.

[Addressed]
WILLIAM GODWIN, Esqr.,
  41 *Skinner Street*,
    Snow Hill,
      London.
Angleterre—
[Postmarks]
LUCCA
[and]
F.P.O
AU. 11
1818

---

[3] Shelley wrote "from the Baths of Lucca to Scott, probably in acknowledgment of the article."—Dowden's *Life of Shelley*, Vol. II, p. 303.

318

LETTERS

Bagni di Lucca,
July 31, 1818.

GENTLEMEN,

I think I excepted especially a note of Fifty Pounds to Mr. Godwin from those which I requested you not to pay. If otherwise I beg you would have the goodness now to pay it, and to explain on my part to Mr. Godwin how the matter stands.

I would thank you also to transmit to me the present state of my accounts.

I remain, Gentlemen,

Your obliged Servant,

PERCY BYSSHE SHELLEY.

[Addressed]
MESSRS. BROOKES & CO.,
By favour of W. GODWIN, Esq.

CCCLXXXVII
TO THOMAS LOVE PEACOCK

Bagni di Lucca,
Aug. 16, 1818.

MY DEAR PEACOCK,

No new event has been added to my life since I wrote last: at least none which might not have taken place as well on the banks of the Thames as on those of the Serchio. I project soon a short excursion, of a week or so, to some of the neighbouring cities; and on the tenth of September we leave this place for Florence, when I shall at least be able to tell you of some things which you cannot see from your windows.

I have finished, by taking advantage of a few days of inspiration —which the *Camænæ* have been lately very backward in conceding

319

—the little poem I began sending to the press in London.[1] Ollier
will send you the proofs. [Its structure is slight and aery; its subject
ideal. The metre corresponds with the spirit of the poem, and
varies with the flow of the feeling. I have translated, and Mary has
transcribed the "Symposium," as well as my poem; and I am proceeding to employ myself on a discourse, upon the subject of which
the "Symposium" treats, considering the subject with reference to
the difference of sentiments respecting it, existing between the
Greeks and modern nations: a subject to be handled with that
delicate caution which either I cannot or I will not practise in other
matters, but which here I acknowledge to be necessary. Not that
I have any serious thought of publishing either this discourse or the
"Symposium," at least till I return to England, when we may discuss the propriety of it.

"Nightmare Abbey" finished. Well, what is in it? What is it?
You are as secret as if the priest of Ceres had dictated its sacred
pages. However, I suppose I shall see in time, when my second
parcel arrives. My first is yet absent. By what conveyance did you
send it?

Pray, are you yet cured of your Nympholepsy? 'Tis a sweet
disease: but one as obstinate and dangerous as any—even when
the Nymph is a Poliad.[2] Whether such be the case or not, I hope
your nympholeptic tale is not abandoned. The subject, if treated
with a due spice of Bacchic fury, and interwoven with the manners
and feelings of those divine people, who, in their very errors, are
the mirrors, as it were, in which all that is delicate and graceful
contemplates itself, is perhaps equal to any. What a wonderful
passage there is in "Phœdrus"—the beginning, I think, of one of

[1] "Rosalind and Helen,/a modern eclogue;/with/other Poems:/By/Percy Bysshe
Shelley,/London:/Printed for C. and J. Ollier,/Vere Street, Bond Street,/1819." 8vo.
Mrs. Shelley says that this poem "was begun at Marlow, and thrown aside—till I found
it; and at my request it was completed . . . during the summer of 1818 at the Baths of
Lucca." It was published in the Spring of 1819, with "Lines written among the
Euganean Hills," the "Hymn to Intellectual Beauty," and "Ozymandias."
[2] Peacock says, "I suppose I understood this at the time; but I have now not the most
distant recollection of what it alludes to." Shelley, who had brought Leigh Hunt's
Foliage with him to Italy, had read in the poem entitled "The Nymphs" of "Oreads,
Napeads, Limniads, Nepheliads," and, as Professor Dowden says, they "probably sug-
gested to Shelley the word 'Poliad,' a city nymph, which appears in this letter." (*Life of
Shelley*, Vol. II, p. 188.) Peacock adds that he abandoned the design of the Nympholeptic tale on seeing the announcement of Horace Smith's *Amarynthus the Nympholept*.

the speeches of Socrates[3]—in praise of poetic madness, and in definition of what poetry is, and how a man becomes a poet. Every man who lives in this age and desires to write poetry, ought, as a preservative against the false and narrow systems of criticism which every poetical empiric vents, to impress himself with this sentence, if he would be numbered among those to whom may apply this proud, though sublime, expression of Tasso: *"Non c'è in mondo chi merita nome di creatore, che Dio ed il Poeta."*[4]

The weather has been brilliantly fine; and now, among these mountains, the autumnal air is becoming less hot, especially in the mornings and evenings. The chestnut woods are now inexpressibly beautiful, for the chestnuts have become large, and add a new richness to the full foliage. We see here Jupiter in the east; and Venus, I believe, as the evening star, directly after sunset.

More and better in my next. Mary and Claire desire their kind remembrances.—Most faithfully your friend,

P. B. SHELLEY.

[3] The passage alluded to is this:—"There are several kinds," says Socrates, "of divine madness. That which proceeds from the Muses taking possession of a tender and unoccupied soul, awakening, and bacchically inspiring it towards songs and other poetry, adorning myriads of ancient deeds, instructs succeeding generations, but he who, without this madness from the Muses, approaches the poetical gates, having persuaded himself that by art alone he may become sufficiently a poet, will find in the end his own imperfection, and see the poetry of his cold prudence vanish into nothingness before the light of that which has sprung from divine insanity."—*Platonis Phædrus*, p. 245a.   Peacock's note.
[4] "There is none other in the world worthy the name of Creator but God and the Poet."

LETTERS

CCCLXXXVIII
TO MARY WOLLSTONECRAFT SHELLEY
Bagni di Lucca

Florence,[1]
Thursday, 11 *o'clock,*
[*August* 20, 1818].

DEAREST MARY,

We have been delayed in this city four hours for the Austrian Minister's passport, but are now on the point of setting out with a Vetturino who engages to take us on the third day to Padua; that is we shall only sleep three nights on the road. Clare's plans with regard to Alba have undergone a good deal of modification, and her present impression is—that I should call on Albè whilst she remains either at Fucina or Padua, so as not to irritate him by entering the same city, but not to conceal—and there I think she is right—her having departed from Lucca. The worst of this plan is that it will not succeed, and that she will never be quite satisfied that all has been done. But we shall see.

Yesterday's journey performed in a one-horse cabriolet almost without springs over a rough road was excessively fatiguing. Clare suffered most from it; for as to myself there are occasions in which fatigue seems a useful medicine, as I have felt no pain in my side— a most delightful respite—since I left you. The country was various and exceedingly beautiful. Sometimes there were those low cultivated lands, with their vine festoons, and large bunches of grapes just becoming purple—at others we past between high mountains,

[1] Although Byron had refused to correspond with Clare, she wrote to him on April 21, to comply with his desire to have the possession of Allegra, notwithstanding that he had made it clear in writing that Clare's farewell to the child must be absolute and final. Soon after the despatch of her letter, Shelley heard at the Milan post-office from a Venetian some sinister reports of Byron's way of life. But Clare, having decided, would not withdraw, although Shelley seems to have warned her that she was in danger of losing the child altogether. Accordingly, on April 28, Elise, Mary's Swiss maid, set out with Allegra for Venice, and remained with the child as nurse. Allegra was subsequently placed in the charge of Mrs. Hoppner, wife of the English Consul-General at Venice. As the months passed, Clare's longing to see her little girl increased, and after the receipt of some letters from Elise, she decided to go to Venice in order to induce Byron to let her see the child. She therefore left the Baths with Shelley as travelling companion, probably on August the 18th or 19th, the day before Shelley wrote this letter. See Shelley's letter to Peacock, October 8, 1818, in which he gives the approximate date of his departure as the "day after I wrote to you" [on August 16]. I have derived this note from Professor Dowden's *Life of Shelley*, in most cases using his words.

322

crowned with some of the most majestic Gothic ruins I ever saw, which frowned from the bare precipices, or were half seen among the olive-copses. As we approached Florence, the country became cultivated in a very high degree, the plain was filled with the most beautiful villas, and as far as the eye could reach the mountains were covered with them; for the plains are bounded on all sides by blue and misty mountains. The vines are here trailed on low trellises or reeds interwoven into crosses to support them, and the grapes, now almost ripe, are excessively abundant. You everywhere meet those teams of beautiful white oxen, which are now labouring the little vine-divided fields with their Virgilian ploughs and carts. Florence itself, that is the Lung' Arno (for I have seen no more), I think is the most beautiful city I ever saw. It is surrounded with cultivated hills, and from the bridge which crosses the broad channel of the Arno, the view is the most animated and elegant I ever saw. You see three or four bridges, one apparently supported by Corinthian pillars, and the white sails of the boats, relieved by the deep green of the forest which comes to the water's edge, and the sloping hills covered with bright villas on every side. Domes and steeples rise on all sides, and the cleanliness is remarkably great. On the other side there are the foldings of the Vale of Arno above, first the hills of olive and vine, then the chestnut woods, and then the blue and misty pine forests which invest the aerial Apennines that fade in the distance. I have seldom seen a city so lovely at first sight as Florence.

We shall travel hence within a few hours, with the speed of the post, since the distance is 190 miles and we are to do it in three days, besides the half-day, which is somewhat more than sixty miles a day. We have now got a comfortable carriage and two mules, and thanks to Paulo, have made a very decent bargain, comprising every thing, to Padua. I should say we had delightful fruit for breakfast—figs very fine—and peaches unfortunately gathered before they were ripe whose smell was like what one fancies of the wakening of Paradise flowers.

Well my dearest Mary are you very lonely? Tell me truth, my sweetest, do you ever cry? I shall hear from you once at Venice, and once on my return here. If you love me you will keep up your spirits—and at all events tell me truth about it; for I assure you I am not of a disposition to be flattered by your sorrow though I should be by your cheerfulness; and above all, by seeing [such][2] fruits of my absence as were produced when [we were] at Geneva.[3] What acquaintances have you [made? I] might have travelled to Padua with a Ger[man,] who had just come from Rome, and paid [——] and scarce recovered from a malarial fe[ver, caught] in the Pontine Marshes a week or two since and I conceded to Clare's intreaties—and to *your* absent suggestions, and omitted the opportunity, although I have no great faith in such species of contagion. It is not very hot—not at all too much so for my sensations, and the only thing that incommodes me are the gnats at night, who roar like so many humming tops in one's ear—and I do not always find zanzariere.[4] How is Willmouse, and little *Ca*?[5] They must be kissed for me—and you must particularly remember to speak my name to William, and see that he does not quite forget me before I return. Adieu—my dearest girl, I think that we shall soon meet. I shall write again from Venice. Adieu, dear Mary!

I have been reading the *Noble Kinsmen*, in which with the exception of that one lovely scene, to which you added so much grace in reading to me, I have been disappointed. The Jailor's daughter is a poor imitation, and deformed. The whole story wants moral discrimination and modesty. I don't believe that Shakespeare wrote a word of it.

[Addressed]
A MADAME
    MADAME SHELLEY
        Bagni di Lucca
[Postmark]
    FIRENZA

---

[2] Letter torn. The words within brackets are conjectural.
[3] When she began to write *Frankenstein*.
[4] Mosquito curtains.
[5] Shelley's two children, William and Clara.

LETTERS

Venise
Sunday Morning,
[*August* 23, 1818.]

MY DEAREST MARY,

We arrived here last night at 12 o'clock, and it is now before breakfast the next morning. I can of course, tell you nothing of the future and though I shall not close this letter till post time, yet I do not know exactly when that is. Yet, if you are very impatient, look along the letter and you will see another date, when I may have something to relate.

Clare changed her plan of remaining at Padua, partly from the badness of the beds which indeed are full of those insects inexpressible by Italian delicacy, and partly from the strangeness and solitude of the place. At present I believe that I shall call on the Albaneser with a letter from her, and without any direct interference on my own part. He will not be up yet, and the interval she proposes to employ in a visit to Mrs. Hopner. All this casts, as you see, "ominous conjecture on the whole success."

We came from Padua hither in a gondola, and the gondoliere, among other things, without any hint on our part, began talking of Albè. He said he was a giovinotto Inglese, with a *nome stravagante*, who lived very luxuriously, and spent great sums of money. He had lately he said had two of his daughters over from England, and one looked nearly as old as himself. This man it seems was one of Albè's gondolieri. No sooner had we arrived at the inn, than the waiter began talking about him—said that he frequented Mrs. Hoppners Conversazioni very much—a contradiction for time to solve.

Our journey from Florence to Padua contained nothing which may not be related another time. At Padua as I said we took a gondola—and left it at 3 o'clock. These gondolas are the most beautiful and convenient boats in the world. They are finely carpeted and furnished with black, and painted black. The couches on which you lean are extraordinarily soft, and are so disposed as to be

325

the most comfortable to those who lean or sit. The windows have at will either Venetian plate-glass flowered, or Venetian blinds, or blinds of black cloth to shut out the light. The weather here is extremely cold—indeed, sometimes very painfully so, and yesterday it began to rain. We past the laguna in the middle of the night in a most violent storm of wind rain and lightning. It was very curious to observe the elements above in a state of such tremendous convulsion, and the surface of the water almost calm; for these lagunas, though five miles broad, a space enough in a storm to sink a gondola—are so shallow that the boatmen drive the boat along with a pole. The sea-water, furiously agitated by the wind, shone with sparkles like stars. Venise, now hidden and now disclosed by the driving rain shone dimly with its lights. We were all this while safe and comfortable, except that Clare was now and then a little frightened in our cabin—Well, adieu, dearest: I shall, as Miss Byron[1] says resume the pen in the evening.

Sunday Night,
5 o'clock in the morn.

Well, I will try to relate everything in its order. After breakfast we took a gondola and went to the Hopner's.[2] Clare went in first, and I, who had no idea of calling sat in the gondola. Soon, a servant came down and requested me to go upstairs. I found Mr. Hopner and Clare, and soon after Mrs. Hopner, a most agreeable and amiable lady who instantly paid Clare the kindest attentions. They received me with great politeness, and expressed the greatest interest in the event of our journey. Soon after—for Mrs. Hoppner sent for them instantly—came Elise and little Ba, so grown you would hardly know her—she is pale and has lost a good deal of her liveliness, but is as beautiful as ever though more mild. The account which they gave of Albè unfortunately corresponds too justly with most of what we have heard, though doubtless with some exaggeration. We discussed a long time the mode in which I

[1] Harriet Byron is one of the characters in Richardson's novel, *Sir Charles Grandison.*
[2] Richard Belgrave Hoppner (1786–1872), second son of John Hoppner, R.A., studied painting with the intention of becoming an artist. He was appointed English Consul at Venice in 1814. His wife was of Swiss nationality.

had better proceed with him, and at length determined that Clare's being here should be concealed, as Mr. H. says that he often expresses his extreme horror of her arrival, and the necessity which it would impose on him of instantly quitting Venise. The Hoppners enter into all this as if it were their own dearest concern.

At three o'clock I called on Albè.—he was delighted to see me, and our first conversation of course consisted in the object of my visit. The success of this is yet doubtful, though certainly the spirit in which he receives the request, and the anxiety he shows to satisfy us and Clare, is very unexpected. He says he does not like her [Allegra] going away to Florence for so long a time because the Venetians will think that he has grown tired of her and dismissed her and he has already the reputation of caprice. Then he said, Why, Clare will be as unwilling to part with her again as she is to be absent from her now, and there will be a second renewal of affection and a second parting. But if you like she shall go to Clare at Padua for a week (when he said this he supposed that you and the family were there); and in fact, said he, after all, I have no right over the child. If Clare likes to take it, let her take it. I do not say what most people would in that situation, that I will refuse to provide for it, or abandon it, if she does this; but she must surely be aware herself how very imprudent such a measure would be.

Well, my dear Mary, this talk went off, for I did not see in that moment how I could urge it further, and I thought that at least many points were gained in the willingness and good humour of our discussion. So he took me in his gondola—much against my will, for I wanted to return to Clare at Mrs. Hoppners, who was anxiously waiting for me, across the laguna to a long sandy island, which defends Venise from the Adriatic.[3] When we disembarked,

[3] Shelley has immortalised this ride with Byron on the Lido, "the bank of land which breaks the flow of Adria towards Venice," in his *Julian and Maddalo*, and has given us a picture of Allegra, now nineteen months old, as she appeared to him at this time:

> A lovelier toy sweet Nature never made;
> A serious, subtle, wild, yet gentle being;
> Graceful without design, and unforeseeing;
> With eyes—oh! speak not of her eyes! which seem
> Twin mirrors of Italian Heaven, yet gleam
> With such deep meaning as we never see
> But in the human countenance. With me

we found his horses waiting for us, and we rode along the sands of the sea talking. Our conversation consisted in histories of his wounded feelings, and questions as to my affairs, and great professions of friendship and regard for me. He said, that if he had been in England at the time of the Chancery affair,[4] he would have moved Heaven and Earth to have prevented such a decision. We talked of literary matters, his fourth Canto,[5] which, he says, is very good, and indeed repeated some stanzas of great energy to me; and "Foliage" which he quizzes immoderately. When we returned to his palace—which

[*The top half of the third sheet is missing here ; this also affects the text after the end of next paragraph*]

[The Hoppners are the] most amiable people I ever knew. Do you know that they put off a journey of pleasure solely that they might devote themselves to this affair, and all with so much ease delicacy tenderness! They are much attached to each other, and have a nice little boy seven months old. Mr. H. paints beautifully, and this excursion, which he has just put off, was an expedition to the Julian Alps, in this neighbourhood—for the sake of sketching, to procure winter employment. He has only a fortnight's leisure, and he has sacrificed two days of it to strangers whom he never saw before. Mrs. H. has hazel eyes and sweet looks—rather Maryish.

[*Paper torn. See above*]

. . . which indeed would do him mischief.

Well, but the time presses; I am now going to the Banker's to send you money for the journey, which I shall address to you at

> She was a special favourite: I had nursed
> Her fine and feeble limbs, when she came first
> To this bleak world; and yet she seemed to know
> On second sight her ancient playfellow,
> Less changed than she was by six months or so.
> For, after her first shyness was worn out,
> We sate there rolling billiard balls about. . . .

[4] When Shelley's children, by his first wife, were taken from him by order of Chancery. See Letter No. cccxiii.
[5] The Fourth Canto of *Childe Harold's Pilgrimage*, published in 1818.

328

Florence, Post-office. Pray come instantly to Este,[6] where I shall be waiting with Clare and Elise in the utmost anxiety for your arrival. You can pack up directly you get this letter, and employ the next day in that. The day after get up at four o'clock, and go post to Lucca where you will arrive at 6. Then take a vetturino for Florence to arrive the same evening. From Florence to Este is three days' vetturino journey, and you could not I think, do it quicker by the Post. Make Paulo[7] take you to good inns, as we found very bad ones; and pray avoid the Tre Mori at Bologna, perche sono cose inespressibili nel letti. I dont think you can, but *try* to get from Florence to Bologna in one day. Dont take the post, for it is not much faster and very expensive. I have been obliged to decide on all these things without you—I have done for the best and, my own beloved Mary, you must soon come and scold me if I have done wrong, and kiss me if I have done right—for, I am sure, I do not know which—and it is only the event that can shew. We shall at least be saved the trouble of introductions, and have formed an acquaintance with a lady who is so good so beautiful so angelically mild that were she as wise too, she would be quite a Mary. But she is not very accomplished. Her eyes are like a reflection of yours. Her manners are like yours when you know and like a person.

Do you know dearest how this letter was written—by scraps and patches, and interrupted every minute. The gondola is now come to take me to the Banker's. Este is a little place, and the

[6] Lord Byron had placed his villa I Cappuccini, near Este, at Shelley's disposal. Hoppner formerly lived at this house, and Byron had now rented it of him, though he never occupied it. In her notes to Shelley's poems of 1818, Mrs. Shelley describes I Cappuccini as "a villa built on the site of a Capuchin convent, demolished when the French suppressed religious houses; it was situated on the very overhanging brow of a low hill at the foot of a range of higher ones. The house was cheerful and pleasant; a vine-trellised walk, a Pergola, as it is called in Italian, led from the hall door to a summer-house at the end of the garden, which Shelley made his study, and in which he began the *Prometheus*: and here also, as he mentions in a letter, he wrote *Julian and Maddalo*; a slight ravine, with a road in its depth, divided the garden from the hill, on which stood the ancient castle of Este, whose dark massive wall gave forth an echo, and from whose ruined crevices owls and bats flitted forth at night, as the crescent moon sank behind the black and heavy battlements. We looked from the garden over the wide plain of Lombardy, bounded to the west by the fair Apennines, while to the east the horizon was lost in misty distance. After the picturesque but limited view of mountain, ravine, and chestnut wood at the Baths of Lucca, there was something infinitely gratifying to the eye in the wide range of prospect commanded by our new abode." Mary set out for Este on August 31. Her little girl, Clara, was taken ill on the journey, and when she arrived the child's condition was serious.
[7] Shelley's servant, who afterwards married Elise.

house found without difficulty. I shall count 4 days for this letter: 1 day for packing, 4 for coming here—On the ninth or tenth day we shall meet.

I am too late for the Post—but I send an express to overtake it. Enclosed is an order for fifty pounds. If you knew all that I had to do!—

Dearest love, be well, be happy, come to me and confide in your own constant and affectionate

P. B. S.

Kiss the blue [eyed] darlings for me, and dont let William forget me. Ca[8] cannot recollect me.

[Addressed]
A Madame
  Madame Shelley,
    Casa Bertini,
    Bagni di Lucca

CCCXC

TO CHARLES OLLIER

[*August* 1818].

Dear Sir,

Oblige me by honouring a draft of £20 that will be presented to you signed A. B. If there should be any mistake with the Bankers it shall be rectified by return of Post, but I earnestly intreat you to pay the draft.

Of course these letters[1] are put to my account.

Sir, yours very truly,

Percy B. Shelley.

I had just sealed my other letter when I discovered the necessity of writing again.

[Postmark]
  F.P.O
  SE. 1. 1818.

[8] Clara Shelley was just a year old, having been born at Marlow on September 3, 1817. She died September 24, 1818.

[1] The postage of which in this case was 1*s*. 11*d*.

LETTERS

CCCXCI
TO LORD BYRON

Este,
September 13, 1818.

My dear Lord Byron,

I have been four or five times on the point of setting out to Venice, and have been always disappointed by some unexpected circumstance. Mary and the children arrived last Sunday, and my little girl has since then been dangerously ill; so am detained an anxious prisoner here for four or five days longer. She is now better, and I hope to be able to see you at the end of the week. We have domesticated ourselves unceremoniously here, and find it, as I think you would find it, a most delightful residence.

Mary desires her kind remembrances. Clara her love. Allegra is quite well, and whenever she is drest calls for papa. William and she are grown fast friends.

Most sincerely yours,

P. B. Shelley.

CCCXCII
TO MARY WOLLSTONECRAFT SHELLEY
I Cappuccini—Este

Padua, Mezzogiorno,[1]
[? *September* 22, 1818.]

My best Mary,

I found at Mount Selice a favourable opportunity for going to Venice, where I shall try to make some arrangement for you and little Ca to come for some days, and shall meet you, if I do not write anything in the mean time, at Padua, on Thursday morning Clare says she is obliged to come to see the Medico whom we missed this morning, and who has appointed as the only hour at which he can be at leisure—$\frac{1}{2}$ past 8 in the morning. You must, therefore,

[1] On September 16 Mary writes in her journal that Shelley and Clare go to Padua.

331

arrange matters so that you should come to the Stella d'Oro a little before that hour—a thing to be accomplished only by setting out at $\frac{1}{2}$ past 3 in the morning. You will by this means arrive at Venice very early in the day, and avoid the heat, which might be bad for the babe, and take the time, when she would at least sleep great part of the time. Clare will return with the return carriage, and I shall meet you, or send you to Padua.

Meanwhile remember Charles the 1st and do you be prepared to bring at least *some* of Myrrha[2] translated; bring the book also with you, and the sheets of "Prometheus Unbound," which you will find numbered from one to twenty-six on the table of the pavilion. My poor little Clara, how is she to-day? Indeed I am somewhat uneasy about her, and though I feel secure that there is no danger, it would be very comfortable to have some reasonable person's opinion about her. The Medico at Padua is certainly a man in great practice, but I confess he does not satisfy me.

Am I not like a wild swan to be gone so suddenly? But, in fact, to set off alone to Venice required an exertion. I felt myself capable of making it, and I knew that you desired it. What will not be—if so it is destined—the lonely journey through that wide, cold France? But we shall see. As yet I do not direct to you *Lady* Shelley.[3]

Adieu, my dearest love—remember, remember Charles the I and Myrrha. I have been already imagining how you will conduct some scenes. The second volume of St. Leon begins with this proud and true sentiment—"There is nothing which the human mind can conceive, which it may not execute." Shakespeare was only a human being.

Adieu till Thursday Your ever affectionate

P. B. S.

[Addressed]
per expresso
MADAME
MADAME SHELLEY,
Capuccini,
Este

---

[2] Mrs. Shelley states in her notes to Shelley's poems of 1822 that he had recommended her to attempt a play on Charles I. This passage evidently related to Mary's work on the subject; and to a translation of Alfieri's *Myrrha*, upon which she was apparently engaged. Shelley's fragments of his drama *Charles the First* belong to a later period.
[3] Professor Dowden suggests that perhaps Shelley had received news which led him to expect his father's death; in which case he would have to return to England.

LETTERS

[*Venice.*] *Mr. Hoppner's, Friday.*
[*September* 25, 1818.]

My dear Clare,

We arrived at Venice yesterday [September 24] about five o'clock.[1] Our little girl had shewn symptoms of increased weakness and even convulsive motions of the mouth and eyes, which made me anxious to see the physician. As she past from Fusina to the Inn, she became worse. I left her on landing and took a gondola for Dr. Alietti.[2] He was not at home.—When I returned, I found Mary in the hall of the Inn in the most dreadful distress.

Worse symptoms had appeared. Another Physician had arrived. He told me there was no hope. In about an hour—how shall I tell you—she died—silently, without pain. And she is now buried.

The Hoppners instantly came and took us to their house—a kindness I should have hesitated to accept, but that this unexpected stroke reduced Mary to a kind of despair.

She is better to-day.

I have sent a message to Albè, to say that I cannot see him to-day —unless he will call here. Mary means to try and persuade him to let Allegra stay.

All this is miserable enough—is it not? but must be borne [one line is here erased]—And above all, my dear girl, take care of yourself.

Your affectionate friend,

P. B. S.

[Addressed]
La Signora Clairmont

---

[1] Mrs. Shelley says in her journal, Thursday, September 24 [1818] : "We go to Venice with my poor Clara, who dies the moment we get there. Mr Hoppner comes, and takes us away from the inn to his house." Clara was buried on the Lido.
[2] Dr. Aglietti died in May, 1836, aged 79.

LETTERS

TO THOMAS LOVE PEACOCK

Este,[1]
October 8, 1818.

My dear Peacock,

I have not written to you, I think, for six weeks. But I have been on the point of writing many times, and have often felt that I had many things to say. But I have not been without events to disturb and distract me, amongst which is the death of my little girl. She died of a disorder peculiar to the climate. We have all had bad spirits enough, and I in addition, bad health. I *intend* to be better soon: there is no malady, bodily or mental, which does not either kill or is killed.

We[2] left the baths of Lucca, I think, the day after I wrote to you, on a visit to Venice partly for the sake of seeing the city and partly that little Alba might spend a month or two with Clare before we proceed to Rome and Naples. We made a very delightful acquaintance there with a Mr. and Mrs. Hoppner, the gentleman an Englishman, and the lady a Swissesse, mild beautiful, and though not very wise unprejudiced, in the best sense of the word. The kind attentions of these people made our short stay at Venice very pleasant. We—I mean Mary and myself, saw Alba, and really we hardly knew him again; he is changed into the liveliest and happiest looking man I ever met. He read me the first canto of his "Don Juan"—a thing in the style of Beppo, but infinitely better, and dedicated to Southey, in ten or a dozen stanzas, more like a mixture of wormwood and verdigrease than satire.[3] The poor wretch will writhe under the lash.—Venice is a wonderfully fine city. The approach to it over the laguna, with its domes and turrets glittering in a long line over the blue waves is one of the finest archi-

---

[1] Mary says in her journal, Tuesday, September 29: "Leave Venice and arrive at Este at night. Claire is gone with the children [William and Allegra] to Padua. Wednesday, September 30. The chicks return. Transcribe 'Mazeppa.' Go to the opera in the evening."

[2] That is, Shelley and Miss Clairmont; Mrs. Shelley having remained at the Bagni di Lucca.

[3] Byron states that he began to write the first canto of *Don Juan* at Venice on September 6, and finished on November 1, 1818. The dedication was not printed with the first edition of the canto, 1819.

334

tectural delusions in the world. It seems to have—and literally it has—its foundations in the sea. The silent streets are paved with water, and you hear nothing but the dashing of the oars, and the occasional curses of the Gondolieri. I heard nothing of Tasso.[4] The gondolas themselves are things of a most romantic and picturesque appearance; I can only compare them to moths of which a coffin might have been the chrysalis. They are hung with black, and painted black, and carpeted with grey; they curl at the prow and stern, and at the former there is a nondescript beak of shining steel which glitters at the end of its long black mass.

The Doges palace, with its library, is a fine monument of aristocratic power. I saw the dungeons where these scoundrels used to torment their victims. They are of 3 kinds one, adjoining the place of trial, where the prisoners destined to immediate execution were kept. I could not descend into them, because the day on which I visited it was festa. Another under the leads of the palace, where the sufferers were roasted to death or madness by the ardours of an Italian sun, and others called the Pozzi—or wells, deep underneath, and communicating with those on the roof by secret passages—where the prisoners were confined sometimes half up to their middles in stinking water. When the French came here, they found only one old man in these dungeons, and he could not speak. But Venice, which was once a tyrant, is now the next worse thing, a slave. For in fact it ceased to be free, or worth our regret as a nation, from the moment that the oligarchy usurped the rights of the people. Yet, I do not imagine that it was ever so degraded as it has been since the French, and especially the Austrian yoke. The Austrians take sixty per cent. in taxes, and impose free quarters on the inhabitants. A horde of German soldiers, as vicious and more disgusting than the Venetians themselves, insult these miserable people. I had no conception of the excess to which avarice, cowardice, superstition, ignorance, passionless lust, and all the inexpressible brutalities which degrade human nature, could be carried, until I had lived a few days among the Venetians.—

We have been living this last month near the little town from which I date this letter, in a very pleasant villa which has been

---

[4] From the gondolieri, who are in the habit of reciting from Tasso.

lent to us, and we are now on the point of proceeding to Florence, Rome, and Naples at which last city we shall spend the winter, and return northwards in the spring. Behind us here are the Euganean hills, not so beautiful as those of Bagni di Lucca, with Arquà, where Petrarch's house and tomb are religiously preserved and visited. At the end of our garden is an extensive Gothic castle, now the habitation of owls and bats, where the Medici family resided before they came to Florence. We see before us the wide flat plains of Lombardy, in which we see the sun and moon rise and set, and the evening star, and all the golden magnificence of autumnal clouds. But I reserve wonder for Naples.

I have been writing—and indeed have just finished the first act of a lyric and classical drama, to be called "Prometheus Unbound."[5] Will you tell me what there is in Cicero about a drama supposed to have been written by Æschylus under this title.

I ought to say that I have just read Malthus in a French translation. Malthus is a very clever man, and the world would be a great gainer if it would seriously take his lessons into consideration, if it were capable of attending seriously to anything but mischief—but what on earth does he mean by some of his inferences?[6]

Pray tell me in your next the name, and all particulars relating to the Ship in which you sent my books—they have not yet arrived.— it is certain we shall never get them without this information.

Mary and Clare send their best regards.

[The signature has been cut away]

[5] "'Prometheus Unbound/A Lyrical Drama/In four acts/with other poems/By/Percy Bysshe Shelley/Audisne hæc, Amphiarae, sub terram abdite?/London/C. and J. Ollier Vere Street Bond Street/1820." The "other poems" in the volume comprise: The Sensitive Plant; A Vision of the Sea; Ode to Heaven; An Exhortation; Ode to the West Wind; An Ode, written October, 1819, before the Spaniards had recovered their Liberty; The Cloud; To a Skylark; Ode to Liberty. Mrs. Shelley says that the *Prometheus* was begun in the summer-house at I Cappuccini (see p. 329). "At last, when at Rome," she continues, "during a bright and beautiful spring, he gave up his whole time to the composition. The spot selected for his study was, as he mentions in his preface, the mountainous ruins of the Baths of Caracalla." On April 6, 1819, Shelley wrote to Peacock that he has just finished *Prometheus*; that is to say, the first three acts. The fourth act was an afterthought that occurred to him while at Florence in the autumn of 1819. This was completed by the end of December, and the book was published in the autumn of 1820.
[6] The following is on a separate sheet, and I am not sure whether it belongs to the foregoing letter. Yet there is no other letter to Godwin in the Bodleian Library to which it can be attached.

LETTERS

I will write again from Rome or Florence—in better spirits, and to more agreeable purpose, I hope. You saw those beautiful stanzas in the 4th Canto[7] about the Nymph Egeria. Well, I did not whisper a word about nympholepsy:[8] I hope you acquit me— and I hope you will not carry delicacy so far as to let this suppress anything nympholeptic.

Do you know if the Hunts have got our things from Russel St. If not when you go to Town, ask for me. Tis no use writing. Hunt never answers letters.—There are two volumes of Lord Byron's poetry left at Hookham's to be bound. Have you received them?— If not pray write for them.

[Addressed]
   THOS. PEACOCK, Esq.,
     Great Marlow,
     Bucks,
       Inghilterre
Angleterre
[Postmarks]
   ESTE [&] F.P.O
     OCT. 27
     1818

CCCXCV
TO THOMAS LOVE PEACOCK

Ferrara,[1]
Nov. 6. 1818.

MY DEAR PEACOCK

We left Este[2] yesterday on our journey towards Naples. The roads are particularly bad; we have therefore accomplished only two days journeys of 18 & 24 miles each, and you may imagine that our horses must be tolerably good ones to drag our

---

[7] Of *Childe Harold's Pilgrimage,* Stanzas CXV–CXIX.
[8] See note about Peacock's projected poem on p. 320.
[1] Professor Dowden says, "The journal shows that the true dates of these letters should be November 6 and 7. In Shelley's *Essays and Letters* they are printed as November 8 and 9.
[2] On October 12 Shelley, his wife, and William were in Venice, where Shelley paid several visits to Byron at the Mocenigo Palazzo on the Grand Canal, and Mrs. Shelley saw her friends the Hoppners. After twelve days, on October 24, they returned to Este, but on the 29th of that month Shelley was again in Venice with Allegra to deliver her over to Byron.

337

carriage with 5 people and heavy luggage thro' deep and clayey roads. The roads are however good during the rest of the way.

The country is flat but intersected by lines of wood trelissed with vines whose broad leaves are now stamped with the redness of their decay. Every here and there one sees people employed in agricultural labours, and the plough, the harrow or the cart drawn by long teams of milk white or dove-coloured oxen of immense size and exquisite beauty. This indeed might be the country of Pasiphaes. In one farm yard I was shown sixty three of these lovely oxen tied to their stalls in excellent condition. A farm yard in this part of Italy is somewhat different from one in England. First the house which is large and high with strange looking unpainted window shutters, generally closed, and dreary beyond all conception. The farm yard and outbuildings however are usually in the neatest order. The threshing floor is not under cover, but like that described in the Georgics, usually flattened by a broken column, and neither the mole nor the toad nor the ant can find on its area a crevice for their dwelling. Around it at this season are piled the stacks of the leaves and stalks of the Indian corn which has lately been threshed and dried upon its surface. At a little distance are vast heaps of many coloured zuche or pumpkins some of an enormous size piled as winter food for the hogs. There are turkies too, and fowls wandering about, and two or three dogs who bark with a sharp hylactism. The people who are occupied with the care of these things seem neither ill clothed nor ill fed and the blunt incivility of their manners has an English air with it, very encouraging to those accustomed to the impudent and polished lying of the inhabitants of the cities. I should judge the agricultural resources of this country to be immense, since it can wear so flourishing an appearance in spite of the enormous discouragements which the various tyranny of the government inflicts on it. I ought to say that one of these farms belongs to a Jew Banker at Venice—another Shylock. We arrived late at the Inn where I now write; it was once the palace of a Venetian nobleman, and is now an excellent Inn. Tomorrow we are going to see the sights at Ferrara.

LETTERS

We have had heavy rain and thunder all night, and the former still continuing we went in the carriage about the town. We went to look first at the Cathedral but the beggars very soon made us sound a retreat, so whether as it is said there is a copy of a picture of Michael Angelo's there or no, I cannot tell. At the public library we were more successful. This is indeed a magnificent establishment containing as they say 160,000 volumes. We saw some illuminated manuscripts of church music with the verses of the psalms interlined between the square notes, each of which consisted of the most delicate tracery in colours inconcievably vivid. They belonged to the neighbouring monastery of Certolda, and are three or four hundred years old, but their hues are as fresh as if they had been executed yesterday. The tomb of Ariosto occupies one end of the largest saloon of which the library is composed, it is composed of various marbles, surmounted with an expressive bust of the poet, and subscribed with a few latin verses in a less miserable taste than those usually employed for similar purposes. But the most interesting exhibitions here, are the writings &c. of Ariosto and Tasso which are preserved, and were concealed from the undistinguishing depredations of the French with pious care. There is the arm chair of Ariosto, an old plain wooden piece of furniture, the hard seat of which was once occupied by, but has now survived its cushion as it has its master, I could fancy Ariosto sitting in it, and the satires in his own hand writing which they unfold beside it, and the old bronze inkstand loaded with figures which belonged also to him assists the willing delusion. This inkstand has an antique rather than an antient appearance. Three nymphs lean forth from the circumference, and on the top of the lid stands a cupid winged and looking up with a torch in one hand his bow in the other, and his quiver beside him. A medal was bound round the skeleton of Ariosto, with his likeness impressed upon it. I cannot say I think it had much native expression but perhaps the artist was in fault. On the reverse is a hand cutting with a pair of scissors the tongue from a serpent upraised from the grass: with this legend *pro bono malum:* What this reverse of the boasted Christian maxim means, or how it applies to Ariosto, either as a satirist or a serious writer, I cannot exactly tell. The Cicerone attempted to explain, and it is to his commentary that my bewildering is probably due, if indeed the meaning be very plain; as is possibly the case.

There is here a Manuscript of the entire Gierusalemmi Liberata written by Tasso's own hand, a Manuscript of some poems written in prison to the Duke Alfonso, and the satires of Ariosto written also by his own hand; and the Pastor Fido of Guarini. The Gierusalemme though it had evidently been copied and recopied is interlined particularly towards the end with numerous corrections. The hand writing of Ariosto is a small firm and pointed character expressing as I should say a strong and keen but circumscribed energy of mind, that of Tasso is large free and flowing except that there is a checked expression in the midst of its flow which brings the letters into a smaller compass than one expected from the beginning of the word. It is the symbol of an intense and earnest mind exceeding at times its own depth, and admonished to return by the chillness of the waters of oblivion striking upon its adventurous feet. You know I always seek in what I see the manifestation of something beyond the present and tangible object: and as we do not agree in phisiognomy so we may not agree now. But my business is to relate my own sensations and not to attempt to inspire others with them. Some of these MSS of Tasso were sonnets to his persecutor which contain a great deal of what is called flattery. If Alfonso's ghost were asked how he felt these praises now I wonder what he would say. But to me there is much more to pity than to condemn in these entreaties and praises of Tasso. It is as a Christian prays to and praises his God whom he knows to [be] the most remorseless, capricious and inflexible of tyrants, but whom he knows also to be omnipotent. Tasso's situation was widely different from that of any persecuted being of the present day, for from the depth of dungeons public opinion might now at length be awakened to an echo that would startle the oppressor. But then there was no hope. There is some thing irresistibly pathetic to me in the sight of Tasso's own hand writing moulding expressions of adulation and entreaty to a deaf and stupid tyrant in an age when the most heroic virtue would have exposed its possessor to hopeless persecution, and—such is the alliance between virtue and genius—which unoffending genius could not escape.

We went afterwards to see his prison in the hospital of Santa Anna and I inclose you a piece of the wood of the very door which for seven years and three months divided this glorious being from the air and the light which had nourished in him those impulses which he has communicated through his poetry to thousands. The dungeon is low and dark, and when I say it is really a very decent dungeon, I speak as one who has seen the prisons in the Doges' palace of Venice. But [it] is a horrible abode for the coarsest and the meanest thing that ever wore the shape of man, much more for one of delicate susceptibilities and elevated fancies. It is low, and has a grated window, and being sunk some feet below the level of the earth is full of unwholsome damps. In the darkest corner is a mark in the wall where the chains were rivetted which bound him hand and foot. After some time, at the instance of some Cardinal his friend the Duke allowed his victim a fire-place; the mark where it was walled up yet remains.

At the entrance of the Lyceo where the library is, we were met by a Penitent; his form was completely enveloped in a ghost like drapery of white flannel, his bare feet were sandalled, and there was a kind of network visor drawn over his eyes so as entirely to conceal his face. I imagine this man had been adjudged to suffer this penance for some crime known only to himself and his confessor, and this kind of exhibition is a striking instance of the power of the Catholic superstition over the human mind. He past rattling his wooden box for charity.

Adieu.—You will hear from me again before I arrive at Naples.

Yours, ever sincerely,

P B S.

Milly wants to give her Aunt and people a 1£ note. Will you some day walk over to Little Marlow, & enquire for one Rachel Nash & tell her that you will give her, or do give her a 1£ from Amelia Shields in Mr. Shelley's services 10s. of which is for herself & 10s. for Amelia Shields' Mother. I think I said this in a letter before.—be kind enough to manage it for me, & tell me how I am to remit you the money.

[Addressed]
    THOMAS L. PEACOCK, Esq.,
       Great Marlow,
          Bucks
    Inghilterra

CCCXCVI
TO THOMAS LOVE PEACOCK

Bologna,
Monday, [Nov. 9, 1818.[1]]

MY DEAR PEACOCK,

   I have seen a quantity of things here—churches palaces statues fountains pictures; and my brain is at this moment like a portfolio of an architect or a printshop, or a connoisseurs common place book. I will try to recollect something of what I have seen; for, indeed, it requires, if it will obey, an act of volition. First we went to see the Cathedral, which contains nothing remarkable except a kind of shrine or rather a marble canopy loaded with sculptures and supported on four marble columns. We went then to a palace— I'm sure I forget the name of it—where we saw a large gallery of pictures. Of course in a picture gallery you see three hundred pictures you forget, for one you remember. I remember, however, an interesting picture by Guido of the Rape of Proserpine, in which Proserpine casts back her languid and half unwilling eyes as it were to the flowers she had left ungathered in the fields of Enna and there was an exquisitely executed piece of Coreggio's, about four saints, one of whom seemed to have a pet dragon in a leash. I was told it was the devil who was bound in that style—but who can make any thing of four saints, for what can they be supposed to be about? There was one painting, indeed, by this master, Christ beatified, inexpressibly fine. It is a half figure, rising from a

---

[1] Shelley's original letter, and a copy of the letter by Mary Shelley, are in the Bodleian Library. The above date was given by Mrs. Shelley when she published the letter in *Essays and Letters,* 1840.

mass of clouds, tinged with an ethereal roselike lustre, the arms are expanded, the whole frame seems dilated with expression, the countenance is heavy as it were with the weight of the rapture of the spirit, the lips parted but scarcely parted with the breath of intense but regulated passion, the eyes are calm and benignant, the whole features harmonized in majesty and sweetness. The hair is parted on the forehead, and falls in heavy locks on each side. It is motionless, but seems as if the faintest breath would move it. The colouring, I suppose must be very good if I can remark and understand it. The sky is a pale and aerial orange, like the tints of latest sunset; it does not seem painted around and beyond the figure, but everything seems to have absorbed and to have been penetrated by its hues. I do not think we saw any other of Corregio's, but this specimen gives me a very exalted idea of his powers. We went to see Heaven knows how many more palaces—Ranuzzi, Marriscalchi, Aldobrandi. If you want Italian names for any purpose, here they are; I should be glad of them if I was writing a Novel. I saw many more of Guido. One a Samson drinking water out of an ass's jaw bone in the midst of the slaughtered Philistines. Why he is supposed to do this God who gave him this jaw bone, alone knows—but certain it is that the painting is a very fine one. The figure of Samson stands in strong relief in the foreground, coloured as it were in the hues of human life, and full of strength and elegance. Round him lie the Philistines in all the attitudes of death. One prone with the slight convulsion of pain just passing from his forehead, whilst on his lips and chin death lies as heavy as sleep. Another leaning on his arm with his hand white and motionless hanging out beyond. In the distance more dead bodies. And, still further beyond, the blue sea and the blue mountains and one white and tranquil sail.

There is a Murder of the Innocents also by Guido finely coloured and with much fine expression, but the subject is very horrible and it seemed deficient in strength—at least you require the highest ideal energy, the most poetical and exalted conception of the subject to reconcile you to such a contemplation. There was a Xt Crucified by the same very fine. One gets tired indeed whatever may be the conception and execution of it of seeing that monotonous and agonized form for ever exhibited in one prescriptive attitude of torture. But the Maddalene, clinging to the cross with the look of passive and gentle despair beaming from under her bright flaxen hair, and the figure of St. John, with his looks uplifted in passionate compassion, his hands clasped and his fingers twisting themselves together as it were with involuntary anguish, his feet almost writhing up from the ground with over sympathy. And the whole of this arrayed in the colours of diviner nature, yet most like nature's self. Of the contemplation of this one never would weary.

There was a "Fortune" too of Guido's; a piece of pure beauty. There was the figure of Fortune on a globe, eagerly proceeding onwards, and Love was trying to catch her by the hair and her face was half turned towards him, her long chesnut hair was floating in the stream of the wind and threw its shadow over her fair forehead. Her hazel eyes were fixed on her pursuer with a meaning look of playfulness and a light smile was hovering on her lips. The colours which arrayed her delicate limbs were ethereal and warm. But perhaps the most interesting of all the pictures of Guido which I saw, was a Madonna Lattante. She is leaning over a child and the maternal feelings with which she is pervaded are shadowed forth on her soft and gentle countenance and in her simple and affectionate gestures. There is what an unfeeling observer would call a dulness in the expression of her face. Her eyes are almost closed, her lip deprest; there is a serious and even a heavy relaxation as it were of all the muscles which are called into action by ordinary emotions. But it is only as if the spirit of a love almost insupportable from its intensity were brooding upon and weighing down the soul, or whatever it is without which the material frame is inanimate and inexpressive.

There is another painter here called Franceschini a Bolognese who though certainly very inferior to Guido is yet a person of excellent powers. One entire church, that of the Dominicans, is covered by his works. I do not know whether any of his pictures have been seen in England. The colouring of his pictures is less warm than that of Guido, but nothing can be more clear and delicate. It is as if he could have dipped his pencil in the hues of some serenest and star-shining twilight. His forms have the same delicacy, and aerial loveliness. Their eyes are all bright with innocence and love, their lips scarce divided by some gentle and sweet emotion. His winged children are the loveliest ideal beings ever created by the human mind. These are generally (whether in the capacity of Cherubims or Cupid) accessories to the rest of the pictures, which are all on *sacred* subjects, and the underplot of their lovely and infantine play is something almost pathetic from its excess of unpretending beauty. One of the best of his pieces is an "annunciation to the Virgin" the Angel is beaming in beauty; the Virgin soft retiring and simple.

We saw besides one picture of Raphael—St. Cæcilia: this is in another and a higher style. You forget that it is a picture as you look at it, and yet it is most unlike any of those things which we call reality. It is of the inspired and ideal kind, and seems to have been conceived and executed in a similar state of feeling to that which produced among the antients those perfect specimens of poetry and sculpture which are the baffling models of succeeding generations. There is an unity and perfection in it of an incommunicable kind. The central figure St. Cæcilia seems rapt in such inspiration as produced her image in the painter's mind her deep dark eloquent eyes lifted up her chesnut hair flung back from her forehead, one hand upon her bosom, her countenance as it were calmed by the depth of its passion and rapture and penetrated throughout with the warm and radiant light of life. She is listening to the music of Heaven, and I imagine has just ceased to sing for the three figures that surround her evidently point by their attitudes towards [her] particularly St. John who with a tender yet impassioned gesture bends his countenance towards her, languid with the depth of his emotion. At her feet lie instruments of music, broken and unstrung. Of the colouring I do not speak it eclipses nature yet it has all its truth and softness.

We saw Domenichino, Albano, Guercino, Elizabetta Sarani. The two former—remember I dont pretend to taste—I cannot admire. Of the latter there are some beautiful Madonnas. Guercino had many pictures which they said were very fine. I dare say they were, for the strength and complication of his figures made my head turn round. One indeed was certainly powerful. It was the

345

representation of the founder of the Carthusians exercising his austerities in the desert with a child as his attendant kneeling beside him at an altar. On another altar stood a skull and a crucifix and around were the rocks and trees of the wilderness. I never saw such a figure as this fellow. His face was wrinkled like a dried snakes skin and drawn in long hard lines. His very hands were wrinkled. He looked like an animated mummy. He was clothed in a loose dress of death-coloured flannel such as you might fancy a shroud might be after it had wrapt a corpse a month or two. It had a yellow putrified ghastly hue which it cast on all the objects around, so that the hands and face of the Carthusian and his companion were jaundiced in this sepulchral glimmer. Why write books against religion, when one may hang up such pictures. But the world either will not or cannot see. [The gloomy effect of this was softened and at the same time, its sublimity diminished by the figure of the Virgin and child in the sky looking down with approbation on the monk, and a beautiful flying figure of an angel.][1]

Enough of pictures. I saw the place where Guido and his mistress, Elizabetta Sarani, were buried. This lady was poisoned at the age of 26, by another lover, a rejected one of course. Our guide said that she was very ugly, and that we might see her portrait tomorrow.

Well good night, for the present. "Tomorrow to fresh fields and pastures new."

[2]To-day Nov. 10 we first went to see those divine pictures of Raphael and Guido again, and then rode up the mountain behind this city, to visit a chapel dedicated to the Madonna. It made me melancholy to see that they had been varnishing and restoring some of these pictures, and that even some had been pierced by the French bayonets. These are symptoms of the mortality of man, and perhaps, few of his works are more evanescent than paintings. Sculpture retains its freshness for twenty centuries, the Apollo and the Venus are as they were. But books are perhaps the only productions of man coeval with the human race. Sophocles and

[1] This is an interpolation by Mrs. Shelley.
[2] This is written by Shelley over Mrs. Shelley's transcript.

Shakespeare can be produced and reproduced forever. But how evanescent are paintings and must necessarily be. Those of Zeuxis and Apelles are no more and perhaps they bore the same relation to Homer and Æschylus that those of Guido and Raphael bear to Dante and Petrarch. There is one refuge from the despondency of this contemplation. The material part indeed of their works must perish, but they survive in the mind of man, and the remembrances connected with them are transmitted from generation to generation. The poet embodies them in his creations, the systems of philosophers are modelled to gentleness by their contemplation, opinion, that legislator, is infected with their influence; men become better and wiser; and the unseen seeds are perhaps thus sown which shall produce a plant more excellent even that [sic] that from which they fell. But all this might as well be said or thought at Marlow as Bologna.

The Chapel of the Madonna is a very pretty Corinthian building —very beautiful indeed. It commands a fine view of these fertile plains, the many folded Apennines and the City. I have just returned from a moonlight walk through Bologna. It is a city of Colonnades, and the effect of moonlight is strikingly picturesque. There are two towers here—one 400 feet high—ugly things, built of brick, which lean both different ways; and with the delusion of moonlight shadows you almost fancy the city is rocked by an earthquake. They say they were built so on purpose, but I observe in all the plain of Lombardy the church towers lean.

Adieu. God grant you patience to read this long letter, and courage to support the expectation of the next. Pray part them from the *Cobbets* on your breakfast table; they may fight it out in your mind.

Yours ever most sincerely,

P B S

Consult Eustace if you want to know nothing about Italy.

[*Written by Mrs. Shelley*]

Keep Shelley's letters for I have no copies of them and I want to copy them when I return to England. When you send another

347

parcel enclose a pair of scissars [*sic*] and a penknife. [The gist of these remarks are repeated by Mary in a postscript on the transcript in which she also says] "I write out Shelley's letter because he has written so wide that it takes up too much room . . .

[Transcript addressed]
  Bologna. Impostata Nov. 10
    THOMAS L. PEACOCK Esq
      Great Marlow
        Bucks
[Postmark]
  F.P.O
  DE 8
  1818